I0095286

CONSERVATIVE VIEWS ON MODERN CAPITALISM IN THE UNITED STATES

DR. JOHN C. BREDFELDT

Copyright © 2024 by DR. JOHN C. BREDFELDT

All rights reserved. No parts of this book may be used or reproduced by any means, graphic, electronic, and mechanical, including photocopying, recording, taping, or by any information storage retrieval system, without the written permission of the publisher except in the case of brief quotations embodied in critical articles and reviews.

ISBN: 978-1-963565-05-8 (Paperback)

Library of Congress Control Number: 2024907268

Printed in the United States of America

Published by

QUIPPY
QUILL

info@thequippyquill.com
(302) 295-2278

PROLOGUE

Conservative Views on Capitalism in the U. S.

It is the Year 1776. A new Country had just been born known as the United States of America. The leaders of the new nation were deeply Christian men and women and believed in concepts like freedom, individual and national honesty and integrity, and the collective wisdom of its leaders to guide the country. That country still exists. Also, in 1776 was a British man who was a sociologist by education. But in 1776 he wrote a book called The Wealth of Nations, that dealt with the first written concept of how a country and its society should document and implement a system of the interchange between among all its individual people and businesses with a singular focus on commerce. With this book, Adam Smith became known then and still is known today as the "Father of the field or discipline known as Economics." Adam Smith included in his book the necessity of practice of Christianity in this new field of economics—not by pounding the word "Christianity" in his book, but by rather by describing Christian concepts in all the dealings among the public within his new comprehensive concept of commerce. He did this by his detailed relationships among the people and the businesses in commerce and he called the new method of organizing commerce in a country, "Capitalism". I cannot tell you a specific date in American history when our U. S. leaders of our Revolutionary War or Founders of our U. S. Constitution said, "Our Economic System will be Capitalism". But, I can tell you that both the Declaration of Independence and U. S. Constitution institute major guarantees of Capitalistic behavior on the part of both government and people.

This book is meant to be read by those who know little or nothing about our U. S. Economic System which is still to this day, almost 250 years after our Declaration of Independence still based on Capitalism. Our Country's economic system still requires Christian behavior on our entire population both as purchasers and producers of goods and services. The USA has made some modifications to its Capitalist Economic System with some, in the author's view, diminishing the effectiveness of capitalism to all Americans. Inherent in all chapters and discussions in this book will be the Christian values of the responsibility we each have towards each other as we act each day during our parts of implementing our U. S. Economic System.

This book has three sections: Section I: Economics Defined and the Foundation of Capitalism, Section II: The Mechanics of Capitalism, and Section III: U. S. Economic Issues. The book is designed to gradually expand your knowledge about the field of economics, understand how the Capitalist Economic System is supposed to work, and then deal with issues where, in the U. S., our governments' policy-makers have implemented economic concepts not in keeping with Adam Smith's concepts of Capitalism. In these chapters, I will provide you with proposed solutions to both correct the current economic policy problems and implement methods to rescind the negative consequences we participants of the U. S. Economy have suffered.

We economists oftentimes have an arrogance about us that you have to be a brainiac in order to understand economic concepts and issues. I am not one of them. I believe that every individual citizen in the U. S. should have a good basic, and in-depth understanding of the U. S. Economic System. Unless we economists unlock the many mysteries about economics, how will our U. S. general population know how to act in it, and understand why its warts, though daunting at times are all solvable, and that Capitalism is still the grand choice of all other economic systems in the world. Finally, particularly in the field of economics, there are always at least a few choices of economic policies that could be implemented. I will always provide you my choices for policy solutions of current day problems. Many will be "conservative," which means that they are usually outside the progressive/liberal policies that you see in today's main-stream media. However, there will be times when my suggested policies for cure(s) to one of our beloved country's economic problems may be widely outside the current realm of conservative economists. To me, I compare my economic policies not to conservatives or liberals/progressives, but rather to Adam Smith's concepts.

So let us begin to explore our U. S. Capitalist Economic System, from its "founding father" through the warts that have developed over the last 250 or so years.

ACKNOWLEDGEMENTS

First, I wish to acknowledge the faculty of Wichita State University's College of Business, and especially those economic professors I had the pleasure to know and from which to learn not just economic theory, but how to use economic theory in practical ways to solve real problems. I used this knowledge throughout my entire 46 years of working in the Air Force as an officer (24 years), and as a consultant to the Air Force upon retirement from active duty (22 years).

I wish to thank all the military leaders for whom I worked who basically turned me loose to determine my own way of how to help the Air Force attain greater efficiencies in mission accomplishment, lower procurement costs of Air Force aircraft and equipment, and the opportunity to conduct strategic plans 15 years into the future. It truly gave my life meaning.

I also wish to thank all the college students I taught for over thirty years both as an Air Force Officer and as a consultant to the Air Force. I told all my students that it was therapy for me to teach them at night after a normally grueling day at the office—and I meant it.

Finally, a special thanks to a very great friend, Billy Smith who read the draft of this book thoroughly and provided not only editing comments, but more importantly found many places in the book where I needed to improve either the wording, add more data, or expand thoughts to provide better, more thorough explanation of concepts. I have known Billy since my junior year in college when he was my roommate for my senior year as well. One of God's major blessings to me was to bring Billy into my life then and kept him close ever since.

SYNOPSIS OF BOOK ENTITLED

CONSERVATIVE VIEWS ON MODERN CAPITALISM IN THE UNITED STATES

By John Bredfeldt

The purpose of this book is to provide a lay reader who knows little or nothing about the workings of the U. S. Economic System a background on its birth, its concepts of operation, its mechanics of operation, and a number of economic issues currently under great scrutiny in the United States. There are three sections to the book. Section 1: Economics Defined and the Foundation of Capitalism discuss the theoretical and conceptual make-up of Capitalism as defined by its creator, Adam Smith in 1776. Section II: The Mechanics of Capitalism, discusses how the capitalistic economic system is designed to work, and particularly how the U. S. Capitalist Economic System has been tailored to work for us as a nation of consumers and businesses. Finally, Section III: U. S. Economic Issues discusses the various economic issues which the American public and businesses face in the U. S. In this section, each chapter deals with one specific issue and addresses the current economic conditions, areas of failures of the government sector to apply capitalism concepts to each of the problems at hand, and one or more recommendations by the author to resolve the issues via better implementation of the capitalist model and concepts originated by Adam Smith.

This book contains two specific elements that many economic treatises fail to provide. One is a relatively vast amount of statistical data in order to provide the reader with facts that support the author's depiction of the issue(s) at hand in each chapter. Then the author will provide what I consider both reasonable and attainable methods of change to greatly improve upon the troublesome issue that is in one or more ways damaging the capability of the U. S. Economy to serve the American public and businesses to its desired potential via its true original concepts. These recommendations are oftentimes considered "conservative economics" in nature because they tend to return to the original concepts envisioned by the founder of Capitalism, Adam Smith. However, there are times in the book where some of my recommendations will, indeed, go outside the normal bounds of Adam

Smith's teachings because the current risks to the American public is too great to use singular and/or non-complex policies to move the U. S. Economy in what the author believes is the necessary direction(s). However, as the author, I admit unequivocally to be a conservative economist at heart and intellectually.

John Bredfeldt

CONTENTS

SECTION I

ECONOMICS DEFINED AND THE FOUNDATION OF CAPITALISM

DR. JOHN C. BREDFELDT

CHAPTER ONE
About Economics and Economic Systems

A generally accepted definition of economics is: The study of the allocation of scarce resources to satisfy unlimited human needs and wants. This definition is composed of a mere 14 words, but they encompass a vast array of possibilities and realities. The first word which opens Pandora 's Box is allocation. "Allocation" denotes the need for a structured system to provide for the determination of which resources will satisfy which unlimited human needs or wants. The words, "scarce resources" introduce the reality that society and its economic system must deal with the uncomfortable condition that we cannot give everyone everything they need or want. This means that within the economic system, methods must exist to determine how and for what output those limited resources will be used. It also necessitates that the economic system must have a method of identifying who will get the limited outputs. The words "satisfy which unlimited human needs or wants" identify three additional realities with which the economic system must deal. First, all needs and wants are driven by humans. This introduces the major imperfection of the economic system in that human beings are always fallible, always fickle, sometimes dishonest and untrustworthy, and oftentimes unpredictable—along with all the other shortcomings of human beings. The second reality is that human needs and wants are unlimited. Thus, humans will never be satisfied with their economic status whether it be in terms of material and financial wealth, or with their personal control over their individual or family economic conditions. The third reality is that no two people will always agree on whether a particular desire for a good or service is a need or merely a want. And if two people will never agree on the definition of whether a particular good or service is a need or a want, imagine the amount of disagreement of needs versus wants when you introduce the reality to a society composed of 330 plus million people.

Imagine if you will, the number of economic decisions and transactions that occur in the United States in a day, every hour, or each minute. To get some idea of the size of the economic activity in the U. S. Economy for just one hour, log your thoughts about economic transactions, or your actual number of economic transactions during that hour and then multiply by 330 million. And remember that an economic transaction covers not just your expenditures for goods and services (known as demand), but also your decisions at work in terms of what projects and output on which you choose to spend your hours' worth of time (known as supply). And, remember to count each decision made for each individual transaction or work effort. For example, when you go to the grocery store, each item that you purchase is a singular economic decision. And, at work, reading each email, and any response to an email each count as an economic decision. This begins to show the enormity of the quantity of economic decisions that an economic system must be able to handle efficiently and effectively just to move goods and services on a daily basis for over 330 million people.

Now, to another reality of every economic system. Every economic system, by its nature is inanimate. Most people would agree with this concept. However, many people have a great deal agreeing with the second factual statement about economic systems—economic systems are amoral. In other words, all economic systems have no elements of morality built into their structure (or construct to use an economic term). This inanimate structure used to allocate limited resources to unlimited human needs and wants does not care, nor can it be designed to care about good versus evil, right versus wrong, or legal versus illegal. Rather, all of the morality (or lack thereof) is introduced into the economic system by humans through their interactions with each other to promulgate economic activity in the form of individual transactions between buyers and suppliers. Thus, when we see religious organizations such as the U. S. Catholic bishops in the early 1980s, or Islamic clerics during the last decade criticize capitalism for their perceived misallocation of goods and services as well as financial and economic wealth in the United States, they are misguided. All any economic system, including capitalism, can do is provide a structure for human beings to interact and determine what is to be produced, who will produce it, the methods of production, and the method of bringing supplier and buyers together to exchange resources and goods and services. No economic system can dictate the morality of the humans involved in the economic system itself. Rather, the morality (or lack of morality) that arises via each transaction in the economic system is a direct result of behavior demonstrated by the humans involved in each transaction. The economic system can enable, or limit the opportunities for humans to demonstrate moral behavior during a transaction, but ultimately, the morality of every economic transaction is determined by the human behavior demonstrated within that transaction. Let me give you a specific example that provides the most relevance to the moral outrages pushed against capitalism by its religious cleric critics. A characteristic of capitalism is that we expect people to act in their own "self-interest." The Catholic bishops translated this concept into stating that self-interest was really a just another name for "greed" and that therefore capitalism was immoral. But if you read Adam Smith's (the creator of the capitalist economic system) explanation of self-interest, he spends a great deal of time discussing how to prevent the powerful good influence of honest and moral self-interest from becoming greed which is destructive not just to the economic transaction at hand, but the capitalist economic system as a whole. In other words, balanced self-interest is a necessary concept of any economic system that promotes freedom of choice (another characteristic of capitalism).

An additional reality of economics is the fact that every economic system must have an orderly process which determines how to distribute resources to make goods and provide services to satisfy the needs and wants of Americans as well as establish a mechanism for efficient distribution of goods and services to all Americans. But, the distribution processes and mechanisms butt against the fact that we have insufficient resources to satisfy the sum total of needs and wants of all 330 plus million Americans. However, the capitalist economic system, like all other economic systems, requires that humans make the uncomfortable decisions of which resources go to produce which goods and services. And the results of these myriads of allocation decisions must knowingly result in some people getting a large share of the goods and services versus others getting a small share. The mechanisms for the allocation of resources can be skewed towards human control (in the case of centrally planned total government-controlled mechanisms) or towards an inanimate control mechanism (limited or no government control). Communism and progressive/socialist economic systems focus on human control while the capitalist economic system has automatic control mechanisms which operate best with little or no government control/influence). However, all economic systems necessitate the establishment and use of a mechanism that implements an economy-wide priority system for the distribution of resources and output. And, whether the priority system is dictated by centrally controlled human intervention or transactions through individual actions and decisions, the human interactions within the economic system must drive towards satisfying the greatest number of needs and wants. Yet, the inevitable consequence, no matter the method of human control (collective versus individual) will always result in disproportionate shares of the output to all members of the American society.

Another economic system reality is that all resources that receive income must become a part of some form of output. A resource not used, but which receives income is a resource wasted. It matters not whether the resource is physical such as a mineral or oil, or a building or road, or whether the resource is human such as the amount of labor to put an auto together, or a manager who solves process problems. Any resource that receives income must provide output or the economy and populace in general will atrophy to a point where no production will be accomplished. Certainly, resources procured without an output reduce the amount of total output available to the economy, and as the quantity of unproductive resources expands, the amount of total output foregone expands with it. This reality eventually becomes woefully apparent in an economy when suddenly the amount of total output in the economy becomes insufficient to satisfy the majority of the people who are served by it. The type of an economy can be either a communistic/socialistic, or a capitalistic economy—it matters not which. What matters is when the country's policy-makers have created the situation where output quantity and quality is substantially low enough to dis-satisfy the majority of the people who are served by the economy. This situation happened in the early 1990s when the Soviet empire collapsed both politically and economically because the people of the Soviet bloc countries were no longer willing to tolerate the low standard of living they had in comparison to the Western European countries and United States which were flourishing due to the half century of successful economic growth under capitalism. But, capitalism is not immune to chronic low standards of living for the majority of its population. As capitalism becomes more and more controlled through an ever-growing insertion of government

6

control, and output of resources becomes either non-existent or greatly limited due to government policies, at some point the populace served by that economic system will revolt. Later in this treatise, I will argue that the United States economy is dangerously close to this trigger.

The final economic system reality is that the structure of the economic system must be compatible with the political system. Where there are major incompatibilities between the two, one will eventually destroy the other in order to generate the necessary compatibilities. Let me provide just a couple of brief examples. First, let us suppose that the economic system employed by a country provides for ownership of property. And, let us suppose that the political system has imposed laws that say the state owns all property. The economic system will not survive in this environment because all economic activity will be based on the free will of the owner, rather than the collective will of government. Since the collective will of government will be enforced by the legal institution (the government itself), the economic system will no longer function—period. A new economic structure that promotes government ownership of property will have to be adopted in order for social order to prevail in that country. As another example, suppose that the government decides that people will be placed in professions or work labor pools based upon their talents as demonstrated during their first 8 years of school. Yet, the economic system employs the concept that people have complete freedom of choice of their professions and/or employee skill sets for work. Again, the economic system will fail because the constraints placed on the labor pool will not be based on individual choice, but rather on government mandate. The economic system will fail because the promise of freedom of choice will not be met by the vast majority of workers. This will promote great dissatisfaction among the work force and when that dissatisfaction reaches a large proportion of the workers, again, a revolt will take place the revolution may be either peaceful or result in war. Russia experienced both where it had a nasty war during the Bolshevik Revolution in the late 2nd decade of the 20th Century and a relatively peaceful fall of the Soviet Union in the early 9th decade of the 20th Century.

Now that we know a bit about definition of economics and the structural requirements of an economic system in general, we will focus on Capitalism as a singular economic system. The reason for this focus, is of course, that the United States Economy is based on the structure of Capitalism as an economic system.

CHAPTER TWO
Characteristics of Capitalism

The United States economic system is modeled around Capitalism. This model was first brought to the general public by its creator, Adam Smith, via his book called ***The Wealth of Nations***, (short title) published in 1776. It was not by accident that Capitalism, an experiment in the field of economic systems was married to the United States Constitution, the great experiment in running a society. Nor was it by happenstance that Capitalism and the U. S. experiment in governing. For, Adam Smith, a sociologist who lived in England watched the growth of the desire for personal freedom both politically and sociologically grow throughout Western Europe and particularly the 13 American colonies. Adam Smith sensed that this sociological change was going to both drive and need a new structure for this revolution towards personal freedom. Thus, like an architect, he created a completely new structure for an economic system that incorporated elements of human behavior, the mechanics of a set of processes designed to incorporate these elements of human behavior, and a recognition of the need to bring the political and legal systems into the economic system as a means to monitor and adjust the economic system towards the social culture of the populace all three systems (economic, political, and legal) were meant to serve. As a conservative economist, I believe that had Adam Smith not engineered Capitalism coincident with the very time that the United States became a nation, we would not be nearly as strong a country as we are today, nor nearly the strong influence in world affairs from the measures of economic wealth, political stock and maturity, cultural strength and influence. In fact, without Capitalism to bolster the greatest political experiment the world has ever seen, it is quite possible that the United States would have failed as a culture, society, and cohesive country before we reached the 20th Century. But there is no doubt that Capitalism was then and is now the only economic system compatible with our society which is oriented strongly towards individual freedom of decision-making, and personal control over our economic, societal, and spiritual well-being. This chapter will provide the characteristics described by Adam Smith as the basis of the formation of the Capitalist economic system.

1st Characteristic: Private Ownership of Property

Adam Smith declared that ownership of property, particularly from the fruits of a person's labor, was absolutely essential in providing the incentives to a worker to provide both the quality and quantity of products or services needed by his customers. The reason was and is quite simple. People will provide their labors to promote their best possible output quality and quantity when they receive the economic (financial) benefits directly through their own desires as to wealth development. When the fruits of their labor are drained from them for the benefit of others to gather the wealth represented by those of the laborers, those who provide the labor have no positive incentive to work hard or to the best of their abilities. Yet throughout the history of mankind, slavery and serfdom have been the two most popular forms of extracting labor from people. But, during the Middle Ages in Europe (from the 14th through the 17th Centuries), individual artisans, and craftsmen became more necessary and plentiful as the needs of society in general became more complex. Additionally, merchants began to emerge as brokers to provide a multitude of goods from the individual producers to the general public. Many economic historians have recognized the 17th and 18th Centuries' emergence of brokers (generally called merchants) by calling this the era of mercantilism. It cannot be denied that great monuments to God and mankind were raised by slaves over the last three thousand years or more. But, neither can it be denied that by our nature, mankind desires to be free from bondage of any sort. Adam Smith proclaimed that the best way to show a person's freedom from bondage was to be able to own property in a manner that represented the wages of his work.

2nd Characteristic: Freedom of Choice

Freedom of choice is a key characteristic that ties capitalism to our political system and culture here in the United States. Politically and culturally, we are a freedom-loving people. We expect to be able to live private lives, and make our daily life decisions with little government intervention. So it is so with capitalism. The capitalistic economic system presupposes that all participants in the economic system make free choices of where to work, what skills to employ and enhance, where to live, what companies to start should we desire, and how hard to work to make our material economic and social lives as comfortable for ourselves and our families as we desire. The government does not tell us what skills to exploit (or not exploit), what goods and services to buy and how much to pay for them, what life's social and economic goals to set, when to retire from work, or when to change employers or vocation. In fact, in the United States, we expect the government to help guarantee our ability to exercise our freedom of choice economically. In short, we can only achieve the characteristic of personal economic freedom of choice when it is NOT inhibited in some fashion by government intervention or influence. No other economic system proscribed by mankind provides for this basic characteristic which so well fits one of the basic desires of every human being.

3rd Characteristic: Freedom of Enterprise

As with people's personal freedom of choice as consumers or laborers in the work environment, so capitalism promotes the ability of people to pursue a business enterprise either individually or collectively for virtually any product or service. Here again, capitalists expect the government to be very limited in promoting red tape which stymies the pursuit of an individual's desire and capability to go into any business that might capture the fancy of the consuming public. The government should only keep people from conducting businesses that harm the consumers or destroy another key element of capitalism that prevents the capitalistic economic system from working properly. In the United States, the federal government has mounds of regulations designed to keep the American public from goods or services that harm them, instituted to protect people while they are at work, and created to protect the American public and workers from blatantly immoral practices that might be conducted by business owners and/or corporate officials/employees. In this characteristic, pure capitalist theorists presume that all business owners and their employees will always produce the best quality product or service for the lowest price and act ethically both internally and with the American public because to do otherwise will ultimately put them all out of a job. Capitalism has protections inherent in its system to discourage business owners from selling dangerous products or having unsafe production environments for their workers because people, having individual choice simply will purchase similar safe products from a different business enterprise, or will choose to work in a business with better working conditions and a higher sense of morality and ethics. Thus, the individual freedom of choice is a major element in capitalism which keeps business owners and workers from becoming monstrous in their business practices. There are other characteristics which we will discuss later that will also help keep bad business practices in check as well.

4th Characteristic: Pursuit of Self-Interest

The individual's pursuit of self-interest is the exercise of freedom to make economic choices that are to the greatest benefit of the individual as measured by the individual. Decision-making for the betterment of one's self or on behalf of others with whom the individual is bonded is a moral characteristic. Yet, of course, a person can go too far in the pursuit of self-interest by putting self above all else. The overzealous pursuit of self-interest, called GREED by many standards, usually occurs when the individual makes economic choices that include behaviors that are dishonest, illegal, or immoral. To use a Biblical standard. Money does not lead one to sinful behavior. Rather, the love of money is what leads one to sinful behavior. There are two major issues associated with the pursuit of self-interest. One will be discussed during the 6th characteristic, and the other will be more greatly examined in Chapter 3, where human nature is the major frailty of any economic system.

However, I do want to make one very important and sage point here. That point is that the overzealous pursuit of self-interest (greed) is not an inherent fault or weakness just with Capitalism. In truth, all economic systems experience this weakness of the human spirit. There has not yet been an economic system devised by mankind that does not bring out the vile evils of greed, oftentimes by a few, but for extended periods of human existence by many in a society. The nature of greed by a few is well known and well publicized in the United States. The corporation that knowingly sells unsafe products to the public in order to save the more expensive cost to make the products safe. The individual who swindles many or all of his/her customers, yet skims large sums of money off the top of their investments for his/her own personal gain. And, of course, during the entire course of the history of mankind the individual criminals, caught and uncaught, who simply steal the money from people. But, we also have, in the course of mankind, large segments of the population who exploit others for profits. In current days and during the last century of the United States, organized crime syndicates have made billions of dollars of profits by selling drugs, prostitution, and illegal gambling to the public as a whole. For 5 thousand years of mankind's history there are documented centuries where one society held an entire ethnic population in slavery for the economic benefit of dictators and their elite populace. Many of the forms of economic enterprise during the first 1900 years of human history after the birth of Christ have held large portions of populations in economic serfdom to the elite few who owned the majority of the land and business enterprise. Only since 1776 with the birth of Capitalism has an economic system been proposed where the majority of a society had true economic freedom. So, when anyone criticizes the implementation of Capitalism as being short on ethics and morals, and long on immorality, it is incumbent on them to define a current economic system that is more consistent morally and ethically, and benefits a larger percentage of the population than Capitalism. I know of no economic system in practice today that meets this challenge.

5ᵗʰ Characteristic: Markets and Price

The mechanism that makes Capitalism work is that of markets and price. The market in Capitalism is any *place* that brings a buyer (consumer) and seller (producer) together to negotiate the price of a specific good or service so that exchange of that good or service takes place. Simply stated, a market is where buyers and sellers exchange goods and services. That place can be a large store such as a department store, a grocery store, or a mega store that sells thousands of products off the shelf. That place can also be smaller in both size and product/services sold such as an auto dealership, an electrician, a plumber, or a specific phone store. Today, in most markets, the store places a price on each item in the establishment and the consumer, by taking that item off the shelf agrees to the price. The exchange takes place at the check-out line where the consumer pays the total bill to the cashier and once the bill is paid, the cashier releases the cart full of goodies out the door. Very seldom do

Americans negotiate prices and quality of goods or services. The only time where direct negotiation between seller and buyer usually takes place is in the purchase of an auto or a house. The internet has promoted more negotiation of goods and services with the advent of eBay and Amazon, but in these markets the buyer can be at a bit higher risk of being dissatisfied with the exchange because they cannot see the items for sale first hand. But, in all cases, an exchange (sale) of a good or service only happens in the market.

The mechanics of the market are what make Capitalism work. The market brings sellers and buyers together, both presumably with the desire to exchange a specific good or service. The seller has a product with specific physical and operational characteristics, or wishes to provide a specific service available to any individual or organization who needs that service. Buyers enter this market because he/she is interested in purchasing the product being offered by the seller that has those specific physical and operational characteristics, or the service being offered by the seller. When the buyer and seller agree on the product or service being offered by the seller, they then must negotiate a price that is considered reasonable to both. Assuming they can reach an agreement on the price, the seller will either give the product to the buyer, or perform the service for the buyer. If they cannot agree on the price, no exchange of the product takes place, nor is the service performed. In a Capitalist economic system, the buyer is said to be in command of the process because the buyer is the ultimate decision-maker of whether or not the exchange takes place since the buyer has the power of the purse. One of the criticisms of Capitalism is that there are many times when buyers are misled by sellers who falsify their claims of the physical or operational characteristics of the product, or fail to perform the service to the satisfaction of the buyer. We will deal with this situation in the next chapter. But, this situation results from one of three root causes. The first root cause is that the seller was indeed, dishonest in the transaction. The second root cause is that the buyer is not dealing with the seller in good conscience. I submit that these first two root causes are no more prevalent in Capitalism than any other economic system. The second root cause could be simply a misunderstanding and/or mis-communication between the seller and the buyer. In this instance, the two should be willing to renegotiate the contract between the two to make the transaction favorable to both.

6ᵗʰ Characteristic: Competition

The sixth characteristic of Capitalism, and an extremely vital element in the successful operation of Capitalism is the concept of competition. Adam Smith, knew the nature of mankind to tend towards greed. But through the establishment of the market mechanism, and the freedom of economic self-interest pursuits, competition keeps greed in check. Why? In the case of sellers, where there are other sellers that provide the same good or service at the same level of quality, the buyer can choose to go to a competitor if he cannot get the product he/she wants at the price they are willing to pay. In the case of sellers, where one buyer may be unwilling to pay the price for the good or service requested by the seller, another buyer may walk through the door who is willing to pay the price for the good or service offered by the seller. Thus, for the vast majority of goods and services, neither a single seller nor a single buyer, can act independently in the market because each has a group of others who either sell the same or similar product or desire to purchase the same or similar product. Furthermore, if a particular seller gets a reputation as being dishonest in their product descriptions or completion of their services, dissatisfied buyers communicate their dissatisfaction to other buyers. Conversely, sellers can get wind of a buyer who develops a reputation of being a reprobate via many "social" internet mechanisms today.

When there is little or no competition in the market place for either a seller or a buyer, such that competition is not fully present, we can expect economic mischief to take place. The result usually ends in greed for either the buyer (in the form of an understated price), or seller (in the form of an overstated price or lower quality of goods or services provided). In either of these two cases, a misallocation of goods and services take place. The lack of competition in any market should always be of concern, but we will learn in later chapters that there are many markets in the U. S. economic system that have become excluded from the disciplines of Capitalism, with lack of competition being a major component in the name of the good of the people.

In fact, Adam Smith considered the presence of competition in the market place so important to the proper moral and ethical operation in Capitalism that he called it the "invisible hand" of checks and balances among buyers and sellers. He understood that when competition is lacking in any market for buyers and/or sellers, greed will probably be the result.

7ᵗʰ Characteristic: Limited Government Intervention

Adam Smith proposed that government intervention in the Capitalist economic system should be limited in scope and dollar impact. His first concern was that the expense of government intervention needed to be as low as possible to keep the government from impacting the decisions of either consumers or producers. The greater the amount of expense of government, would require a greater amount of taxes to pay for government, which in turn would limit the decision-making capability of consumers and producers due to lower income and profits. Second, the larger the intrusion of government in the Capitalist economic system, the larger the role of government in the total decision options available in the economic system as a whole. In short, larger government would lead to less freedom of economic decisions for both consumers and producers, thus inhibiting the mechanical workings and natural checks and balances within the Capital economic system as a whole. Finally, Capitalism was designed to promote individual freedoms of choice which would result in maximizing the incentives of both consumers and producers to exploit their skills to the maximum extent in pursuit of the greatest economic gains. Government, by its very nature is the antithesis of individual initiative by forcing each individual to relinquish some of their personal freedoms for the sake of the collective public.

We will more thoroughly discuss the role of government in the Capitalist economic system both as proposed by Adam Smith and as practiced in the U. S. today in Chapter 6.

8ᵗʰ Characteristic: Extensive Use of Capital

In the first 7 characteristics of Capitalism, Adam Smith constructed an economic system that could exist in his time of 1776. But, his vision of the Capitalist economic system could not be realized until three other characteristics became a reality. In other words, Adam Smith predicted three additional economic conditions that would happen in the future and become major drivers in the development of and full execution of the Capitalist economic system. The first of those future characteristics was the extensive use of capital.

Adam Smith defined capital generally as we economists define it today. Capital is the physical means of production used by labor to produce a good or a service. In other words, it is the set of tools, equipment, and/or supplies which an individual uses to produce a good or service, and the building or facility in which the person conducts the production process. In Adam Smith's days, virtually all means of production were of a "hard good" nature. This means that all the tools of production and the place of production were almost always something tangibly touchable. However, with the advent of the electronics age, such things as electricity, telephones, radio and television, and most recently, computer software have revised the term capital to be means of production that cannot be physically seen or touched by humans. Furthermore, the electronics age has also changed the place of production from a physical facility to an electronic wave of some sort through use of email, electronic transfers, and even 3D printer systems.

However, the physical characteristics of capital do not change its function—the means of production where a person uses an inanimate item to produce a good or service. There were definitely means of production in the days of Adam Smith, but they were to be greatly outmoded less than 100 years later when the industrial revolution began and tremendous production efficiencies arose from the implementation of the new massive production capacities available for use by mankind. By the turn of the 19th Century into the 20th Century, America had created the production line which permitted an explosion of production activity capable by one worker on a production line. And, of course, since the early 1980s, the personal computer has made all workers tremendously more productive.

Adam Smith did not predict the specifics of the advances that capital would play in the growth of an economic system, but he accurately predicted that the additional implementation of capital in the economic system would greatly expand its total output and consumer and producer choice. It is this concept of the importance of capital in an economic system that provided the namesake for Adam Smith's proposed economic system—Capitalism.

9th Characteristic: Specialization of Resources

Both as a result of the 8th characteristic, the development of capital, and because of the very expansive growth of the output of the U. S. economic system, people became more and more specialized in what they did in order to gain the expertise and experience needed to work in a more complex production process. Additionally, capital resources also became more specialized so that production processes could be broken into smaller and smaller tasks in order to promote productivity—the act of getting more output for the same or smaller number of resources used to get that additional output.

Again, Adam Smith foresaw this economic phenomenon long before it was realized. In fact, the specialization of labor became a major emphasis of management theory in the United States beginning in the early 20th Century. It was at this time in the U. S. history that the concept of the production line was beginning incorporation in some of the most complex production processes in the country such as automobiles and steel. Specialization of resources continues today throughout the world and has become so entrenched in economies throughout the world that people have to make more specific decisions on education and training paths to take to prepare them for what seems an ever-expanding list of life-work areas of specialization.

10ᵗʰ Characteristic: Substantial Importance and Use of Money

Money was of course used in the days of Adam Smith. But Adam Smith realized that as economic activity expanded, money would be the key factor in either promoting or limiting the volume of economic activity. In fact, for Capitalism, money became a key element in the success or failure of the Capitalist economic system to work. As we will see in the next chapter, the basic mechanical workings of the Capitalist economic system demand the ready availability of money in order for the exchange of goods and services to occur between producers and consumers. It is, in fact ***THE SINGULAR MEDIUM*** by which exchange between producers and consumers can and will take place. And, particularly, the growth of a Capitalist economic system occurs when the number of exchanges between producers and consumers take place. Thus, in order to meet a fast and sustained expansion of a Capitalist economic system, money must be available for those exchanges to take place.

So, Adam Smith predicted that the importance of money, in particular its availability, would grow as the expansion of the economy grew. In Chapter 8 we will discuss the importance of money in the U. S. Economy, as well as the overarching financial system.

CHAPTER THREE
The Frailty of All Economic Systems

Before we delve into the U. S. economic system, we need to address the frailty of all economic systems. That frailty, simply put, is the recognition that operation of every economic system is based substantially on the behavior of the human beings within that economic system. All economic systems by their nature are amoral—meaning that the economic system cannot be designed to be prone to either moral or immoral character or results. The morality of every economic system is based on the behavior of the human beings that operate within the confines of the amoral, inanimate dictates of the economic system. Nor does a characteristic or collection of characteristics of any economic system dictate the behavior of human beings. Granted, those characteristics may provide greater opportunities or perhaps tendencies towards moral versus immoral behavior (or vice versa), but it is always the human beings in their individual decisions and behaviors that result in either moral or immoral results.

It is critically important that we understand this because ultimately it results in the attitudes that the general public will have about the type of economic system they desire and role of government in their economic system. To a major degree, I believe that the divisions within the United States between conservative and liberal economists, pro-capitalist versus pro-socialist/communist economic system proponents, and conservative versus liberal political people center on the understanding of this very basic truism. The morality immorality of economic outcomes, the economic outcomes that help or harm individuals or groups of people, and the consequences of economic decisions are all based on the behavior of the individuals or collective groups of people—not the economic system. Let us then explore some of the major determinants of morality within the U. S. economic system.

1ˢᵗ Determinant: Moral Authority

The first and perhaps the most important determinant of the success or failure of an economic system to result in moral behaviors is whether or not there is a generally accepted definition of the moral authority of the country or the public within the United States. Moral authority has two elements that must be present. First, the moral authority must be a generally accepted document that a majority of the population identifies as the written guidance for moral, and ethical behavior. The second element is that this specific moral authority has to be recognized as applying to the people in a specific area of land space—usually a country such as the United States. The answer to the question of moral authority in the United States statistically is considered our Judeo-Christian heritage. According to the most recent data listed in Wikipedia, roughly 63% of the American public consider themselves Christians, and another 2% or so of the American public consider themselves Jewish. Thus, as a society we should judge the moral and ethical behaviors of people in their participation in the U. S. Economic system based on our Judeo-Christian heritage and the principles of our Judeo-Christian theologies and standards.

In the early 1980's a number of Catholic Bishops in the United States criticized a number of behaviors and results in the U. S. Capitalistic economic system as immoral and inconsistent with the Judeo-Christian principles that guide the United States. I generally did not disagree with many of the situations they cited against our country's basic principles of moral behavior. But, I did (and still do) disagree with their assessment of the cause. Their general statement was that the cause of the immoral results or conditions of immoral economic behavior in the United States was the Capitalist economic system. I categorically disagree with this assessment. They often cited the characteristic of practicing self-interest as the cause because they interpreted self-interest as nothing but another concept of greed. Yet, I challenge anyone to find a statement by Adam Smith that he supports greed as an acceptable substitute for the concept of self-interest. Rather, I believe that Adam Smith goes to great lengths to define the difference between the moral high-ground of decisions of self-interest versus the immoral grounds of decisions based on greed. What the Catholic bishops needed to do was condemn the human nature to make an economic decision based on the immoral psychological concept of greed rather than a decision based on self-interest that is based on considerations of what will happen to others as an outcome of that decision. No economic system can prevent greedy or evil people from making economic decisions to reach economic success at the expense of others. Nor is there any economic system known to man that provides an individual a greater opportunity to make economic decisions that provide for economic success both to himself/herself and others than Capitalism.

2nd Determinant: Reason for Human Existence

The reason for human existence provides a necessary insight to acceptable versus unacceptable human behavior in an economic system. Furthermore, as long as the economic system does not inhibit acceptable behavior that promotes the moral reason for human existence, I contend we should not kick about the economic system. In the United States, using the Christian Bible as a reference, let me provide some short passages that, to me, define the purpose for human existence.

In 2nd Thessalonians, Chapter 3, Verse 10, Paul states, "For even when we were with you, we gave you this rule: If a man will not work, he shall not eat."

In 1st Thessalonians, Chapter 4, Verses 11 and 12, Paul comments, "Make it your ambition to lead a quiet life, to mind your own business, and to work with your hands, just as we told you, so that your daily life may win the respect of outsiders and so that you will not be dependent on anybody."

In Romans, Chapter 12, verses 10 and 11, Paul states, "Be devoted to one another in brotherly love. Honor one another above yourselves. Never be lacking in zeal, but keep your spiritual fervor serving the Lord."

In Ephesians, Chapter 4, verse 28, Paul says, "He who has been stealing, must steal no longer, but must work, doing something useful with his own hands, that he may have something to share with those in need."

In Proverbs, Chapter 21, verses 25 and 26, the statement is: "The sluggard's craving will be the death of him, because his hands refuse to work. All day long he craves for more, but the righteous give without sparing."

Finally, in Ecclesiastes, Chapter 9, verse 10, the writer says, "Whatever your hand finds to do, do it with all your might…"

These passages delineate a number of specific imperatives for living as a Christian. First, work so that you produce for others, earn their respect, and get your life sustenance in return. Second love and serve the Lord, and love and honor others as ourselves. Third, share our economic blessings with others. And finally, when you work, put your entire ability and heart into it. It is pretty obvious to me that a major Christian mandate towards personal behavior in our economic system is to work so that we provide goods and services to others. Other comments from Christian authorities that I have heard and read over my last 55 years or so is that we should provide an honest day's work for an honest day's pay. We should also conduct our economic lives in honest dealings both as workers (producers) and as consumers. I am not aware of any passages in the Bible that state that any civilian organization is to develop an economic system that will force human beings to conduct their lives in their economic endeavors in a completely moral fashion as compared to God's high moral standards. That feat is simply impossible because the nature of mankind is to sin. To the contrary, God always lays the cause of sinful behavior on those committing the sin. It is therefore preposterous for anyone, especially a group of men who are supposed to be the most knowledgeable Christian theologians to state that Capitalism is the cause of the shortfalls of morality demonstrated in economic activity within the United States of America.

3rd Determinant: Capitalism Depends on Complete Honesty of All Individuals

The Capitalist Economic System requires complete honesty in each and every transaction among sellers and buyers. Wherever complete honesty is absent, the buyer will be displeased with the product or service quality for the price paid, or the seller will feel cheated for the price charged due to his inability to satisfy the buyer. We all know of people within every society who tries to swindle others in financial and material ways to gain at the expense of others. Trust is a necessity in all transactions between a buyer and seller. When trust becomes visibly absent before or during the conduct of the exchange process, the exchange of the good or service most likely will be terminated. When trust is violated after the transaction, the relationship between the buyer and seller at best gets testy, and at worst completely disintegrates.

But, complete honesty is not the only obvious pitfall to capitalism. A dissimilar situation can create the appearance of dishonesty and/or mistrust. That situation is an accurate understanding between the buyer and seller as to the complete and exact characteristics and quality of the product or service transacted between the buyer and seller. Many transactions happen between a buyer and seller where the buyer does not take the time to fully understand the technical characteristics and/or quality of the product or service offered by the seller, even though the seller has done a good job of describing both to the buyer. For every transaction, it is the responsibility of the buyer to fully understand what he/she is buying, and often more importantly, to understand what they are not getting with the specific product or service offered by each and every seller. Being a good consumer, who gets the fewest disappointments on anything bought be it a product or service requires a good deal of research on the part of the consumer. The seller can provide the consumer a product with a completely accurate description of the specifications of the product or service, both verbally and in writing. But, if the buyer fails to ask all the detailed questions necessary to fully understand what he/she is buying, that is not the fault of the seller.

On the other hand, the seller needs to assure himself/herself that the product or service they are offering the buyer will satisfy the need or want of the buyer. So, the responsibility of the seller during the transaction process is to ensure that the product or service offered will, in fact, meet the need or want described by the buyer. Thus, the seller needs to get as much detailed information from the potential buyer as to product/service specifications desired, and quality desired to be coupled with the price the buyer is willing and able to pay. The seller needs to understand that the statement, "The buyer is always right," is blatantly wrong. Not all buyers are reasonable in their expectations. A buyer who walks into a Mercedes showroom expecting to buy a brand-new Mercedes for less than $20,000 has unrealistic expectations of being able to leave the dealership with a new Mercedes. A buyer who expects to walk into a respectable jewelry establishment and purchase a brand new perfectly cut one carat diamond in a platinum setting for $300 will leave the jewelry shop with nothing in his or her hand. The stories of purchasers with unrealistic expectations are numerous and happen every day. The role of the seller is to bluntly tell the potential buyer early in the discussion that the seller cannot/will not be able to satisfy the buyer.

Alternatively, a buyer who is offered a deal that sounds "too good to be true" needs to run from the seller and the deal offered as quickly as possible. We are, as consumers, all familiar with the number of scams that potential sellers will throw at potential buyers. All of us have had some of those scams attempted on us. Unfortunately, in every society there are dishonest people who make a living by making money in a dishonest fashion either as a seller or a buyer. None of the dishonesty is caused by the economic system employed by society—in this case Capitalism. The dishonesty is caused by human nature.

4ᵗʰ Determinant: Individual Responsibility

Once you accept that one of the major mandates of living on this Earth is to work so that we can each contribute to the well-being of other people, one set of individual responsibilities immediately arises. First, if you can work you should work. But, suppose you cannot find a job, does your responsibility to work end there? Not by a long shot. For, if you cannot find work, society in the United States provides you many opportunities to improve your opportunities to find work. You can get a higher education. You can learn a specific skill through a job training program. You can volunteer for any number of government programs that will give you work experience and provide you additional skills. Such things as the military, the peace corps, and the job corps provide training and work experience. People should also understand that they must get a high school education in order to have a good possibility of living above the poverty level of income during their lives. Without a high school degree, individuals pretty much doom themselves to an entire life of poverty until they take action to get out of that lifestyle. By the way, every state in the United States provides a public education system designed to ensure that every American has access to a high school education. Yet, in many inner-city school systems across the country, the high school graduation rates hover around 50%. It is the responsibility of every individual in the United States to attend school and earn a high school degree. Our society simply cannot hire enough truant officers to seek and find people who are ditching high school. Nor can society force an individual to study and complete the work necessary to earn a high school diploma.

But, back to one of the Bible verses quoted in the 2nd Determinant, "If a man will not work, he shall not eat." Society has no responsibility to provide sustenance for an individual who will not do the preparation necessary to get the skills necessary to obtain a job. Beyond the ability to find a job, society has the right to expect people to ensure that they do not commit behaviors that prevent them from leading productive lives. Becoming a drug addict, having a child or children out of wedlock, becoming an alcoholic, or conducting a life of crime all prevent an individual from becoming a productive member of society. It also prevents an individual, and any children or other immediate family members from living a life in anything other than economic squalor.

In the United States, our Capitalist economic system provides every individual the option to make decisions that help prepare him/her to be a productive member of society and earn a good living economically and enjoy the benefits thereof. On the other hand, that same Capitalist economic system provides every individual the option to make decisions that inhibit or utterly destroy their opportunities to make a good living economically and live a life of poverty. It is hoped that the personal psychological drive for self-interest will strongly encourage each individual to do everything he/she can to exploit their talents to their best income generating advantage. But, Capitalism does not force you to make the right decisions in your own honest self-interest.

The liberals and progressives in our society today and for the last 5 decades have implemented economic and political policies that dimmish, if not erase the bad personal decisions millions of Americans.

In fact, many Americans have forgone getting an education or committed behaviors that have limited or destroyed their ability to get a good paying job, if any job at all so that they can live a decent life economically. These welfare programs have cost working Americans trillions of dollars during those 5 decades, and yet, the number of people who made the decisions to commit the bad behaviors that have resulted in people going on welfare has increased.

As a conservative economist, it is quite apparent to me that these economic welfare policies have exacerbated the problems of poverty rather than solving them. We will discuss the policy options that could/should change this trend in Chapter 11.

For those who might believe that a reasonable alternative to Capitalism is a Communistic economic system, you should consider this. Under a Communistic economic system, everyone will work, because it does not allow anyone to collect benefits from the government without working for them. And, yes, the pay for the majority of the population is very similar. But there is no real middle class in a Communistic economic system. There is the ruling/government administrator class of people of approximately 10% of the population who get pay and benefits similar to the top 10% of Americans. But the remaining 90% of the population lives much closer to the poverty level of the United States than to the median income level of the American middle class. Furthermore, under a Communistic economic system, you do not get to determine what your life's work or job will be. You don't even get to choose the level of schooling you receive. The government tells you what job you will do, what level of education you will receive, and where you will live. So, if you like freedom of choice of any aspect of your life, you do not want a Communistic economic and political system. It will not improve your economic lot. Rather, it most probably will degrade your economic well-being below whatever level of misery you currently think you live. If you do not believe this, do a bit of research on the way the major Communistic economic systems currently function or did function before they self-destructed.

5th Determinant: Individual Needs versus Individual Wants

One of the major conflicts in any economic system is the determination of true individual true needs versus individual wants. Every person in a society and economic system has both elements in their daily decision-making of what goods and services to purchase or not purchase, and in their determination of what goods and services are affordable and those that are not affordable. As an economist we would hope that each individual maximizes or completes the satisfaction of all their needs before he or she begins to purchase goods or services to satisfy any of their wants. Similarly for a society, economists would want all of the needs of each individual in society to be satisfied before we divert any resources to goods and services that merely meet wants. Where individuals achieve the full and complete satisfaction of their needs, economists would say that those individuals have optimized their economic decision-making. Where a society achieves the satisfaction of all the collective needs of all the members of its society, the society (and the associated economic system) has also optimized their economic decision-making.

The problem that arises in every society and economic system is that the determination of what goods and services are true wants versus those goods and services that are mere needs. A significantly greater complication in that determination process when we add either quality and/or quantity to the equation. Let us take one simple example. Every human being has to eat food in order to survive. Suppose we send 5 people to a food market to purchase meat for their family of four for one week. Let us say that each of the families has one father, one mother, one son, and one daughter and that the adults and children in each family are of equal height and weight. And let us further assume that each family will consume 10 pounds of meat in one week. At this point, hopefully, the reader and all 5 families agree that 10 pounds of meat is a reasonable total of quantity to purchase for one week. So, when the five representatives of each of the families go to the meat counter, would we reasonably assume that, given several choices of types of meat, cuts of meat, family meat taste preferences, and anticipated menus for the week, that each of the representatives will buy precisely the same quantity and type of meat for their families? Of course not. But suppose one of the five families has a budget of $50, one family has a budget of $150, and the other three families have a budget of $100 for the 10 pounds of meat. Will all five representatives buying meat at the counter have the same perception of what type and quality of meat is needed to feed a family of 4 otherwise identical human beings? Probably not. And, in fact the family with the $50 budget for meat may decide that the 10 pounds of meat they buy does not satisfy their needs because it is all hamburger, sausage, and canned meats, versus a variety of steaks, fish, and seafood that the families with $100 a week to spend on meats can purchase. And, it is also possible that the 4 families who do not have $150 to spend for meat may think that the lobster and steak and fresh fish diet the four members of that family eat each week is a splurge of expense to the point of being at least partly a want because the high-income family is buying high priced meat that is meant to satisfy not the need for survival, but rather to satisfy a mere taste of high-priced meat. It is even possible that those four families could envy the higher income family because the higher income family does not have to make the hard financial trade-off and prioritizing decisions that lower income families have to make. And, what of the three families with the same weekly budget for meet? Do we expect all three of those families to purchase the same types of meat for the week? Certainly not, because we can reasonably expect that each of the three families has differing tastes and/or menus for the week which will drive differing meat purchases for them. But, what we know for certain is that the perceptions of the definition of a need in terms of the total meat package purchased for the week will be different for all five representatives and their families.

A need can be dictated to an individual in broad terms such as the three survival needs of food, shelter, and clothing, or in more specific terms such as minimum supplies for grade school, high school, or college. The vast majority of Americans must have some form of transportation to get to and from work from and to their place of residence. Belonging to many organizations such as Boy or Girl Scouts, the military, police, and fire personnel may require specialized equipment and uniforms. In the United States, the federal government establishes a basket of goods that every household should have to meet minimal requirements of an adequate "standard of living." But, to a large degree, the demarcation between a good or service that is a need versus crossing the line to becoming a want is an accumulation of perceptions by each individual within the society and every economic system.

The differences in the individual perceptions of needs versus wants creates a tremendous amount of tension among individuals and groups within a society. Every economic system has to contain a method of distributing the resources to the goods and services in the correct priorities and amounts to first meet all the needs of its citizens, and then to address the production and distributions of goods and services that are more appropriately defined as wants. Within the Capitalist economic system, the mechanism that provides for the allocation of resources to goods and services and distribution of goods and services to needs and wants is the market mechanism. This mechanism will be addressed in Chapter 5.

6ᵗʰ Determinant: Individual versus Societal Benefits

Adam Smith certainly meant for the satisfaction of individual needs and wants to be the major driver of the capitalist economic system. He looked upon the role of government to be limited to facilitating the attributes of the capitalist economic system and to ensure the safety of all participants. Government's role was to ensure that the mechanics of the system were encouraged to work easily and efficiently towards each individual's opportunity to maximize his/her personal economic well-being. In Chapter 6 we will discuss the role of government in the U. S. Capitalist economic system by comparing what government does now versus the roles for government articulated by Adam Smith. However, the conservative view is that government's involvement in the U. S. Capital economic system should be very limited. Looking at the current involvement of government in the lives of all Americans, particularly by the federal government, conservative economists consider government collectively as being far too intrusive in the U. S. Capitalist economy. Generally, Adam Smith expected the society as a whole to be most benefitted when individuals succeeded economically, rather than when society, through the government tried to define and dictate that which was most beneficial to individuals and the collective populace. Clearly the current situation in the U. S., is that the federal government in particular has thousands of tentacles stretching to the far reaches of economic activity throughout both business and individuals.

Oftentimes, and particularly in the United States, all levels of government have taken it upon themselves to act either as an arbitrator among the citizens, or in some instances a dictator over their citizens by defining specific goods or services as needs or wants. Conservative economists today shudder at the vast intrusion of government in the economic decision-making by business as sellers and individuals as consumers or labor today. And, this government influence has caused many of the major adjudged societal shortcomings. Worse, by its increasing intervention government has not only failed to fix the stated U. S. Capitalist economic shortcomings, but has exacerbated them. Indeed, to conservative economists, the government intervention in the U. S. Economic system has become the number one "most wanted" on our hit list. Governments always state that their involvement in the economic lives of business and individuals is for the benefit of all Americans, even if it be at the expense of targeted businesses or individuals. Yet, much of the American public and many liberal/progressive economists fail to understand that every expense experienced by an American to provide benefits to others in our economy erodes the freedom of individual decision-making by those providers. The result is that oftentimes, the net effect of individual liberty through government intervention in the U. S. economy reduces the sum total of economic freedom and wealth benefits rather than boosting them. More in Chapter 6.

7ᵗʰ Determinant: Corporate Morality versus Societal Needs

There are many people in the United States who look with great disdain at the corporations of America as evil, greedy, and unresponsive to the needs of individual consumers and our society as a whole. They cite examples on a daily basis of overpricing the American public for particular goods and services, providing products of poor quality and safety, providing unsafe working conditions to their workers, providing insufficient wages to their workers, and swindling money from the general American public in the ever-increasingly complex corporate finance schemes through Wall Street and banking institutions. Well, this might shock you—I AGREE!!!!!! Where I disagree is that our Capitalist economic system is the cause of these ills. Remember that I earlier said that all economic systems are amoral. Every business, no matter its size of a family-owned corner grocer or a mega-corporation with tens of billions of dollars in sales each year, is operated and managed by—PEOPLE. All decisions made in the name of a business are made by the people who work within its confines. So, yes, GM autos that have individual and fleet-wide design and manufacturing defects which result in inconvenience, extra cost, and sometimes the death of GM owners. But, the GM logo and corporate name did not design and build those GM vehicles—*people* did. So, when we as members of society or as individuals experience a problem with a business, don't blame the company name or logo, blame the individuals running that company name or logo. Additionally, because those who cheated you were part of our economic system, don't blame capitalism, our economic system, for your pain, blame the people who brought the pain to you. The evil-doing is not inherent in the capitalist economic system. Rather, evil-doing is singularly a human characteristic, and every human being is not only capable of cheating others, but is expected to cheat others because it is our nature from the day we are born until the day we die. Conservative economists realize these facts and we have no difficulty defending Capitalism as the preferred economic system of the United States because we understand that all other economic systems create a far more limited environment of individual choice and economic decision-making.

Something else, I want to address shortly here. Most Americans spend the vast majority of their time thinking of themselves as consumers, yet most of us spend 40 hours per week or more dealing with others in the form of a structured environment known as a job. We spend our years from ages 6 through 18 working as students where we have to satisfy the "whims" of teachers and the education system in order to graduate from high school. If we fail to meet all these whims, we do not graduate from high school and our job opportunities and wealth potential are greatly limited for the rest of our "working lives." After reaching the age of 18, our U. S. society pretty much declares us adults and expects us to find work that will make us productive members of society where we get a wage or salary for a defined type of work that produces a defined output. In fact, we spend a minimum of 12 years of our lives learning how to be a producer of a package of goods or services. Yet, the vast majority of American workers give little thought to their responsibility to provide an honest day's work for their pay. So, when I teach a course in micro-economics where the focus of our economic deliberation is more as a business/supplier, the first hurdle I force the class to clear is the mindset that spending most of their waking hours worrying about being a consumer is both morally/ethically incorrect, and hazardous to their life-long economic well-being. Let us pose this situation. It is 3:00 PM. You sit at your desk after having just talked to a GM technician who said your car would be in the shop for three days getting 3 recall notice repairs done, fuming at GM and the technician (who had nothing to do with the design flaws requiring the repairs). Suddenly, you get a phone call from someone in a sister office who needs you to develop a spreadsheet on the cost of sales for one of your company's new products in order for them to develop a comparison of planned expenses versus actual costs as the new product is introduced into production. The individual on the phone says she needs the information by 9:00 the next morning to present a comparison to the VP of finance at 11:00 AM. You figure it will take you at least five hours to complete the spreadsheet, thus forcing you to work beyond your normal work hours in order to meet her deadline. Do you react as the technician reacted to you where, your interpretation for what he said was, in effect, "Tough, you'll get your car at my convenience of workload and work time, no matter what your needs are." In which case your response to your sister employee is something like, "I can't possibly provide the information by the 11:00 AM time for your meeting, let alone the 9:00 time you requested, so get your meeting time changed or go it alone." Or, do you respond as an employee who desires to give good service, accept the fact that you will have to work late this evening and say, "OK, I'll try to email the spreadsheet to you by 9:00 AM tomorrow. Is there a preferred format in which you need me to submit the data?" We all have these kinds of requests and deadlines frequently each week of our entire working lives. At the time, none of us as whether our response has anything to do with the U. S. being a capitalist, socialist, or communist economic system. How we react to the situations leaves an impression on how we as individuals are perceived in terms of quality of workers. But, it also provides part of the impression of how your organization performs—the quality of your company, organization name, and its logo. How you, individually, and we American workers collectively act as sellers has nothing to do with a reaction to the structure of a capitalist economic system. Rather it has everything to do with our personal and collective willingness to help others, do our jobs with high (or low) quality, and meet/exceed our customers' needs and wants.

One final comment, for all the liberal/progressive economists and political leaders in the U. S. who think that capitalism should be replaced by some form of a socialist economy, characterized by an economy with much greater central control by government entities or agencies, remember this—remember those governmental agencies are also run by people. And a characteristic of all organizations is to grow in stature and power which ultimately leads to greater decisions and control of activity at that centralized location of power. As government grows, and becomes more and more, the central planner and decision-maker of economic decisions, individual and business economic and personal decision-making authority and autonomy is diminished. All non-capitalistic economic systems place more central economic decision-making on the government, thus reducing the personal and economic decision opportunities to individuals and businesses. Loss of economic decision liberty is as harmful to individuals and society as the loss of non-economic personal decisions. In fact, as a conservative, capitalist-loving economist, I submit that loss of economic decision autonomy is worse than loss of any other personal decision autonomy, because people are most easily blackmailed or coerced into submission when their and/or their family's economic well-being is threatened. You don't believe it. Think about the times in your life when your boss plainly stated, or implied that failure to accomplish a specific task in a specific manner to get to a specific conclusion would result in economic recrimination in your job—either through poor performance appraisal or through outright loss of your job. How did you feel?

8ᵗʰ Determinant: Source of Moral Authority versus Human Law

The final determinant of the frailty involved in all economic systems has to do with the source of moral authority versus human law in a society. The issue is simply this: are the laws governing the society based on a moral authority above and beyond the human capacity for understanding or through and from human thought? In the United States, as a conservative economist, and an avowed Christian, I propose the second sentence of our Declaration of Independence as the answer to this question for the United States.

> "WE hold these Truths to be self-evident, that all Men are created equal, that they are endowed by their Creator with certain unalienable Rights, that among these are Life, Liberty, and the Pursuit of Happiness—That to secure these Rights, Governments are instituted among Men, deriving their just Powers from the Consent of the Governed, that whenever, any Form of Government becomes destructive of these Ends, it is the Right of the People to alter or to abolish it, and to institute ne Government, laying its Foundation on such Principles, and organizing its Powers in such Form, as to them shall seem most likely to affect their Safety and Happiness."

Coupled with the argument given in the First Determinant above, that the United States is a predominantly Christian country with a Judeo-Christian heritage, it seems clear to me that laws in the United States were meant by our Founding Fathers to be derived from the moral authority as annotated in the **Bible**. This means that, in the United States, the moral authority is a higher being than humans (God and Jesus Christ) and that the moral standards delineated in the Bible are the laws by which mankind should live and from which all laws of man should originate.

This is not unique to the United States and Western Europe whose societies and laws are based on the Judeo-Christian heritage. It is, indeed the dominant theme throughout the majority of the world's population and nation-states. China and parts of South-east Asia have a triumvirate of the religions of Buddhism, Taoism, and Confucianism as the major religions upon which their societies are built and laws are based. India and the surrounding countries have based their laws on a diversity of four major religions—Hinduism, Buddhism, Jainism, and Sikhism. And in the Mideast and African nations, Islam is the basis for their cultures and laws.

I propose that, within the United States, during at least the last 50 years of our history, we have begun a philosophical and cultural struggle of whether to base the operation and principles of implementation of our economic system on our Judeo-Christian heritage guided by the moral imperatives stated in the ***Bible***, or on the federal government whose moral and cultural tenets are based to a great degree on the intellect of man. Again, as a conservative economist guided by the Christian teachings, I have received during the last 60 years or so of my 67 years of age, I firmly believe that the U. S. economy is much better when based less on the rules of government established by the intellect of man than when based on the enduring cultural values based on our Judeo-Christian heritage. In short, for this (and I hope most) conservative economist, the U. S. Economy will necessarily serve the American public better with limited government intervention that it would with the current insidious encroachment and growth of government involvement in our Capitalist economic system.

With the background of the human and cultural frailties that affect all economic systems under our belt, it is now time to discuss the mechanics of the U. S. Capitalist Economic System. In other words, let's learn the mechanics that make the U. S. economic system work.

SECTION II

THE MECHANICS OF CAPITALISM

CHAPTER FOUR
The Circular Flow Model

The Circular Flow Model provides the three major sectors (or players) of the Capitalist Economic System. It describes the roles played by each of the three sectors, identifies the ways each sector engages and interacts with the other two sectors in the model and provides the methods of interaction through markets and laws.

Sector One: Households

Households in the capitalist model are as we would describe them today. A single household is as we would currently visualize it. It can be comprised of a group of family members that have a father, mother and children. It could be comprised of a single parent with children. It could also be comprised of one adult. Or, it could be comprised of a couple of generations of a family of people all living under one roof or living separately, but who have common goals and interests that bring them together to make collective decisions that affect those common goals or interests. And, economic decisions tend to be some if not many of those collective decisions that affect the common goals or interests of the household. In the United States, we tend to look upon a household as a family, but in doing so, we often emphasize the role that families play in the promotion of common social goals or interests. As economists, we emphasize the role that households play in the individual and collective decisions for the common economic goals or interests.

There are two major economic interests that a household has which affect our capitalist economic system. First, households own all the resources that are used to produce goods and services within the U. S. Economy. The most directly owned resource by households is the labor pool which all families sell to themselves or employers to make goods and services. Today, in families that have two adults, oftentimes both adults have jobs where they sell their labor to a business. But, there are some families who have one or more adults and perhaps some of their children who work in a family-owned business. The first labor example, where an individual works for some-one else is simply called a laborer. The second labor example, where an individual works for his/her own family is called an entrepreneur. A third resource owned by households is land. Land is composed of two major types. The first is simply called land space. This is the land surface that is owned by a household. In the U. S. it is usually translated into a defined plat of land that has specific dimensions of size and boundaries. Besides the land surface, there exists all that lies above and below the land surface. If you are a farmer and own one square mile of land and oil, or coal, or iron lies below the surface of your land space, you can sell that oil, coal, or iron to any business who wishes to mine it. If you have a spring-fed pond on part of the surface of your land, you can sell it to any business who needs water. If you have timber or grow wheat on the surface of your land, you can sell it to a business that wants to create lumber or grind your wheat into flour. And, of course, you can sell your land space to a business. All of these are examples of the ownership of land. The final (of four) resource owned by households is capital—that is the plant and equipment used to produce goods and services. Capital is oftentimes defined by economists as the means of production. Capital ownership is also the namesake of our U. S. economic system, Capitalism. It is not immediately obvious to most people that the physical capital is owned by households. After all, aren't most products produced in the U. S. made in buildings on machines owned by companies? The answer is: Well, not really. First, a large portion of production facilities owned by large corporations were purchased through loans made by financial institutions. Those financial institutions got their money from the American public in the form of bonds bought by people and savings by people. Secondly, the value of capital is degraded every year by the quantity of products and services produced. This degradation of capital is called depreciation and decreases the value of the capital each year. For the small family-owned companies, usually called entrepreneurships, the physical means of production are already owned by a household in order to produce the goods or services offered by the family-owned enterprise. Thirdly, homes owned by households are, in the U. S., called a capital good because homes provide a more stable environment for the household laborers to be more productive-at least, so the theory goes.

Thus, we have the first major function of households defined. Households provide the four resources within the U. S. Capitalist

Economy from which goods and services are made. The question is, how is it that households who own the resources, get together with businesses who need the resources? The answer is simple—through their interaction and interchange within the Resource Market.

Sector Two: Businesses

The singular goal of a business is to sell goods and/or services to the world public—but principally, the U. S. public. All businesses operate within a very simple model. They purchase resources, put the resources through a production process which results in the final good or service to sell. Graphically, the model looks like this:

Resources → *Through Production Process* → *Results in Good or Service*

Each good or service produced requires a consistent quantity and quality set of resources to be combined in a singular repetitive process to produce the same quality product or service. Where the quantity or quality of resources changes and/or the repetitive process changes in any fashion will necessarily result in varied quality and/or quantity of the good or service produced. Businesses purchase the resources from households (who own the resources), use the resources (land, labor, capital, entrepreneurship) to produce the good or service, and sell the good or service to the public.

There are three major structural forms of business. The simplest structural form of business is called a sole proprietor. This is a business that is owned by a single individual—or perhaps a single family. Usually, a sole proprietorship has a small sales base as a percentage of the total product sales both in the local area and certainly within the United States as a whole. There are millions of sole proprietorship businesses in the United States, and examples abound. Virtually all family-owned enterprises such as family farms, main street shops owned by families or individuals, and hard goods production and repair businesses owned by an individual or family meet the structure of a sole proprietorship. Sole proprietorships usually sell a single product or service, or a limited range of similar products or services. For example, a farmer may grow and sell wheat, corn, and sorghum crops and expand into selling cattle, chickens,

43

and hogs for meat. A family main street store would generally sell a variety of a narrow type of product such as baked pastries, cakes and cookies, jewelry, liquor, or drugs. An individual or a family service company might be a roofing company or a general contractor, a plumber or more expansive plumbing and environmental control systems contractor, a painter or more expanded siding, sheetrock and painting service.

The second major structural form of business, which is also relatively simple, is called a partnership. A partnership is a small group of individuals who have created a business enterprise to provide a narrow range of goods or services. Generally, today, the vast majority of partnerships are in the "professions" such as accountants, medical clinics, legal offices, and computer specialties. In a partnership the business enterprise is owned by the major players and decision-makers in the organization such as the senior accountants, medical doctors, and senior lawyers. Partnerships can be fluid organizations in terms of ownership and scope of products/services. One reason is that most partnerships have an ebb and flow of individuals into and from the partnership. Sometimes partners leave one firm for another due to monetary rewards, opportunities to expand or limit work scope, or a simple change of work or living environment. Additionally, partnerships may want to expand their business opportunities by bringing more people into the business as partners, or shrink their liability and business exposure by shrinking the number of partners. Finally, partnerships can have a major flux of partners due to the financial, liability, and/or reputational risks or damage from one or more of the partners. Many of the risks customary with partnerships a half century ago have been greatly mitigated by the fact that most states now allow partnerships to form legal corporations with the benefits of limited liability. This means that only corporate finances and assets are eligible in litigation suits and awards, which exclude the finances and assets of each of the partners either individually or collectively.

The third and final business structure is that of a corporation. A corporation traditionally sells a relatively large array of products and/or services related to a major business sector, usually called an industry. Thus, for the auto industry we have three major auto makers—Ford,

General Motors, and Chrysler. These three companies not only build the autos, but provide company-owned or licensed dealerships to sell and repair the autos. The defense industry has major sub-sectors such as ship builders; aircraft builders; electronics manufacturers; gun, armor, and combat vehicle manufacturers, and various military equipment logistics support and maintenance firms. Most corporations (outside those formed for sole proprietorships and partnerships) are also publicly owned. This means that the corporation has offered stock to the public for purchase at a market price per share. Stock is essence is a formal certificate of ownership certificate in exchange for money, and the exchange happens usually through one of the three major stock exchanges in the United States. Many U. S. stocks may also be offered for purchase via international stock exchanges.

Oftentimes corporations try to expand their sales and profits through a strategy known as horizontal integration. For example, the manufacturers of defense equipment hope to obtain a long-term logistics and maintenance contracts to ensure their ability to improve the quality of the product through improved maintenance techniques and parts reliability. And, of course, the logistics and maintenance contracts last well beyond the hardware production period. Thus, the corporation helps guarantee its long-term sales and profitability for perhaps 30 years beyond its production sales and profits. Another kind of corporate expansion results when a company purchases the entire production phase of a product or service from obtaining the resources, manufacturing the product or service, selling the product or service, and distributing the product or service. Oil corporations oftentimes are vertically integrated. They purchase the land and equipment to explore for oil. Once oil is found, the same company collects the oil and transports it to a distribution port that it owns. Then, that distribution port may send the oil to a refinery, again owned by the oil company. Finally, the oil is distributed from the corporate-owned refinery to a company owned retail gasoline station via a company owned pipe line or trucking company for ultimate sale to the consumer. The same oil corporation has total control over the product from resource discovery and resource generation through production, and then direct sale to the public. The oil company may go even further in that it may develop, manufacture, sell and distribute the distillate byproducts of oil waste via the oil corporation's totally owned chemical products subsidiary. A third type of corporate expansion of sales and profits is through conglomeration. In this situation, a corporation expands its ownership to a multiplicity of diverse products or services that have little if any relationship to each other. In other words, corporate conglomeration is the expansion of a company into multiple industries with very little relationships to each other. Conglomerate corporations were particularly popular in the 1960s and 1970s, but have fallen out of favor the last thirty years or so because many companies who tried this diversity found that they failed to maintain the sales and profit status of some or all of the diverse companies in the corporate portfolio. The major reason for this is that boards of directors and corporate headquarters staffs simply found it difficult, if not impossible to keep up with the quick changing technology of each of the industries in which they dabbled and even more difficult to find the multi-industry individual expertise for an entire board and corporate staff necessary to deal with the major issues that arose each week/month/year for the multiple companies participating in the multiple, unrelated industries. Thus, by the end of the 20th Century, many corporations that went into conglomeration had such bad experiences that they discarded companies in multiple industries to re-establish themselves in a single industry. Big, simply was not better when it involved a corporate expansion by buying or merging with companies in dissimilar, unrelated industries.

One corporate growth/expansion characteristic remains alive today as it has been for well over a century. That characteristic is the purchase or merger with one or more corporations (companies) in the same or very similar industries. In a later chapter, we will deal with this topic in some detail from both a theoretical and practical implementation standpoint. For now, we simply need to recognize that there is a major trend in the United States for the last quarter century for corporations to merge and in the process form a company that has a larger share of sales, customer base, and geographical area served by that particular industry. This results in companies that have outright de facto monopolies, or an increase in monopolistic power over consumers in geographical areas or specialized product/service offerings within the industry. Theoretically, monopoly power almost always results in less competition that ultimately provides the consumer with fewer choices, lower product/service quality, and higher prices. There are instances where the economic or social effect(s) of a monopoly may be of generally positive benefit to the consumers and/or the U. S. society. However, I contend that the public certainly perceives that most of the monopoly activity of the last 25 years or so has proven to be detrimental to industry customers in specific and U. S. society in general. Again, we will deal with this topic in more depth in a later chapter.

In summary, all business enterprise, no matter their form or size get resources from households which they put through processes to produce a good or service to present for sale to the American and/or international public.

Sector Three: Government

The role of government in an economic system does much to determine and establish the type of an economic system that exists for every country. In fact, I contend that the economic system and political system must indeed work towards the same goals for households and business in order for the economic system to work well. Where the economic system and political system are at odds with each other in their goals or their policy implementation of the relationships between households and business, chaos will arise to the point that a revolution will take place. If you don't believe this statement, I simply point you to the recent downfall of the USSR in the 1990-1991 time frame where they lost both economic and political power over a vast number of satellite countries as well as their general populace in their mother land. In short, the USSR had a repressive economic system that necessitated a repressive political system to be implemented against both their households (people) and businesses. As a result, their economic performance was so poor that not only the people of the satellite countries, but the Russian people began to openly revolt against the USSR government. The USSR government finally had to adjust both the economic and political systems to provide individuals greater decision-making in both their individual and collective political and economic choices. In short, the USSR, but particularly their satellite countries became more democratic politically, and more capitalist economically.

Unfortunately, putting the U. S. Constitution aside, the United States Economy has become decidedly more government-controlled and more restrictive of individual economic decision-making than it was 7 years ago, 20 years ago, and certainly since 1946. The government controls have been instituted with intent by past and present Congresses and Presidents. These government controls have driven the U. S. Economic system away from the free enterprise, Capitalism as described by Adam Smith to an economic system fraught with federal and state government controls well beyond anything that Adam Smith would have deemed acceptable to characterize our Economic System as Capitalism in his eyes. Federal and state government tax policies, spending programs and policies, regulations, and laws have severely restricted the capability of individuals, households, and businesses to make economic decisions that promote or even permit freedom of economic choices that are not only good for them but good for society from an economic viewpoint. It isn't so much that we are marching towards socialism and even communism. Rather, it is that we have greatly departed from the documented and intended characteristics of capitalism which has done grave damage to our economy, and in turn, to our citizenry. This will be discussed to a much greater degree in future chapters, but let me provide a bit of a summary structure for the later discussion here.

First, I admit that I am not a legal scholar, nor would I necessarily be accepted as a scholar on the U. S. Constitution. But, I can read, and I will herein comment on that which I know to be factual from that which is or is not contained in the U. S. Constitution about our U. S. Economic system. However, before we go to the Constitution, I want to raise a short discussion on the Declaration of Independence. As I read the Declaration, I see it with three general parts. The first part is a philosophical discussion about the right of revolution and the timing and conditions under which a revolution can be justified and should be executed. The second part is a list of grievances that the colonists had against the King of Great-Britain. There are many grievances cited, but three pertain to economics. The first is that the King's representatives "cut off our Trade with all Parts of the World." The second is that the King's representatives "imposed Taxes on us without our consent." The third is that the King himself "has plundered our Seas, ravaged our Coasts, burnt our Towns, and destroyed the Lives of our People." The third part of the Declaration is the formal statement of independence of the colonies from the King and Great-Britain. So, I conclude that economic grievances were a formally declared part of the reason that the colonies revolted. I would also remind not only the reader, but the Congress, the President, and the Supreme Court that an event during that time frame, called the Boston Tea Party, was driven by the British tax system and the resulting taxes on tea and virtually all imported and exported items of U. S. individuals and businessmen. This being the case, frankly, I am disappointed that the United States Constitution remains totally silent on the type of economic system to be used as the basis for our new country, any basic economic principles by which the people and our governments (federal, state, local) must follow, or any economic protections of the people from our federal government. But, that is the one immutable fact of our Constitution. It says absolutely nothing about our economic system in either type or structure. Because of this, the United States is in a miserable state of economic affairs. I defy anyone to give an accurate portrayal of our economic system by name, description, and consistent policy development or implementation. I further defy anyone to declare a consensus of the governed of the United States, what the structure of our economic system is or should be, and the policies that need to be developed for us to reach them. Finally, I have to ask why we have a Congress with only a handful of members educated in economics (at most), and, only one or two (if any) professional economists in the Congress for any session. Finally, I really want to know how it is that 9 members of the Supreme Court can make major economic policy that is in direct conflict with the most basic principles of our Capitalist Economic system as recently when the Supreme Court upheld Obamacare? A major economic principle violated by Obamacare was and still is that it did away with people's right and ability to choose the coverage they wanted. Rather, Obamacare forces all Americans to purchase a singular comprehensive plan that covers all medical risks. As a result, the insurance premiums all Americans using private insurers experienced a sudden significant increase in both their annual insurance rates and their co-pays. With the implementation of Obamacare, and the approval of Obamacare by the Supreme Court, the American public lost the ability to make a major economic choice on 18% of the total Gross Domestic Product of the United States. I did not read one sentence in the majority report of the

Supreme Court on Obamacare that indicated the court even considered this critical structural economic issue. A sizable portion of Capitalism in the U. S. died on that day.

All levels of government in the United States, but the Federal Government in particular have consistently and persistently violated many of the major principles and tenets of the Capitalist Economic system as described by Adam Smith. And the effects have had nasty, disastrous results. But, our Washington leadership in the form of past and present presidents, congresses, and Supreme Court justices have worked very hard to destroy the heretofore assumed economic system known as capitalism. In fact, these three branches of the federal government have so incredibly damaged our economic system that they have collectively managed to convince as much as 25% of the American population that capitalism is an inferior economic system to communism in just the last 15 years. For the last 80 years congresses have passed major legislation that was completely economic in nature, and in every aspect violates both the U. S. Constitution and basic principles of Adam Smith's capitalist economic precepts. Example 1—Social Security. It is by implementation and by structure an insurance system with an implied, if not written guarantee to the American public of promised payout for a given premium. For at least 20 years, through the middle 1950's the congresses and presidents had to justify it as a tax system with a non-guaranteed benefit in order to convince Supreme Court justices on several occasions that it looked like a duck, quacked like a duck, swam like a duck, and walked like a duck, but was really a cuddly fiber-filled teddy bear. And our Supreme Court justices bought that garbage hook, line, and sinker. Of course, the Supreme Court forewarned the congresses and the presidents that an insurance system was unconstitutional because a current congress could not obligate a future congress for expenditures from the U. S. Treasury. Example 2--And what of the recent new government insurance system, Affordable Health Care? The supreme court, once again, bought the argument that a premium paid to the government for health care insurance, or a fine paid to the government for failing to purchase health care insurance, or a subsidy paid by the federal government to an individual to make the health care insurance "affordable" were all taxes, even though the law itself never used the word, "tax." And furthermore, the Supreme Court decided that the basic characteristic of capitalism, the individual freedom of economic choice to purchase or not purchase health care insurance, was not supported by the U. S. Constitution, but a federal government directive to force the purchase of a federal government designated-content health insurance plan which utterly destroyed any individual economic freedom of choice WAS allowed by the U. S. Constitution. Example 3--The democrats in previous and the current congress constantly and loudly criticize the republicans for proposing general revenue tax systems that are a single rate for all taxpayers, known as a proportional rate because such a tax system is "unfair" to low-income Americans because they can't afford to pay the same tax rate as wealthy Americans. The democrats never use the economic term for that situation—called regressive, nor have they provided any real economic analysis to prove just how regressive such a tax really would be. On the other hand, the democrats have kept the republicans from making any structural changes to the Social Security System because any change would be throwing grandmother over the cliff. Yet, the current Social Security system promotes economic regressivity to a huge extent because wealthy income earners pay no Social Security taxes above an income ceiling of around $160,000 in 2023. A person who makes $320,000 per year pays no Social Security tax on income above $160,000. This makes the high-income person pay an effective tax rate of only 6.2 per cent. Compare that to a middle-income worker who earns $100,000 and pays the full standard Social Security Tax Rate of 12 per cent against his entire $100,000 salary/wages in 2023. Furthermore, Social Security benefits are not currently "means tested" which means that guys like Donald Trump can collect Social Security—at the maximum amount paid to an individual. The Social Security System is going broke. Two immediate revisions to at least make the system fair to all is to delete the income ceiling which could bring in as much as $80 billion or more each year in Social Security revenue, and put a maximum retirement earnings from all sources to keep those who do not need Social Security benefits from collecting Social Security benefits upon retirement.. But, once again, with a major economic crisis already upon us for Social Security, past and present congresses will not deal with the problem. Example 4-- Here's the last, but simple economic question. Why isn't a $32 plus trillion debt and trillion dollar plus annual deficit a major economic problem and issue, and why haven't presidents and congresses solved the annual problem for all but 4 years out of the last 50 and 12 years out of the last 90?

Now notice that I haven't even discussed federal, state, and local government regulations that greatly affect our U. S. economic system and economic performance. Nor have I addressed any state and local taxes or expenditures that violate and/or affect our U. S. economic system and economic performance. There is plenty of meat on the proverbial bones for discussion there as well, and we will deal with some of them in later chapters.

Here are my bottom lines about government intervention in the U. S. Economic system. First, if capitalism is our desired economic system, all governments in the U. S. have to support it through developing, legislating, implementing, and enforcing programs, public policies, laws, regulations, and court decisions that promote capitalism rather than destroy it. Second, the United States economic system is very ill and it affects every American, every household, and every business in a seriously negative fashion albeit to different degrees for each and every individual situation. Third, all levels of government, but particularly the federal government senior policy and decision-makers must immediately recognize the grave economic ills that face this country, especially those that are government made, and fix them. Fourth, any economic policy inconsistent with capitalism will have a negative effect on the economic performance of the United States and will spare neither individual Americans nor business. Finally, the body politic in this country has to make a clear, unequivocal statement that the singular economic system in the United States today and for the life of this country is capitalism. We can no longer afford to argue that modified capitalism, heading towards socialism, heading towards communism is acceptable public policy. An economic system is like getting pregnant—you either are or you are not, there is no in between—at least in terms of the long-term economic performance and benefits to its people.

The Role of Markets

The resource market is simply a place where households meet with businesses to exchange resources. That place may be a physical place where the prospective buyer of the resource (business) and meets face to face with the owner of the resource (household). But the business and household do not have to meet face to face in order to be in a market. The market could be the internet, a newspaper ad, through email, via a document transfer system (U. S. Postal Service, FedEx, UPS, or other physical document delivery carrier), or over the telephone. The market could be through an intermediary such as a real estate agent, a human resource firm, a catalog, or a sales person. But, generally, the transfer of resources from households to a business eventually involve a signed bilateral contract, and that occurs in at least one physical location. The contract document defines what resource quantities and qualities, a schedule of delivery by the households to the business. In turn, the business provides the household with financial remuneration called income to the household for the exchange of those resources. The payment made by the business is recorded on their internal financial records as a cost. The income received by households is defined differently for each of the four resource categories. Labor income is defined as wages or salaries. The income for land is defined as rent. The income for the use or purchase of buildings and equipment (capital) is defined as interest. Finally, the income for the entrepreneur is defined as profits. The federal government and most state governments collect data at least quarterly, and often monthly by each of the 4 major resource income definitions in order to determine if any of the resource categories are trending abnormally high or low against history. If abnormal trends are identified, the government will often attempt to determine the causal factor(s).

The product market is similar to the resource market. The major difference is that the product market is the place households (as consumers) go to purchase goods and services from businesses (as suppliers). The product market can be defined in the same numerous entities as described for the resource market. However, particularly in the United States, consumers oftentimes go to a place that acts as a physical inventory exchange house called a retail sales store. Consumers make hundreds of purchasing decisions in these stores by deciding to purchase or not to purchase specific items based on the quality and price of the good or service offered. Rarely does a price negotiation take place for any good or service in a retail sales store. The goods are on the shelf where the consumer sees the price of the item and either takes it off the shelf and pays for it at the cashier register prior to leaving the store. It is at the time that the consumer pays for the item at the register that exchange takes place and the consumer can leave the store with the item. In the United States, consumers and producers are uncomfortable and inexperienced at negotiating the price for an item because 99% or more of our purchases are made in a fixed retail price environment. The two major markets where true negotiation takes place in the U. S. are for automobiles and real estate—especially homes.

The final distinction for exchange of goods has to do with capital equipment. Capital equipment is purchased by a business to enable them to produce goods and services for consumers. Thus, capital goods are usually purchased by one business from another business who specializes in building structures for business enterprise or equipment specialized for business use in the production of consumer goods or services. The one single item purchased by consumers that is considered a capital equipment or investment item is a home. All other purchases made by a consumer for use in their non-business household is considered a consumption item. And, although most capital equipment items and buildings are produced by an intermediary business, that physical means of production is still considered under the ownership of one or more households.

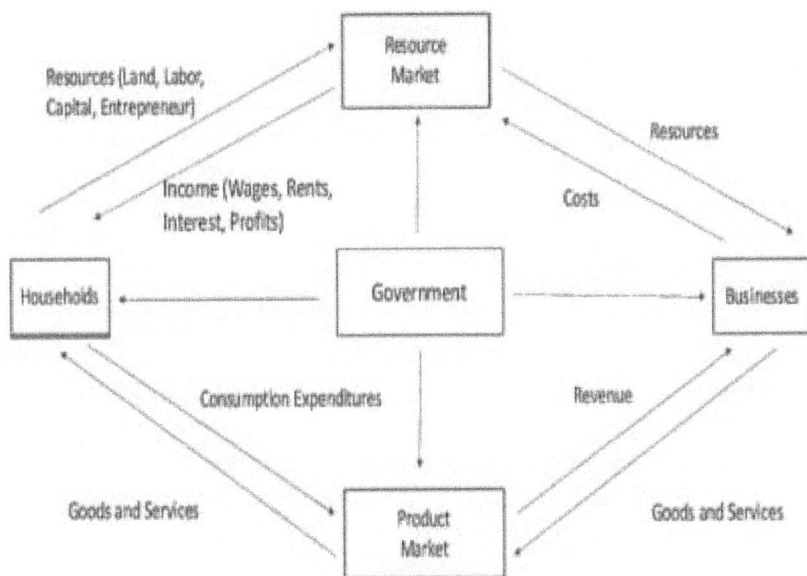

Resource Market

Resources (Land, Labor, Capital, Entrepreneur)

Resources

Income (Wages, Rents, Interest, Profits)

Costs

Households

Government

Businesses

Consumption Expenditures

Revenue

Goods and Services

Product Market

Goods and Services

CHART 1

The Circular Flow Model Explained

Chart 1 shows the flows of resources and goods and services between households and business. It also shows the points in the model where government intervenes in the United States Economy.

The Resource Market

At the top of Chart 1 is the Resource Market. The resource market is the place where households, as the owners of resources meet with businesses who need the resources to produce goods and services to exchange the resources from households to businesses. In the Resource Market, businesses seek to find the specific resources they need to produce their products or services. Those resources are of various qualities of land, labor, capital, or entrepreneurship. A negotiation takes place between the businesses and households to reach a price of exchange for the resources. Usually, a contract between the households and businesses are drawn to document the exact resource quantities, qualities, and schedule of resource deliveries. If the discussion is for labor, an individual may negotiate for his separate pay and benefits with a business representative, or may simply go to work for a business due to the fact that the business has standard wage rates or salaries for specific experience and grade levels. Most government jobs at all levels of government (including the military), most jobs covered by labor union agreement, and many of the trades (such as construction, and repair services) have pre-negotiated wage rates/salaries with standard benefits which require no or little negotiation between the job-seeking laborer and the business representative. Other jobs such as higher-level management and professional positions often involve much more negotiation between the job seeker and the business in order to fill the empty position in the business. Once a contract is signed between the household and business for specified resources, households receive income and the business incurs cost. Two important outcomes of this exchange of resources are the fact that household receive income. The type of income is defined by the type of resource. Wages go to laborers (including salaried personnel). Rents go to the owners of land for the purchase of land space or resources above or below ground. Interest goes to the households that own capital (the physical means of production including buildings and equipment). Finally, Profits go to entrepreneurs, or people who are the sole owner their businesses. The costs of the resources are important to a business because those costs determine the profits or losses to a large degree.

Let me make one final point about the resource market, because we will touch on it throughout the remainder of this book. People who are employed by another, be it a large corporate business or a small business owned by an entrepreneur, rarely remember that they spend at least 40 hours per week in the labor market. And, in the labor market it is important to remember that your worth to the organization with whom you are employed depends on your personal quality and quantity of work produced. If your quality or quantity of work falls below the expectations of the business, or worse yet, below the quality and quantity of the work specified in your contract, then from an economic sense, the employer should replace you with someone who will provide either improved quality and/or greater quantity of work output each week. Notice that I did not say work effort. For in the end, your employer is paying you for high quality and high quantity of output. Work effort that produces no output is both costly and useless to the employer.

The Product Market

Most people spend much of their time outside the work environment focused on the product market. Or more simply put, when people are not working they tend to be thinking about purchasing something. The act of a person purchasing a good or service is called consumption. And, generally speaking, in the Capitalist Economic System, there is no free lunch. Thus, in order to obtain a good or service, a person has to go to the product market and search out the availability of a good or service, find it, contract for it, and then pay for it. The product market is the place where a person searches for a product, or a person or organization to provide a service. The Product Market tends to be more complex than the Resource Market because quality has a high degree of variability and the quality variability is greatly exacerbated by the fact that sellers and consumers often miscommunicate with each other about the quality of the product for the price paid. The quality of the product or service often becomes a source of consternation between both the seller and the consumer. When the quality of a product or service fails to meet the expectations of the consumer, the consumer generally will become greatly disappointed. The consumer will almost always react negatively about a producer/seller who disappoints him/her (consumer). This may arise in the form of a direct comment about the quality to the producer from the consumer, or it may arise in the "word of mouth" negative statements about the producer by the consumer. It may ultimately result in the filing of a formal complaint by the consumer to a government "consumer protection" agency. The important thing to remember about the interaction between the consumer and producer in the Product Market is that the exchange of the good or service is not really over until the consumer is completely satisfied. An important part of any business is to receive feedback on the consumer satisfaction to ensure that there are no surprises that will show up later due to a dissatisfied customer.

The Role of Government

Much of the remainder of this book will be about "the role of government" in any Capitalist Economic System, and specifically in the U. S. Economic System. Within the U. S. today, government plays prominent roles in seeking to affect and successfully affecting the behavior of people, institutions, and businesses throughout the country and our economy. Governments can affect the economic behavior of people in a direct manner by making certain activities illegal. An example of this behavior control is making it illegal for people to steal, or to discriminate against other human beings. Government directly controls business by implementing safety regulations, preventing negative environmental pollution, and preventing fraudulent sales practices. Governments can indirectly affect the behavior of people and business by tax policies that promote some types of behavior or discourage other types of behavior. In the U. S., federal and state governments provide tax deductions for interest on home loans in order to encourage/enable the general American populace to purchase personal family dwellings. Tax subsidies are granted certain businesses in specific market situations in order to encourage a business to embark in particular markets. Governments' tax policies can also be used to discourage behavior of people and business such as high excise taxes for alcohol and tobacco products for people, and higher import/export taxes for some goods or services produced by U. S. or foreign businesses. The government can greatly affect business and consumer activity through greater government regulations and laws aimed at the interpretations and structures of contracts (known as tort law). In short, in the United States, governments at all levels have tremendous influence in the behavior of people as consumers and laborers, and businesses as organizational entities and producers of goods and services. The involvement of governments in the U. S., and indeed, any Capitalist Economic System is in great debate on many fronts at one time, all the time in the U. S. The approach to government involvement in the U. S. Economic System is perhaps the greatest divide between conservatives and liberals/progressives. These differences will be addressed throughout the remainder of this book.

CHAPTER FIVE
The Mechanics of the Market System

In this chapter, we will explore the heart of the Capitalist Economic System—the mechanism that makes Capitalism work. It is called the Price Mechanism or, alternatively, the Free Market System. It is composed of three basic elements: a market for each good and service, people who produce each good and service, and people who need or want each good and service.

We have already discussed the basic characteristics of the marketplace, so I will not reiterate them here. But, we have not discussed why the market exists in the first place. It's really quite simple. A market for a good or service exists because there are people who want a particular good or service. In addition, the market exists because there are people, in the form of business enterprise, who produce the specific good or service desired by people. The final reason that a market exists is because the price asked by the seller is within the affordable reach of the buyer (consumer) and both the seller and buyer are willing to negotiate a price acceptable to each which permits the exchange of the good or service from the seller to the buyer. There is also one very critical question of which comes into the market first, the seller or the buyer. We will discuss this at the end of this chapter as it has tremendous economic policy implications. But first, let's discuss the remaining two elements to the market system rather thoroughly.

The Concept of Demand

Demand is generally defined by economists as a schedule or line which represents the quantity of a good or service a consumer is both willing and able to purchase at various given prices. The behavior of a buyer is stated via the law of demand. That law simply states that generally, for most goods and services, a consumer will buy more of each good or service as the price decreases. The opposite of the postulate of the law of demand is generally true as well—a consumer will buy a lower quantity of a good or service as the price increases. The law of demand accurately describes the natural behavior of consumers which is to pay as little for each good and service as possible. This "law of demand" is true for two reasons. The first, which is strictly economic, is that people can simply afford to purchase a larger quantity of a good or service because their limited budgets allow them to purchase more goods and services as the prices for them decrease. The law of demand is true for a psychological reason as well. Because the vast majority of consumers have a limited budget to spend on a cornucopia of goods and services, they must prioritize their purchases on the most important goods and services first. For human beings, the three necessary expenditures are food, shelter, and clothing. Once these absolute human needs are met, if the consumer has additional budget (or income) remaining, the consumer can buy goods or services that are important on his/her list of wants (the needs having been already satisfied). Oftentimes the importance of one of those remaining goods and services will vary with the price of the other goods. This priority in association with the many other goods and services competing in his/her mind for highest priority may be totally psychological in that the person simply will not spend more than a self-imposed ceiling price on each of the remaining goods and services—no matter the priority. To prove this point, just ask yourself how many items you decided not to purchase in the last week simply because the price of the item or service was outside your psychological barrier of the ceiling price. In other words, it became unaffordable not because it necessarily took too much of your income, but rather because the price exceeded the value of satisfaction you felt you would receive in return for the expense of the good or service. These two conditions illustrate the boundaries in definition of demand—the ability to pay, and willingness to pay.

The Concept of Supply

Supply is generally defined by economists as a schedule or line which represents the quantity of a good that a producer (or alternatively called, a supplier) is both willing and able to sell at various given prices. The behavior of a supplier is stated via the law of supply. That law simply states that generally, for most goods and services, a supplier will sell more of each good or service as the price increases. The opposite of the postulate of the law of supply is generally true as well—a producer will sell a higher quantity of a good or service as the price increases. The law of supply accurately portrays the natural behavior of a producer—that is to sell his/her goods or services at the highest possible price in order to make the highest profit possible. This "law of supply" is true for two reasons. The first, which is strictly economic, is that people can simply afford to produce a larger quantity of a good or service because the increased revenue allows them to incur the greater costs of producing a higher quantity of goods and services as the prices for those goods and services increase. The law of supply is true for a psychological reason as well. The greater the price a supplier can charge for his/her good or service, and the greater unit profit a supplier can make for each item produced, the greater the psychological incentive for a supplier to produce a greater quantity of the good or service. The law of supply and its economic and psychological incentives are true not just for the business owner, but everyone in our economy who is gainfully employed. Every one of us desires to work for an employer who will pay us the most for our talents. Generally speaking, we will work under extremely unpleasant conditions for a short period of time as long as we believe there is a reward for greater income through a promotion, job series change, or geographic move. Also, we generally understand that as we achieve better education, training, and experience, we greatly enhance our opportunities to make more income from virtually every company or organization that might need our services. Thus, we ensure that our resumes reflect our complete education and training levels achieved as well as the details and content of our work experience. So, when we seek employment, we may be employees rather than a business owner, but we behave (act) exactly as a supplier. The major reason, as workers, that we act like suppliers where we will produce a greater quantity for greater income is the fact that we have household expenses. As we get older, we initiate life changes that increase our expenses (otherwise known as costs). We get married, we have children, which in turn increases the size of the home we need, the amount of the three necessities we must buy, and to meet the human desire to increase our standard of living the longer we live. As employees, we may not see a promotion as providing a greater quantity of our talents, but employers do because each promotion involves adding more and usually broader responsibilities than you had previously. I won't belabor this point, but the critical thing you need to understand is that however much time each week that you spend at your job, you are a supplier, not a consumer. This is a fact that many employees fail to understand and remember.

The Concept of Exchange

Remember that every economic system must provide for the exchange of goods and services. The Capitalist economic system provides for the exchange of goods and services through bringing suppliers of each good and service and those who demand those same, exact goods and services into this place called "the market." In Capitalism, the market is designed for the negotiation of price for each good and service to be conducted by suppliers and consumers. In the market, the supplier must try to negotiate the buyer to as high a price as possible to make maximize his/her profit while the buyer must negotiate the price as low as possible to fit the expenditure into their budget. If the supplier and consumer cannot agree on price, no exchange of the good or service takes place. The supplier must then seek other people to purchase his/her good or service, and the consumer must seek another supplier in order to successfully negotiate a price for which the new/alternative seller will exchange the good or service. The negotiation between seller and consumer, in the United States is generally silent because the consumer is given a take it or leave it price on a store shelf, via a catalog, or over the internet. If the buyer accepts the price and pays for the good or service, exchange takes place. If the buyer does not accept the price, exchange does not take place. In Capitalism, the consumer has the upper hand as long as he/she is willing to leave the market place when the lowest price offered by the seller is still too high for the consumer to willing and/or able to pay to take the item or obtain the service being sold by that particular seller.

But, just because the buyer has the upper hand does not mean that the buyer can be unreasonable. Consumers cannot have unrealistic expectations of how low the price for a good or service should be if their expected or affordable price for the good or service is so unreasonably low as to cause the seller to incur a loss rather than a profit on the sale. The term, "The consumer is always right," is abundantly untrue in Capitalism, because a consumer who insists on a price that forces a seller to take a loss is simply unreasonable. And, the exchange should not take place because the Capitalist economic system cannot long operate where a large number of exchanges between sellers and consumers result in losses to the sellers. Unfortunately, the negotiation activities between the seller and consumer in the market are fraught with opportunities for dishonesty and fraud both for sellers and consumers. Here, every day in the United States, we see items in news sources, consumer trade magazines, and government advisories where sellers have deliberately defrauded consumers or where consumers have stung sellers. This condition is NOT a characteristic or failing of the Capitalist economic system. Rather it is a failing of the morality of the humans dealing in the market exchange process. For the fraud or dishonesty in the exchange or the good or service is not driven by the process, but rather by the moral/ethical fiber of the individuals concerned.

Additionally, the negotiation process provides a great deal of opportunity for simple miscommunication. Most often the miscommunication involves the quality of the product or service, the schedule of delivery of a product or the schedule of completion of a service, or oftentimes, the warranty of the product or service. In these instances, an exchange takes place, but if the consumer is disappointed in the future, he/she has little leverage to get the seller to provide full satisfaction from the exchange. Nor, usually can a producer be fully compensated if a consumer, through no fault of his/her own cannot ultimately pay the negotiated price for the item purchased or the service rendered. Consumers often purchase items under a credit agreement with every intention of making the payments. But in today's society, the economic plight of millions of individuals changes for the worse each year. People lose their jobs or keep a job only through a demotion. The family situation changes through divorce and the split households keep both adults, even if both are working, from meeting all their joint financial obligations when they were married. And, of course key breadwinners in a household can become ill, disabled, or die leaving the remaining family members unable to live the same standard of living before the death of the family member. No consumer can foresee and mitigate all the financial hazards that can befall them, and so these unforeseen financial calamities usually effect both the consumer and some past sellers.

The point here is simply that exchange in the market place is full of risk both to the consumer and seller. Consumers are going to have many times in their lives where they spend money for goods or services and simply will not receive the quality that they anticipated for the price they paid. Sellers, also are going to have instances in their business operations where consumers will not meet their contract obligations (usually financial) negotiated in good faith with the consumer in the market place for a specific good or service. But in no instance, is the Capitalistic economic system at fault.   Where fraud occurs in the transaction the failure is simply human nature. Where unforeseen events occur negating the full completion of a market negotiation transaction, the human condition of physical or emotional human frailty, or simple inability to mitigate all contingencies come into play. Later on, we will discuss what the role of government might be as a hedge against all these risks inherent in the market place and the transactions conducted therein between buyers and sellers.

CHAPTER SIX
The Price System--United States Model

The operation of every economic system requires a structure to make it work. The structure of the economic system is generally dictated by the type of economic model selected by the country to allocate the scarce resources to meet the total human needs and wants of the society the economic system serves. There are five fundamental questions that each economic system's structure must answer. They are:

- *How does the economic system provide for the decisions of what will be produced?*

- *How does the economic system provide for the decisions of who will get the output?*

- *How does the economic system provide for the decisions of resource usage levels?*

- *How does the economic system provide for the decisions of how items will be produced?*

- *How will the economic system provide for modification required by external changes in order to keep the economic system viable and robust in operation?*

The Functions of the Price System

For the United States Capitalist Economic System, the structure that answers these five fundamental questions is call the "price system." In essence the price system relates all five of the economic questions to dollar costs and/or prices through which individual and collective human decisions are made. These dollar translations of the economic behavior of people to answer the five fundamental questions are as follows:

- *The dollar votes of consumers tell what will be produced.*
- *The income of consumers tells who will get the output.*
- *The costs of resources determine the resource usage levels.*

- *The profits/losses of businesses tell how items will be produced.*
- *Relative product prices and resource costs will reflect the changes in the economic system required to retain its viability and keep it robust.*

Now that we know how the U. S. Price System structure translates human decisions to economic outcomes, let's delve a bit deeper into how this structure applies to the various major sectors of the U. S. Economic System. A sector within an economic system is a large conglomeration of human organizations that have relatively common goals and behavioral traits and attitudes. In the United States, we have three major sectors of the U. S. Economy—Households, Businesses, and Governments. Households, and businesses are composed of individuals who will react to economic stimuli in similar fashion given similar or identical circumstances. Governments are composed of individuals who are supposed to react to economic stimuli not in their normal personal mode of self-interest, but rather react to economic stimuli by considering the benefits to society as a whole. Let us first consider the Household sector of the U. S. Economy.

The Household Sector—Income

The Household sector owns all the resources in the economy. Households sell these resources to generate income which they use to purchase goods and services. It is this income that enables households to dictate which goods and services will be produced by the economy by what they buy and conversely by what they do not buy. Those four resources are land, labor, capital, and entrepreneurs.

The owners of land (whether land space or raw materials) receive income in the form of rent. Rent is meant to denote the short-term nature of the ownership of land and the household's capability to receive income for it. Short term ownership of land is derived from the fact that an individual's or a family's ownership of the land is anticipated to be for a period of time far less than the life of the existence of the land space or the raw materials. Indeed, we may purchase land space and its raw materials contained therein, and the modern deed to the land indicates that we own it in perpetuity. However, the ownership of land by an individual is only good for as long as those individual lives. We can pass the deed to our heirs, but those heirs may decide to leave the land at some future generation. Indeed, an individual can sell land at any time in the future and, in the process, lose the rental income inherent thereof. Finally, in the history of mankind, no land has been inhabited by the same families and their heirs for more than a number of centuries. The native Americans that owned and inhabited the entire continental United States at the beginning of European habitation in 1492, now own only a small portion of that land, as mostly European immigrants pushed further and further west through the 19th Century. In any event, the term, "rent" as the type of income for land would seem to correctly define the non-permanence of the income for land.

The household own the most familiar resource which is labor. Each household usually has at least one "breadwinner"—an individual designated to earn sufficient income through employment of their labors meet the needs of all the people within the entire household. These days in the U. S., many households have two working adults or two working people in order to earn sufficient income to provide for the total needs of the household. Individuals sell their time and their skills to an employer to produce a set of outputs designated by the employer for which the employer provides an hourly or salaried stipend known simply as wages. To an economist, there is no distinction between white-collar and blue-collar workers, or managers versus production line laborers. All are simply called labor and all collect wages because each is doing the same thing—trading their time and their skills for wage income.

Capital is the "means of production," or more precisely, the buildings, machines, and equipment which people use in the production of goods and services. Capital is absolutely NOT the finances or financial instruments used by businesses to purchase capital goods. Businesses purchase these buildings, machines, and equipment usually by borrowing money to pay for them over time. The money borrowed is not free, the lender(s) of that money must be paid interest in order to convince those money-owners (otherwise known as investors) to loan their funds to that business for the output purpose of that business. The interest paid by the business must be sufficiently high to keep the prospective investors from spending their money at a place and purpose other than that desired by the business seeking their funds. The investors are households in that they provide the dollar finances through bank checking and saving deposits translated to loans, or directly purchase stocks or bonds that become the financial instruments used to transfer the money from the households to the businesses needing the capital goods. The interest paid on the loans, dividends paid on stocks, and interest paid on bonds are the income that passes to the households for the use of their money by the business who purchased the capital goods. The final resource used in a business operation is also a person known as the entrepreneur. An entrepreneur is a special person who owns and operates a business. This special person is a business owner who takes all the risks of financial losses or profits of the business. The profits of the business must be sufficient to keep the entrepreneur from going to another income alternative such as an employee of a different business, or a different enterprise as an entrepreneur. Losses of the business must not be sufficient to drive the entrepreneur from his business either through bankruptcy or psychological frustrations of failure. There are millions of entrepreneurs in the United States Economy. Many are owners of small businesses such as family farms, corner retail stores, and single product line skilled tradesmen. A few entrepreneurs grew from small businesses to giant corporations. The U. S. has a great history of such people from men such as Henry Ford who invented the mass production of automobiles, to Steve Jobs who created the personal computer and various models of the "smart phone", to Bill Gates the founder of Microsoft computer software. Although these men are the most famous of successful entrepreneurs, the truth is that there are millions of successful small business entrepreneurs who provide a vast array of goods and services not just to the American public, but to the world.

The Household Sector—Expenditures

The members of households spend their income on three things—consumption, taxes, and saving (or dissaving). Taxes are mandatory expenditures directed on households to pay to various levels of government. Taxes are come in many types, structures, and purposes. We will deal with tax structures and systems in Chapter 12. But for our purposes now, we merely need to understand that households have little to no influence on the amount of taxes that they pay each year. Nor can they escape all taxes by making major changes in their lifestyles. Virtually every living American will pay taxes during his/her life. And, every dollar of income spent on taxes is money that cannot be spent on a need or want of any member of the household.

Saving in a household can be either deliberate or accidental. Deliberate saving occurs when one or more individual in the household decides to place a certain amount of money into savings on a periodic basis. People who place a specific amount of money into individual retirement accounts or a workplace retirement saving plan have a deliberate saving plan. Some people may place a certain percentage of all income brought into the household into a saving account on the day that the income arrives in the household. Or, some people may place a certain amount of money per month into a saving account targeted for a future event such as a vacation, purchase of a home, or payment for college. These deliberate savings require discipline and determination to ensure that the payments are scheduled, defined in amount, and then accomplished faithfully. Accidental saving is saving that is neither preplanned, nor scheduled for accomplishment. It usually occurs because an unexpected, higher amount of income arrives and some part of it can easily be set aside with no pain of reducing the planned purchase of goods or services. Or, on rare occasions, a planned expenditure may not occur and some part of the unspent funds can painlessly be placed in a saving account. Deliberate saving, if maintained for a long period of time—say the entirety of your adult working years, will be painful sometimes, because you will have to forego purchase of a good or service for which the household seems to have a great need or greatly desired want. But, true deliberate saving is as sacrosanct as taxes. That is, the failure to save is as painful as the repercussions of failure to pay your taxes. Accidental saving is never planned, or painful and so is decidedly not a mandatory expenditure.

Households purchase goods and services each month. This act of purchasing goods and services is called "consumption." The wherewithal to purchase these goods and services usually comes from the income they earn. However, that is not always the case. Today, with the widespread availability of credit cards, people can purchase goods and services beyond their income. In fact, a household can purchase beyond their income up to the total dollars of the combined credit limits of their credit cards. The total dollars of the combined credit limits of their credit cards becomes an additional income source—so long as they do not reach the credit limits in their purchases, or fail to pay the minimum balances on the credit cards and have them cancelled by the company who issued the card(s). It is fun to purchase goods and services with credit cards, but, just like taxes, the future monthly payments (which usually include healthy additional interest charges) become a mandatory expense that reduces your income available for necessities. The ease of immediate credit card income access for purchases can quickly turn into tenacious long term financial burdens.

At the beginning of any household accounting cycle such as a month, 3 months (a quarter), or a year, economists can predict the amount of income a household should have to purchase goods and services. This income is calculated by determining to expected income to be earned from the four resources (land, labor, capital, entrepreneur) and subtracting the expected expenses for taxes and deliberate saving. This income is defined by economists as disposable income and relates to the amount of income that is in the discretion of the members of the household to determine the goods and services they wish to buy for that period. At the end of the accounting cycle, economists can calculate the dollar amount of saving or dissaving a household has accumulated by simply subtracting total purchases of goods and services from income earned from the four resources (land, labor, capital, entrepreneur) and excluding temporary income generated from debt instruments such as short-term loans and credit cards (but still including the goods and services purchased via those short-term loans and credit cards). Where the income earned exceeds the purchases made by the household for that period, the household has incurred a net saving. Where the income earned is less than the purchases made by the household for that period, the household has incurred dissaving.

The Business Sector Model of Operations

Whereas the first two fundamental economic questions are addressed solely by the households by their roles as consumers, the second two fundamental economic questions are addressed solely by businesses. The business sector has a singular model of activity or operations that applies to every business in the U. S. Economy no matter how large or how small. That model is as follows:

Resources → *Processes* → *Outputs (Goods or Services)*

At every business enterprise, the business obtains resources that are combined together through processes to make outputs in the form of goods or services. The business purchases the best quality resources possible within the budgeted cost of the company, combines those resources into the lowest cost processes possible given their level of technological prowess to produce the highest quality, lowest priced goods and services they can in order to make their products and services as competitive as possible in the market for sale to consumers. The combination of the costs of the resources and production processes matched against the price received for the output determines the profits or losses of the firm. The firm can cut production costs by either obtaining lower cost resources or establishing processes that combine the resources more efficiently (and thus, lower their costs). The firm may also be able to improve their quality as they lower costs when they change their production processes as well. Firms that have an environment of better matching resources to need and continuously improving production processes are the most successful at making higher profits than their competitors and retaining or increasing their sales year after year. Businesses that fail to improve resource matching to production needs and increase efficiency/productivity as well as product or service quality through process improvement will see their sales and profits diminish over time to the point that they will no longer be competitive enough to survive. In short businesses that fail to change with the times both technologically and qualitatively will simply go out of business to the joy of their competitors who will gain that company's former sales base.

The United States is littered with entire industries where the U. S. dominated the world's production, which either no longer exist in the U. S. or have greatly dwindled in size and breadth of production.

The Business Sector—Expenses

Business secures and purchases resources in order to put them together in a specific mix to produce a good or service. In virtually all instances today, this mix of resources, called process, involves the interaction of labor with capital resources to produce a good or service. And, of course the production process occurs on some land space, or under or over land space (in mines, under water, or in the air). Finally, these production activities result from an idea of purpose established by an entrepreneur. The entrepreneur may be directly involved in the daily production activity such as a farmer or corner grocer, may be a chief executive officer or chairman of the board of a corporation like Bill Gates.

All of these resources procured by a business entity to accomplish production result in expenses (or costs) to the business enterprise. These costs, when accumulated in total are matched against the total revenue received by the company. Where the total revenue matches or exceeds the total costs of producing the good or service by the company, the company will remain in business because they receive profits which encourage them to continue to produce. Where accompany faces a condition of continued excess of costs over revenues for the good or service produced (losses), the company will quit production either voluntarily or through force by the households who own the resources they are no longer paid their worth for their resources. The total revenue collected by the business enterprise is calculated by multiplying the total quantity of the good or service sold to consumers by the unit price paid by consumers. The total expenses incurred by the business is calculated by multiplying the total quantity of each resource by the total cost of each resource and summing the total cost of each resource. The total revenue is matched against total cost to determine whether a profit or loss has been incurred by the business enterprise. The business calculates profits and losses on a monthly, quarterly, and annual basis.

A company who produces at a loss must either reduce total costs or increase total revenue in order to remain in business. To reduce costs a business must reduce the quality or quantity of their resources. Reducing the quality of the resources generally decreases the unit cost of the resource which translates into lower total costs of production. Decreasing the quantity of the resources used results in lower total costs of production because fewer resources are used. Usually, decreasing the quality of resources results in a decrease in the quality of the product or service provided for sale to the public. Oftentimes the public rejects the lower quality, especially if the price is not reduced because they can get a higher quality product for the same or slightly higher price. The best way to reduce costs is to change the production process in such a manner that it lowers cost while at the same time retaining, if not increasing the quality of the good or service.

Virtually all production results from a human interacting with a machine. A company can train its people how to use the machine more efficiently to get more quantity per hour of labor expended. For example, suppose a company brought a new software system in for all its workers to use, but did not train the workers on how to use the new software. The workers will struggle at least for weeks to learn how to use the new software and while they are learning, their output quantity and quality will deteriorate. Why, because every time the individual has to learn something new about the new software, output suffers from the time it takes for the individual to determine how to use the software for the particular application. Additionally, people won't immediately become proficient on the software once they begin to use it. They will make more errors and thus, the quality of their output will diminish. The other alternative that a business might employ to increase productivity or efficiency is to replace outdated technological equipment with new technology equipment. As an example, when I first came into the business world after graduation from college in 1969, the modern equipment I used to calculate costs and revenues was a tape-printing calculator. I used this equipment for my first 15 years of adult employment. But in 1984, my business organization purchased a personal computer for me to use. Along with that computer came a wondrously new technology called spreadsheet software. My productivity increased by several hundred percent because I could calculate current costs and revenues by changing the quantity and unit costs/prices of the resources and units of output sold while the spreadsheet completed the entire set of calculations against all the resources and outputs in a blink of an eye. Additionally, I could model

73

future scenarios of budgets and costs by merely changing input and output quantities and letting the software do all the calculations—again, at the speed of the blink of an eye. For me and those in my profession it was like going from the stone ages to Nirvana in a matter of weeks. I also bought my own personal computer in 1984 with spreadsheet and word processing software so that I could learn to use the software more quickly and apply its use to household needs. Since 1984, computer technology has improved in terms of speed of calculation and breadth of applications, but the basic major jump in productivity for me happened in 1984 where I no longer had to hand-crank hundreds of numerical calculations of addition, subtraction, multiplication and division each day—all with a significant reduction in calculation errors at the same time.

Companies that fail to reduce costs and enhance the quality of their output on a continuous basis will become non-competitive at a fairly fast pace and will be forced to catch or surpass the prices and quality of output of competitors or go out of business. It is profits that reward a company for its increased efficiency and higher quality output and losses that encourage a company to accomplish increased efficiency and higher quality output or cease to exist.

The Business Sector—Revenue

Success in sales and a resultant high level of total revenue in the business world depends on three things. First, the product or service must be deemed of high value to the people who consume the product. Additionally, the larger number of people who desire that specific good and service provides a greater opportunity for sales and revenue. Second, the product or service of your particular firm must be deemed reasonable and fair for the quality provided by the individuals who seek to purchase the particular good or service you sell. But, you must realize that most of the potential buyers of your product or service will look to other companies who produce and sell similar or identical products. So, you cannot price your product in a vacuum. Rather you must be aware of the prices charged by your competitors. Third, your product must be of high quality and perceived to have at least as high a quality as that of your competitors. Today, quality may not be as high a priority for sellers on their initial purchase of an item of the type they have never purchased before. But, if they purchase and item or service that is of lower quality or particularly significant lower quality than anticipated and desired, quality will definitely be a major determinant of their future purchases of the same or like item or service. I postulate that Americans, more than any other consumers throughout the world, are the most quality-conscious in the world. And when Americans purchase goods and services, the quickest way for a business to get a bad reputation nationally, is to produce goods or services that disappoint a large number of consumers.

The long-term viability of a company depends on providing a family of products or services that satisfy the needs and wants of a large segment of the U. S. consumers, not just for the present, but in the future as well. Thus, any company that wishes to be successful for decades into the future must be willing and able to develop new products or services that will meet the needs and wants of the future generations of Americans. I get very amused at advertisements that declare a product "new" AND "improved." If ever there was an oxymoron, this is it. A product that is truly new—meaning having some characteristics completely unique to that product for the first time in the history of mankind, cannot possibly be improved at the same time. For the concept "improved" denotes that the product or service has a history of customers and use against which the product has recently been modified for an enhancement in its quality or use.

Business Structure in the United States

Business enterprise is defined in three separate structures for production of goods/services. We'll start at the most robust level of organization for production, called an industry. An industry is composed of several companies that produce like, or similar products or services. Within our definition, I will restrict the companies that compose an industry to those that are chartered within the USA. So, the auto industry would be composed of General Motors, Ford, and Chrysler and would exclude Toyota, Kia, and Hyundai even though those companies have factories in the United States. The telecommunications hardware industry would include Apple even though their I Phones are mostly produced in China and Motorola where most of their products are manufactured in Brazil and China, but exclude Samsung, LG, and Sony. The inclusion of companies considered within an industry often depend on the definition of the industry. For example, the auto industry could include not just the original equipment manufacturers of autos, but also the after-market auto parts makers and distributors. Or, the computer industry could limit only the computer hardware manufacturers, or include software and ancillary computer interface equipment. So, it is important when talking about an industry that we specifically define the industry and then accurately assign the companies within the industry that we have defined. The next lowest level of business enterprise structures of production is the firm. It would seem on the surface that it is easy to define, determine, and name a firm. After all, it should be obvious that a firm is the owner of the logo and company name. However, that is not always the case. Oftentimes today, a named company may, in fact be owned by a corporation with a different name. At one time in recent history, for example, Chrysler was owned by Daimler-Benz of Germany. And, major business parts of Motorola have gone through several buyouts and resales by other corporations including Nokia and Google in the last eight or so years. Boeing Aircraft Corporation has absorbed many other aircraft industry giants over the last twenty or so years--McDonnell and Douglas aircraft manufacturing companies being two. Within the United States, mergers and consolidations of companies, including many large corporations has been a trend for the last thirty years or so. These consolidations have generated several mega-corporations that provide opportunities for monopolistic behavior of restricted output and/or higher prices because of limited, if not non-existent competition. This situation will be addressed in Chapter 7 in a summary fashion.

The major determining factor of this level of business enterprise structure is who is the senior decision-making individual or board members on behalf of that company's name. For example, suppose a company has a president and a staff of vice presidents whose singular responsibility and sole authority rests in making the day-to-day operating decisions of the company. Yet all policy and strategic decisions of the company are made by a higher organizational structure, although of a different company name. In this case, the lower business enterprise, even though it retains the logo name of the company, is not the true business enterprise structure. Rather, the business enterprise making the strategic and policy decisions on behalf of the lower company is the true firm.

The lowest level of business enterprise structures of production is a plant. This is a physical entity where the good is manufactured, or a service center where people answer telephones or emails to provide a service. A plant may have a familiar subservient name to a company logo, such as a Ford Escape final assembly plant. And these plants may, in fact, be located on foreign soil. We have already stated examples of American logo named products that are produced on foreign soil. The key thing to remember here is that a plant is at a fixed location to produce specific goods and or services on behalf of the second level business enterprise structure.

Legal Forms of Business Enterprise in the United States

The legal forms of business enterprise describe the type and complexity of a business entity that has a government-endorsed and approved capability to conduct business within the legal limitations described by that legal form of business conduct approved.

The first legal form of business enterprise, which is also the simplest is called a sole proprietorship. The characteristics of this kind of business enterprise are that the business is owned by a single individual and usually has a small number of employees. Additionally, the liabilities faced by sole proprietorship oftentimes exceed the limits of the business enterprise itself. Indeed, the liabilities of a sole proprietorship can extend to the entire personal and family assets owned by the owner and his/her family members. Usually, these sole proprietors are granted permission to do business (meaning provide their goods or services for sale to the general public) through licensing by a local government entity such as a city or county. You see these businesses everywhere in the USA. They are usually easily identified because the business name often embellishes the family name. There are millions of sole proprietorships in the USA. From the so-called corner grocer, local restaurant owner, local plumber or electrician, and hair stylist shop to the family farm, we all come across and use a sole proprietorship to satisfy a need or want virtually every day of our lives. Sole proprietorships may not only be licensed by a local government, but also chartered by the state, usually through a limited liability corporate (LLC) charter. The LLC has become a popular, and often necessary aspect of conducting business as a sole proprietor in order to protect personal and family assets from liabilities that result from their business activities.

The second legal form of business enterprise is called the partnership. A partnership is composed a group of individuals who provide a like or similar good or service to the public. Partnerships are usually formed in order to provide a broader range of the like or similar good or service. Additionally, partnerships are also formed in order to spread the high overhead costs of administration and facilities among a significant larger number of customers. Partnerships face the same liability issues as sole proprietors in that liabilities incurred by the business can be expanded to the personal assets of all the partners in the business. As with the sole proprietor, this business liability exposure to personal assets can be mostly solved by acquiring a LLC from the state. Partnerships tend to be established in the "professions" with medical doctors, lawyers, and accountants being the majority of today's partnership businesses. As with sole proprietorships, partnerships usually have to get licenses from a city or county government in order to conduct business.

The third legal form of business enterprise is called a corporation. A corporation is a business entity that is created to provide specific products or services to the public. Corporate charters to conduct commercial business operations are granted by a state, usually through the Department of State organization. The corporation also has a specific, singular, unique name that must be used as reference in all business operating activities. Furthermore, the business cannot adjust its business operations to expand the type of products or services to the public without seeking and being granted a change in its corporate charter from the state. And finally, perhaps the most beneficial aspect of a corporate charter versus a sole proprietorship or a partnership is that the corporation is treated as an individual entity—just as if it were a person in the room. Thus, those who have ownership of the corporation and those who work for the corporation are usually not deemed as legally responsible for any adverse results that occur from actions or decisions taken or made by corporate officers. Even when adverse results are due to illegal activity conducted by corporate officers, employees, or owners, it is very difficult to bring criminal charges against them because, legally, it is the "corporate entity" that drove the results. This situation, where people who work for the corporation take the stance that all decisions they make are for the good of the corporation, rather than through due consideration to the resultant effects to the corporation's customers has resulted in many harmful effects to the American populace. U. S. history is replete with products causing harm to large number of Americans and few, if any, criminal charges being brought against the corporation's workers and/or officers who knowingly allowed those harmful results to occur because they made their decisions to perceived benefit of the corporation. Usually, corporations are fined or directed through a court order to make financial restitution to any damages they cause consumers. But, their officers rarely face any criminal charges even though people are killed or handicapped for life because of their callous decisions. This, too will be addressed in summary fashion in Chapter 13.

The Public Sector (Governments)—Revenue

As we saw in the Circular Flow Model, governments at all levels in the USA influence the U. S. Economic System at all four entry points—households, businesses, the product market, and the resource market. Governments justify this influence either as a way to affect the behavior of people or corporate entities, or as a way to defray the negative impacts resulting from the perceived structural economic activity of Capitalism. The various levels of government use tax systems, categorical programs of expenditure, fiscal policy, and regulation to influence the behavior of people towards "acceptable" and more "predictable" behavior and to alleviate the negative economic impacts to individuals due to perceived structural deficiencies of the Capitalist economic system.

There are 5 revenue sources for the three major levels of governments in the USA. The highest level of government, the federal government, receives its revenue from three types of tax sources. The personal and corporate income taxes bring the greatest percentage of revenue to the federal government. Social Security and Medicare taxes (called payroll taxes) are paid a percentage of wage and salary earners pay with and equal contribution by the employer. The final federal government's revenue comes from indirect business taxes (mostly excise taxes). The federal government attempts to affect household and business human behavior in the income tax system by providing favorable or unfavorable tax treatment to thousands of specific individual or business actions. For example, the federal government encourages people to purchase homes by making home loan interest and home property tax deductible from their income each year. On the other hand, the federal government discourages ordinary personal saving because it charges income tax on the interest earned. The current federal income tax rate discourages businesses from even conducting business operations in the United States because we (the USA) have among the highest, if not the highest corporate income tax rate in the world. Conservatives, especially, believe this is a major reason that many U. S. corporations are shifting vast amounts of production offshore to other countries. The 15.3% tax rate Americans pay on their wages earned into Social Security and Medicare is a major reason that we see such a low saving rate in the U. S. as compared to many of the modern western economies. And, even though most excise taxes are levied to discourage behaviors that cause a large cost to society, they seem no to be effective. For example, the federal excise taxes on tobacco and liquor seem not to deter their use. Additionally, the excise taxes placed on businesses to discourage various types of pollution have not had the desired decrease in pollution as well. The point here is that federal tax policies implemented to affect behavior of household and business have often been ineffective, and in many instances have had major deleterious economic consequences.

For state and local governments, their revenue sources are significantly different from the federal government. Each state usually has a combination of revenues from several of the following sources. The first revenue source for state and local governments come from fees and licenses. Payroll taxes, mostly in the form of state and local government employee retirement contributions bring the states a large source of revenue. Many states have sales taxes, property taxes, and/or income taxes. State and local taxes and fees seem to affect household and business behavior more in terms of making a state a place of business enterprise, accepting or rejecting a job, or deciding for or against retiring in a particular state. Once in the state, as long as the original state or local tax and fee factors that brought the households or businesses to the state do not change, people seem to be relatively benign to a desire to change their state of business production or residence.

In conclusion, there is no doubt that the current federal tax structure has had major effects on the economic behavior of households and business. In many instances, the major economic effects seem to have been much more negatively than positively consequential to the overall U. S. economic performance. The state tax and fee revenue systems certainly have an impact on the decisions of businesses and households to take residence in a state. However, unless significant revenue factors change in a state once the residence decision is made, most businesses and households seem not to be influenced significantly enough for them to voluntarily change a state of residence.

The Public Sector (Governments)—Expenditures

Federal Government revenues and expenditures will be addressed in detail in Chapters 11 and 12 of this book, so I will not address them here.

I know of only two states who do not have a balanced budget clause in their constitutions that prevents the state government from spending more than it takes in revenue each year. There are a few states who can issue bonds for structural (real property) construction. However, all states must keep their annual expenses within their annual collected revenues. So, budget deficits, if they arise have to be dealt with swiftly by the governor and legislature. States expenditures tend to be by far the highest for public education which includes as much as roughly two-thirds of all K-12 public schools in the states, and significant support to state colleges and universities. The next highest expense usually goes to retired state employees with the largest group of them being teachers. State roads and highways are probably the third largest expense of the states each year. Finally, all states have a public welfare system that adds to the federal welfare subsidies that come into the states. But the bottom line for states is simple from a financial perspective. Each year, the state legislators and governors must abide by a balanced budget law based from each state's constitution.

CHAPTER SEVEN
The Role of Government

As we saw in Chapter 6, the three levels of government, particularly the federal government have major influences in the behavior of households and businesses. Before we discuss the full array of government roles in the U. S. Economy, we will first address the role of government in a capitalist economy as prescribed by Adam Smith.

The Role of Government Envisioned by Adam Smith

Adam Smith stated the first role of government as follows: "The First Duty of the Sovereign, that of protecting the society from the violence and invasion of other independent societies, can be performed only by means of a military force." The statement in and of itself is pretty self-explanatory. Simply put, the first role of government is to establish a military force, presumed sufficient to protect our society—in this case, the United States of America. The protection of our society includes not just its population, but its natural resources and infrastructure by which we provide the goods and services which will preserve our standard of living and our culture.

Adam Smith declares the second role of government to be: "that of protecting as far as possible, every member of the society from the injustice or oppression of every other member of it, or the duty of establishing an exact administration of justice…" Here, Adam Smith included the necessity for government to promote justice from one person to another. But, he also included the need for government to ensure the establishment and enforcement of the economic liberties of individuals and the protection of the capitalist free market. Furthermore, he committed government to assure that contracts between individuals, between individuals and an organization, and contracts between organizations were enforced to assure order and certainty in the economic system and its processes. Finally, he included the government's role to assure that competition in the marketplace was maintained because as previously noted, competition to Adam Smith was the major force that kept economic civility and personal and organizational integrity integral within capitalistic markets.

Adam Smith identified the third role of government as follows: "The third and last duty of the sovereign or commonwealth is that of erecting and maintaining those public institutions and those public works, which, though they may be in the highest degree advantageous to a great society, are, however, of such a nature, that the profit could never repay the expence to any individual or small number of individuals, and which it therefore cannot be expected that any individual or small number of individuals should erect or maintain. Adam Smith further defines this third role into only two specific areas when he states, "After the public institutions and public works necessary for the defence of the society, and for the administration of justice, both of which have already been mentioned, the other works and institutions of this kind are chiefly those for facilitating the commerce of the society, and those for promoting the instruction of people." The point that Adam Smith makes in this proposition is that there are goods and services with a cost so high that an individual or small group of individuals simply cannot afford to accomplish within the meager means of their own individual or small collective incomes. Thus, government needs to collect the revenue from a sufficiently large number of people to bring the high infrastructure cost down to a level affordable by all the people governed. Adam Smith greatly emphasized that these "public works" programs initiated and operated by governments had to be limited to the two purposes of promoting the commerce of economic activity and education. He condoned no other public expenses of government, save one—to preserve the dignity of the sovereign. Here, he meant that government should be considered as a body of organizations meant to provide the governmental programs and the institutions of government should protect the reputation and role of government, knowing that particular individuals holding government offices would sometimes disappoint the general populace in carrying out the duties inherent in the government office. Adam Smith did not want the government structure destroyed because of human frailty—as long as the purposes of the government office remained within his confines of the limited roles of government.

A Brief History of Federal Government Spending In the USA

We will take a quick romp of the expansion of government spending in the United States using the government operations and establishment of government programs as the benchmarks of how and for what purposes that expansion took place.

The truth of the matter is that government roles had already begun in the colonies long before the colonies declared their independence from King George of England or Adam Smith published the Wealth of Nations, both of which happened in 1776. Several cities had grown and were of sufficient size to need a government to establish justice and keep domestic order and to develop and provide for basic infrastructure necessities. Most of the thriving cities of the colonies had police and courts, city administrators and governing bodies, and public works such as water and sewer systems, perhaps port authorities, certainly wharves and docking facilities for ships, and roads with street names. Oftentimes these colonial cities had government halls where governing bodies would meet—particularly courts, and where city administrators would work. The functions of these city governments were limited to the functions stated by Adam Smith above. The defense of the colonies was provided to a large degree by England, with each colony having a loosely organized group of volunteers, minimally paid by any government (if at all) usually called the militia. One other organization, loosely tied to government in terms of formation and function was the postal system. The first vestiges of a postal system in the colonies appeared in 1673 when a postal route was established between New York and Boston. In 1683 William Penn established the first post office. The First Continental Congress established a postal service, with Benjamin Franklin appointed as the first Postmaster General.

When the 13 colonies declared their independence, the first and pretty much the singular major governmental operation they established was the Continental Army. Another major function was to establish and print a monetary currency known as the Continental Dollar. The Continental Army won our Revolutionary War. The Continental Dollar became next to worthless by the end of the Revolutionary War because

85

its purchasing power was no greater than one-fortieth of its original value when issued in 1776. The federal government of the United States was formed with the signing of the U. S. Constitution by the delegates from the 13 Colonies (known as the Constitutional Convention) on 17 September 1787. Upon the formal ratification of the 9th Colony/State on 21 June 1788, the United States became the central governing body of the 13 Colonies/States. The federal government relatively immediately established an army and navy, a central banking mechanism including the minting of federal coins and printing of federal currency, the equivalent of a federal postal service and federal state department, and the beginnings of a justice department to prosecute to uphold federal laws, and a federal judiciary to interpret the constitutionality of laws passed by any governmental institution. Except for times of war, where the extensive and expensive use of the army and navy was involved, the federal government focused on maintaining and sustaining these limited governmental operations. However, the federal government did play a role in the establishment of roadways, waterways, and railways during the 19th century as the United States population explored and gradually moved westward from the original 13 states to the Pacific Ocean states. Transportation was recognized as a major factor in the development and sustainment of commerce in the United States.

Beginning with the industrial revolution from the mid-1800s on, there became a significant centralization of wealth in the control of a few people and their dominant companies to the point that the federal government determined that they needed to play an oversight and regulatory role in what became the fairly obvious formulation of monopolies. The effects of these monopolies became fairly rampant restriction of quantity and quality of goods and services at unreasonably high prices. These few wealthy individuals did indeed provide great economic progress to the United States as a country, but at the same time they tended to direct and distort economic activity in directions that became noticeably disproportionate to favored industries, customers, and employees. The monopolistic behavior of these few giants of wealth were so powerful in their decision-making that they could often challenge and thwart the goals of western movement and progress desired by the federal government. The federal government, via the Congress passing anti-monopoly laws, and the federal attorneys prosecuting monopolistic behavior tried to enhance the competition held so necessary to the Capitalist economic system. The first major anti-monopoly legislation was passed in 1890 (called the Sherman Anti-trust Act) with another major anti-monopoly bill passed in 1914 (known as the Clayton Act). The federal government, during the entire 20th Century and the first two decades of the 21st Century have monitored, and have, on occasion threatened, or outright denied mergers and corporate pricing and production behaviors that have patterns of large price increases with little increases in either output or quality of product or service.

The American public, and particularly the framers of the U. S. Constitution wanted no part of a central bank controlled by the federal government. The experiences of national bank systems in Europe were abysmal in that the central controls greatly stifled individual personal choice and business initiative or rather systemically failed leaving both businesses and the public in the cold for conducting exchange of goods and services easily and quickly. During the time from its birth in 1787 until early in the 2nd decade of the 20th Century, the United States resisted the creation of a central bank run by the federal government. This all changed with the Federal Reserve Bill, signed into law on 23 December 2013. We will discuss the Federal Reserve as an institution more in the next chapter. However, for the topic of this chapter, the creation of the Federal Reserve is probably the first major institution of the U. S. federal government that may violate the general purposes of government intervention in the Capitalist economic system envisioned by Adam Smith. A centrally controlled banking system, which has, in the last 30 years or so, morphed into a centrally controlled financial system by the federal government is certainly not mentioned by Adam Smith as a function appropriate for government. We will discuss this topic much more thoroughly in the next two chapters.

The United States government gets severely out of line with Adam Smith's guidance on government involvement in the Capitalist economic system beginning in the early 1930s. The Stock Market crash in late October 1929 took just 4 working days to take virtually all dollars out of the U. S. Stock Exchange making most stocks in the United States literally worthless. Thus entered the Great Depression of the 1930's--a decade of dire economic performance. In 1933, the unemployment rate approached 25% of the workforce, prices decreased by 5.1% for the year, and the total output measured by the Gross Domestic Product in 1933 was half that of 1929. When Franklin Roosevelt took the office of President of the United States in 1933, he immediately flooded the Congress with several programs which together composed "The New Deal." The New Deal Programs made government mandated structural reforms to the U. S. Capitalist Economic System, created a number of work programs designed to put Americans back to work, established federal government grant programs meant to place money in the pockets of the poorest Americans, and created the Social Security System. President Roosevelt did not seem particularly concerned about how the federal government was going to pay for all these programs, although most of his economic and federal budget advisors were. However, in an open letter published on 31 December 1933 in the New York Times by a British Economist named John Maynard Keynes, President Roosevelt got a major economic policy boost. In this rather lengthy letter, in Paragraph 17, Keynes finally gets to his major policy recommendation. He states, "In the field of domestic policy, I put in the forefront, for the reasons given above, a large volume of Loan-expenditures under Government auspices. It is beyond my province to choose particular objects of expenditure. But preference should be given to those which can be made to mature quickly on a large scale, as for example the rehabilitation of the physical condition of the railroads. The object is to start the ball rolling. The United States is ready to roll towards prosperity, if a good hard shove can be given in the next six months...." Keynes suggested that the federal government should deliberately and decisively go into debt in order to increase employment, income of the general populace, and demand for goods and services. This deficit spending on the part of the federal government would increase the total output of the U. S. Economy in the form of Gross Domestic Product. From 1933 through 1941, the federal government implemented Keynes' suggested policy of deficit spending each year, greatly expanding the welfare programs and domestic infrastructure programs funded by and administered by the federal government.

On 7 December 1941, with the attack on Pearl Harbor, the need for welfare and domestic infrastructure programs disappeared because the entire country's economy became focused on the effort to support and win World War II. Of course, the war caused the annual federal budget deficit to soar for the years, 1942 through 1946. The federal government experienced surplus federal budgets for 6 years from 1947 through 1959. Welfare expenses by the federal government in 1947 were more than 5 times the welfare expenditures in 1945. The welfare expenses grew steadily each year from 1947 through 1964. In 1964 President Lyndon Johnson established his "War on Poverty" initiatives. His War on Poverty expanded existing welfare programs and created new welfare programs. The two most expensive and far-reaching laws were the Food Stamp Act signed into law on 31 August 1964. This law made permanent a pilot program to provide millions of low-income Americans "food stamps" which were the equivalent of cash for food purchases. The second law was the Social Security Act, signed into law on 30 July, 1965, which created the Medicare and Medicaid programs and provided a substantial one-time increase in Social Security benefits. Medicare was to be funded by a fixed annual tax levy on the wages of all people paying into Social Security and by a monthly premium paid by Americans age 65 and over who were registered for Medicare benefits, and Social Security was to be paid by the continuation of the annual tax levy on the wages of people. Medicaid was to be paid from general federal government revenues. Largely because of the implementation and sustained continuation and/or annual increases in the programs of the War on Poverty, the federal government had only one surplus budget year (1969) from 1960 through 1997. The federal government had a surplus budget for the years 1998 through 2001, and has had annual federal budget deficit each year (beginning in 2002) since. In summary, since the implementation of the New Deal in 1933, the federal government has had surplus budgets in only 11 years. We will talk more specifically about the expenditures on welfare and entitlement programs in Chapter 11.

However, at this time, I want to draw the reader's attention back to the topic of this chapter, the tenets proposed by Adam Smith that governments in general, including the federal government, should spend public funds for only limited government activities. None of the welfare or entitlement programs begun under the New Deal, nor the War on Poverty meet any of the criteria for expenditure of public funds stated by Adam Smith. In fact, the impact of John Maynard Keynes' proposal that there is economic justification for spending public funds on these types of programs created an entirely new and separate school of economic thought, greatly modifying the Adam Smith concept of Capitalist Economics. That school of thought is appropriately called "Keynesian Economics," and as you might guess has become the bedrock of economic policy thinking for the political and social liberals and progressives as well as the U. S. Democratic Party. Just as predictable, I suspect, are we conservative economists who believe that Keynesian Economics," has been grandly misinterpreted and mis-implemented in current federal government public policy by the democratic U. S presidents and congresses since 1933 insofar as government spending is concerned. Additionally, we conservative economists believe that Keynesian Economics, proposes public policies for government influence in a capitalist economy that is seriously flawed in theory, apart from being in conflict with Adam Smith in terms of appropriate government expenditures.

A Discussion of Federal Government Regulation in the USA

Adam Smith does not spend much time discussing the role of government in terms of directive regulation in his book. Certainly, his discussion of the necessity of government to provide public services, enhance and encourage commerce, provide for justice and the enforcement of contracts, and to ensure an economic system environment to ensure competition all necessitate laws and regulations to implement those government functions. However, the history of the United States, particularly in the 20th Century and our current Century have seen a major expansion of government regulation well beyond those necessary to achieve the basic foundations of government intervention in a capitalist economy as envisioned by Adam Smith. Rather than talk about specific regulations of which there are thousands in the United States, I will address a limited number of regulations by broad purpose. I will do this by addressing the regulations in the product and resource markets.

The Public Sector (Governments)--Regulation

The three levels of government, but particularly the federal government use regulation as a means to force households and business to behave in a particular fashion through legal mandates. These legal mandates provide government the direct control of outcomes, normally through processes. Thus, most government regulations are focused at the resource and product market processes. Government then anticipates that properly controlled processes through regulation will result in the desired outcomes in product output or resource utilization and income. Let us first address the resource market. The resource market is replete with laws and regulations which affect the hiring, firing, and promotion processes of human labor. Child labor is not permitted in the United States. "Sweat shops" which employ large numbers of people in cramped quarters with wide variations in temperature and ecological conditions are illegal. The Civil Rights Act of 1965 established a number of human characteristics that could no longer be a part of the consideration to hire and fire individuals. Generally, the federal government has passed laws making labor unions a preferred labor pool in a number of industries throughout the USA. Additionally, federal labor law dictates how an employer must deal with individual members of a labor union and a labor union itself. In short, the federal government has, for longer than a century, passed laws to govern how employers must deal with their employees or potential employees.

The federal government is at least as intrusive, if not more so in the product market. Here again, the federal government has passed many laws during the last century defining safety standards in production, insisting on safety equipment for workers, and preventing certain resources and products from being used in the production process. All these actions of involvement in the production process are meant to protect workers from hazards that could cause serious injury or death. Additionally, the federal government has passed many safety and environmental laws meant to protect consumers from faulty or products of inferior quality that could cause consumers serious injury or death. Also, the environmental laws are designed to help protect the general public from air, water, and soil pollution that could cause mass injuries or death. Finally, the federal government has developed an entire specialty of consumer and product market protection via antitrust laws. The goal of antitrust laws is to preserve competition in the market to preclude monopolies. Monopolies are particularly egregious in the product market because they have the ability to dictate the quantity and quality of output in order to drive prices up to consumers at unreasonable levels. In the next chapter we will briefly discuss how successful this area of regulation has been.

Households, to have restrictions on their behavior as well. For example, they have to represent their skills, education, and experience accurately when talking to a potential employer. Additionally, people must adhere to quality and quantity work standards at the workplace. Finally, and most importantly, people have the responsibility to tell the truth in their relationships with other employees, their employer, and any customers with whom they come in contact. Additionally, governments are greatly intrusive in the financial well-being of households. On the negative side, households pay a plethora of taxes to each of the three major levels of government (federal, state, and local). The tax burden to households with wage or salary income generally reaches 40% or more of the annual income of the household. If you don't believe it I encourage you to determine your effective income tax rates for your federal, and state and local income taxes (where applicable). The effective rate is determined by dividing your income tax liability for the year by the adjusted gross income (AGI) on your Form 1040 (and its derivatives) and the equivalent on your state and local income tax forms. Add to that rate the combined FICA taxes you and your employer pay (generally 15.3% of your salary or wages paid). Then add to that, your state and local sales tax rate, and your property tax (total property taxes paid divided by AGI. It does not take long to get to 40% of your income going to taxes. Another way that at least one level of government can affect your income is by the establishment of a minimum wage. Taxes definitely have a serious impact on the behavior and ability of people to purchase goods and services. Increasing taxes on anyone decreases their ability to purchase goods and services. When you decrease the ability of a significant number of households to purchase goods and services, those reductions result in decreased demand, and ultimately a decrease in GDP follows.

Minimum wages at the federal level have been around since at least the early 1960s. Additionally, Obamacare drove companies to pay for mandated medical insurance for all full time and some part-time employees. These two mandated income expenses oftentimes drive employers to reduce their total number of employees to keep total labor costs stable from year to year. In the process, the quality of the product may diminish, or greater inconveniences to the customer may arise. I remember the fast-food days of the late 1970s and early 1980s. When I walked into a fast-food joint, such as a McDonalds, there would be a half dozen registers at the counter, each of them with a person at the register. They would take your order, go to the food warmer directly behind them and take the already made burger and fry from the warmer, place it into a bag, get your drink (often previously made and in the cup during peak dining hours), and you would be out the door in a matter of a couple of minutes. And, your order would usually be correct. Today, during peak hours, you are lucky to see three registers fully attended, you usually stand several deep in line to get to an attended register, you place your order and you wait for a few minutes for it to be completed and handed to you. Also, frequently your order is either incomplete or incorrect in some fashion. Why has fast food changed so much in the last 30 to 40 years? Mostly because, fast food places face stiff competition from each other to keep their meal prices low. In order to keep meal prices low even in the advent of increased minimum wages or the added burden of Obamacare, the company can only afford to hire the number of employees that fit last year's total labor costs. If the labor costs double, as some currently propose for a new round of minimum wages, the fast-food companies must fire enough employees to meet last year's labor expenses. This means longer waits for food, and fewer orders done correctly because people are being forced to work at a faster pace to try to meet the workload with fewer people. The alternatives are two: increase prices for the food, or make the customer complete their own orders using a computer-like register. Now you make your orders and probably receive your orders with no human contact. Getting an order error corrected will take much more time and effort. At some point, people simply quit going to that fast food provider because the low price is simply not worth the customer's frustration, time, and inconvenience. At that point, the economic impact of the minimum wage or addition of Obamacare for that employee becomes totally moot—for that person/those people become unemployed and without the level of income they anticipated they would receive. The point here is simple. Public policies that deal in economic activity have economic consequences. Unfortunately, those consequences are often ignored as unsubstantiated or as pure theoretical poppycock. Yet, once consumers are driven away from the company and/or the product/service, for some reason, no one searches out past customers to ask why they quit buying the product/service from that particular company.

Regulations directly imposed on employers will almost always have a negative impact in that the imposition of those regulations will cause the company to spend more money to implement those regulations. The question that must be asked from a public policy standpoint is whether or not the social cost benefit to society is greater than the cost of implementation to the businesses who are forced to implement a particular regulation. Unfortunately, rarely are truly credible cost/benefit analyses performed to accurately and fully measure the costs of implementation against the anticipated benefits to be received. In reality, reasoned public policy proposals are virtually impossible to be defensibly computed in a financial sensing.

The debate of global warming is a perfect example of this. On the one hand, those who claim that global warming is a problem, predict no less than cataclysmic results of billions of people killed, an entire upheaval of the world's capability to produce food, severe flooding of significant parts of the world, and other major catastrophes if we don't impose tremendous restrictions in the product market. Most of the restrictions proposed for global warming are simple—no more use of carbon-based fuels. This would bring the entire world to a virtual standstill since all transportation, most electrical power, and all heating and cooling systems depend on carbon-based fuels. The world economies would stop dead in their tracks if we suddenly stopped using fossil fuels. So, the anti-global warming proponents argue vociferously that global warming has not been scientifically proven, and therefore does not exist. There has been little discussion about a middle-ground solution because neither side has presented true cost/benefit analyses. Nor has the root cause been discussed, because it too, has nasty doomsday implied solutions. The root cause of global warming has been much more a factor of world population growth than the use of fossil fuels. World population in 1900 was less than 2 billion people, while in 2000 it was in excess of 6 billion people. Think of it, what would the world's use of fossil fuels would be if the world population were cut by two-thirds. Would it not be somewhere close to one-third the total fossil fuels burned today? The problem is that the discussion on global warming is nothing but a point, counter-point reciting nothing but doomsday proposals with certain doomsday results. Yet, certainly there are current alternative non-fossil fuel alternatives that show promise of being able to replace the use of fossil fuels substantially in the future. It's just that none has been developed technologically to be able to replace its fossil-fuel component as a lower or even equivalent cost/price alternative. And, I have seen no studies on either side of the global warming debate that provide a truly competitive country-wide or world-wide cost/benefit analysis that supports transitioning from carbon-based energy sources to non-carbon-based energy sources. Everything I have seen in the debate to date has been whether or not the scientific evidence shown for global warming is credible. And, because of that, the world is pretty much at a standstill. Certainly, I have seen little discussion about the undeniable root cause of global warming—the substantial increase in world population discussed much at all, let alone in terms of economic impact to the planet. My recommendation is that we stop debating the unfathomable apocalyptic absolutes of both sides of the discussion and begin technological development and exploitation of current known alternatives for power by fossil fuels with the intent of making the alternatives economically attractive to individual consumers and industries who are the major users of fossil fuels. Once the cost/benefit analyses become favorable to non-fossil fuel alternatives as compared to our current fossil fuel alternatives, the market place should kick in and provide the technological revolution desired to both parties. I would state, that the world population issue needs to be addressed, because this planet simply will run out of resources sufficient to meet the bare necessity demands of the majority of the population sometime in the not-so-distant future.

A fine example of how the capitalism markets ultimately overcome perceived inequities in a particular area of economic distress is the recent very quick change in the market minimum wage in the U. S. Before the COVID crisis, a large number of people were clinging to the

U. S. legal minimum wage of $7.65 an hour. A large number of people had to quit work because they were ill and the labor market in the U. S. became hugely critical in virtually every industry be it private or public. For all of 2019 and the first half of 2020, no organization knew who was going to be able to work each day or for how many hours.   Many businesses couldn't keep enough workers at their worksites to keep their places open for more than a few hours. Suddenly people who could work, with or without needed experience became a hot commodity. I remember in early 2019, there were throngs of people throughout the United States that were demanding the U. S. minimum wage go to $15.00 an hour. Well, beginning in the second half of 2020, help wanted signs went up in virtually every store in our part of Northeast Georgia from 40 to 60 miles north of Atlanta. The advertised starting wages were from $12.00 per hour at fast food places, to $15.00 plus per hour at the more prestigious restaurants. Virtually all the retail outlet stores have desperate help wanted signs. The labor data today is in great flux and seems greatly inconsistent with what I know is happening where I live. The national unemployment rate has been below 4.0% for aa year or so today, and the number of help wanted signs for low-skilled labor are still prominent. The labor statistics also say that real wages in the U. S. have not moved up much, if any from the pre-COVID days. But, I don't necessarily believe that either, because I know the lowest wage-earning jobs in the U.S. have grown dramatically. However, what probably hasn't happened is that the many labor-intensive desk jobs in the U. S. still have a lot of stay-at-home workers earning less pay than those workers who have returned to the office. There are employer trends that indicate that some part of our labor force will remain as stay-at-home labor for the foreseeable future if, not permanently. I know the largest employer in the U. S. is contemplating designating a sizable number of their jobs as work-at-home.   Another area where the U. S. has yet to see much absorption is all the illegal aliens we are getting in the U. S. Ultimately these folks will either have to find a job, or the U. S. welfare system will crumble around us all. What we don't know is how many of them are skilled in any type of job we need in the U. S. and how long it will take them to learn English, find a job, and a home for themselves and their families. I do not trust the current unemployment rate calculation in the U. S. because I am convinced that most of the adult illegal aliens have yet to be included in the labor force counted within the U. S.

unemployment statistics. I fear that the unemployment rate in the U. S. is 3 to 4 percentage points higher than currently calculated. But, the bottom line is simply this. The U. S. labor market structure is in an era of major reinvention. I feel we are in for some rough times as a country, but I am also sure that Capitalism has the means and methods to help us adjust both faster and in a more complete fashion than any other system. I just hope the federal government won't get in the way of our natural capitalist process adjustments.

As for all other public policy decisions on regulation, I believe that a thorough, credible cost/benefit analysis, complete with financial data, should be required for all proposed regulations and that whenever the benefits are shown to be less than the costs, the regulation not be implemented.

I will briefly mention taxes and fees on businesses here as well. Essentially, taxes and fees are not an expense in that they have not been incurred to procure resources that will produce a good or service. The sole purpose of a business is to provide a good or service that they can sell to consumers in order to make a profit. Taxes and fees are, at a minimum, a disincentive for businesses to exist since it detracts from their capability to produce output, or to a greater degree taxes and fees become prohibitive for a business to achieve sufficient profitability. In either case, the business, at some point may decide that producing that good or service is no longer worth the loss of efficiency or profits to make it worthwhile for that business to continue to exist. However, another major impact to the U.S. Economy that we have experienced greatly in the last half century is that we have had major portions of various industries in the U.S., find our homeland corporations unprofitable as compared to foreign competitor producers and we have simply lost a large market share of producing that particular product, or in some cases entire product industries to companies in other countries. Examples are the home electronics industry that includes televisions, stereos, radios; the computer chip industry; much of the steel industry; telephones be they cell or land line, the entire home small appliance products industry. These are just a few of American industries that lost our corporations either into non-existence, or producing their name brands overseas. This is a national destructive Having now covered the price system and the three major sectors of the U. S. Economy, we now go to a bit of a deeper discussion about the role of government in capitalism.

From an economics viewpoint, there is one single, unarguable conclusion about government regulation. It costs the resources, and businesses money. The most recent estimate of the costs of regulation of all sectors of the U. S. Economy was conducted by the Competitive Enterprise Institute (CEI) in early 2018. According to the CEI, their estimate of the annual cost to the U. S. Economy for all four private sectors (Households, Business, Resource Markets and Product Markets) is $1.9 trillion dollars. This estimate has been the most widely accepted recent estimate by business publications in the U. S. Those costs get passed to the consumer in the form of higher prices. As a conservative economist, the first order of evaluating regulatory impacts on the economy is to get an accurate, complete, picture of the cost of each of the regulations. Secondly, we need to make a complete, accurate estimate of the dollar amount of the benefit received for each regulation. Then, we need to determine the ultimate value of implementing or not implementing the regulation based upon the cost of implementation versus the dollar value of the benefit(s) received. Also, as part of the evaluation, we need to consider any catastrophic consequences to the households, businesses, resource market, or product market to assure ourselves that we are not putting a sector of our society at grave risk of a fatal, unconscionable loss. As a conservative economist, I recognize that Adam Smith would probably have apoplexy over the amount of regulation placed on our society by government. But, as a conservative economist, I also recognize that in our complex economy with complex production processes and complex goods and services being consumed by the American public, there are risks that have catastrophic costs to individuals and society. Every time that a catastrophe occurs, the cost is generally unacceptably high. I believe that we should prevent catastrophic loss and costs as much as possible by regulating the risk mitigation for the prevention. I also believe that where there is no probable risk for catastrophic loss, that regulation probably is not needed as interference in the U. S. economic system.

The American Judicial System versus Adam Smith

Today, I can safely say that the federal government of the USA has overstepped its bounds in that no less than the Supreme Court of the USA has recently gravely degraded the individual freedoms and rights of economic self-determination. The most egregious recent example of the failure of the federal government justice system to uphold fundamental capitalistic principles as stated by Adam Smith is the Supreme Court decision in King versus Burwell on 25 June 2015. In this decision, the Supreme Court upheld the structure of Obamacare which has two major elements that violate and individual's right of choice. First, Obamacare forces all Americans to have medical insurance. It is no longer voluntary. Second, Obamacare dictates a singularly universal coverage for every insurance policy. Thus, consumer choice is prohibited and destroyed for healthcare in the United States. Because of the universality of Obamacare, fully 18% of the annual Gross Domestic Product in the United States no longer allows for consumer choice either in terms of the decision to purchase or not purchase a service, or choice in terms of scope of medical spectrum coverage. But, Obamacare is only the most recent flagrant violation of the basic right of consumer choice.

First on the list is Social Security. The vast majority of American workers are automatically enrolled in Social Security. Individuals and their employers each pay 6.2 % of an employee's wages/salary up to $160,200 for 2023. This totals 12.4% of an employee's salary that the federal government deducts as if it were a 401K or IRA personal retirement account. Next on the list is the additional 1.45% paid by individuals and their employers each which goes into Medicare hospital insurance. Neither of these two programs are voluntary either in terms of choice of participation, or amount of participation. Nor, are there levels of participation or choices of program content for either Social Security or Medicare. No, the structure of each program is singularly defined and the program content is the same for one and all. However, in the case of Social Security, the payout per individual is defined by a rather complex formula that is heavily weighted by the number of quarters paid into Social Security, and the total annual wages/salaries earned each year. The formula provides a lower percentage of payout for each additional increment of wages/salaries earned, meaning the payout is theoretically "means tested." Furthermore, a monthly insurance fee of a minimum of

$100 for medical doctors' expenses are deducted from each individual's Social Security. Although this is a "voluntary" fee approved by the individual on Social Security, it is next to impossible to get primary doctor's health care insurance once a person reaches the age of 65. Thus, the federal government coerces Americans age 65 and older to participate in the monthly Social Security medical doctor's insurance fee. Additionally, the expected retirement period payout for baby boomers entering their days to collect Social Security is at best, anticipated to be equal to the amount of Social Security deposits they made during their entire lifetime. In other words, for baby boomers, the rate of return on their "investment" of their Social Security funds is 0% for the entire 40 years plus that most of us worked and paid into this account. Imagine what our monthly payouts might be had the federal government had to provide us all a reasonable rate of return on our IRA/401K equivalent accounts. An additional point about the social security tax structure is that it penalizes the lower income people in favor of the wealthier people. Once an individual reaches the ceiling of $160,200 the employee and employer pay no more social security taxes for that year. So, suppose a person earns a salary/wage of $320,400 during 2023. He/she only pays an effective rate of half the 12.4% or 6.2%. This type of a tax system is categorized as a "regressive" tax and is frowned upon by economists as being blatantly unfair.

One last point to this as well. Economists and public policy wonks decry the low savings rate of the American public in general. I contend that one of the largest reasons for such a low savings rate is the fact that the federal government already reduces our earnings by 15.3% each year by this forced "investment". The combined expenditures for Social Security and Medicare paid by the federal government for Fiscal Year 1940 through Fiscal Year 2022 will be provided in Chapter 11. Again, the United States Supreme Court has upheld both the Social Security and Medicare systems as legal economic program structures within the Constitution of the United States. However, declaring them legal under the United States Constitution does not make these two programs consistent with the principle of freedom of choice of consumers held so dear by Adam Smith and we conservative economists, nor does it validate the concept of "means testing" the payout of Social Security as consistent with Adam Smith's economic principles.

The Total US Federal Government Impact on the US Economy—A Summary

The federal government of the United States through its regulation and its massive welfare spending programs has a tremendous economic impact on the annual U. S. Economy as shown by the proportion of expenditures of the GDP. For Fiscal Year 2022, the total federal government welfare expenditures were $1.768 trillion. Additionally, the estimated cost of federal government regulation is $1.9 trillion. That makes the total federal government influence on the U. S. Economy in areas not considered valid by Adam Smith for a capitalist economic system to be $3.6 trillion. This, in turn equates to slightly less than 15% of the total GDP (of $24.3 trlllion) worth of federal government mandates which are outside the intended interaction of government in the U. S. Economic System. As a conservative economist this is, indeed an egregious interference of government in our economy and our economic system. The damage to individual economic freedom and the significant increased prices paid for all goods and services by American consumers is staggering. These trends can simply not be allowed to continue lest the U. S. Economic System inevitably morph from capitalism into a communist economic system.

CHAPTER EIGHT
The Role of Money and Banks

The Functions of Money

Before we get to the definition of money, it is helpful if we first determine the three major functions of money—especially in our modern-day society. In our modern-day complex society money provides three services (functions) to individuals, organizations, and to the U. S. Economy as a whole.

The first function which really makes any modern-day economic system work, and quite notably, our U. S. Capitalist Economic system, is that of a medium of exchange. Each day in the United States, there are billions of exchanges of goods and services among our consuming population and business enterprises. In order for these billions of transactions to occur, there must be a quick and efficient way for them to be completed. If we were dependent on the barter system (negotiating goods for goods, labor for goods, or goods for labor) the number of transactions completed in a single day would be greatly reduced. In our modern-day world, this situation would simply shut down our economic system. Money provides us, as consumers, the opportunity to buy several products from one retail store with no quibbling at the checkout counter. We simply go to the store, pick out the items we want, and "pay" for them at the checkout counter. During a single day, we can go to several stores, purchase a myriad of different items and drive home with a large quantity of varied goods—all from an afternoon's efforts. Similarly, a business can hire hundreds of employees, of significantly different skills and capabilities, and of differing skill levels simply by paying them different wages or salaries. Simply put, money permits these billions of daily transactions to occur because it is the singular common denominator in the conduct of all economic activity. The alternative to this singular common denominator, call money, is to have individuals and businesses negotiate an exchange of the skills or output of an individual for the services or products of a specific business enterprise. An ancillary, but decidedly important by-product is that it greatly amplifies the freedom of people and businesses to exercise economic choice. Imagine, for example, that you went to a Kroger grocery store to purchase a cart full of groceries necessary to feed your family for a week. You get to the negotiation station with your cart, and offer your skill as an accountant to keep that store's accounting records for a week. And suppose the Kroger store manager told you that she wanted you to contribute two weeks of your accounting skills to keep the store's accounting record. But, you could only "spare" a week's worth of your skills to Kroger because you needed that second week free to provide your accounting efforts in exchange for products from Home Depot to make repair your roof and other external damage to your house due to recent storm damage. Nothing good can come from the Kroger negotiations because you will either take home fewer groceries which means you cannot feed your family for as long as you needed, or you may decide you have to buy those groceries at the expense of getting your house fixed. Of course, even with money, we all have to make trade-off decisions such as this every day, but the bartering will take a lot of time. One further choice you have is to buy fewer groceries that would last you just a few days, and hope that negotiations with other merchants will free up enough time to provide more of your accounting services to Kroger for additional food very soon. But, here is the truly frightening situation. Suppose the manager of that particular Kroger store tells you she already has accounting services and does not need your skills and that no trade for food can take place at all. Now, you must find another grocery store and start over. Multiply these negotiations by every stop in every store that you make in a week. Would you be able to complete all the purchases you need or want? Would you be able to develop a work schedule that would satisfy all the merchants in order for them to agree to the transaction of exchange? The answer to both questions is that a satisfactory settlement between yourself and all the merchants will not occur in terms of your labor commitments, the time taken for less than desired negotiation outcomes, and the high probability that some negotiations will result in no exchange at all.

Compare this barter situation with your ability to walk into any establishment, reach agreement on price, and walk out the door with the good in hand or a promise for a service to be rendered to you for an agreement on price permitted by the use of money. Additionally, think of the amount of time, frustration, and anxiety saved on your part because you don't have to negotiate for a cart-full of products every time you go shopping. The truth is, that the U. S. Economy could not function as it does today without a monetary system in use for all economic transactions.

The second function of money is to provide a standard of value. By translating all economic transactions to a stated, universal money base, people and businesses are able to compare the relative value of resources for producers and goods and services for consumers provided by all competitors of each of the resources, goods, and services. Additionally, businesses are able to decide the relative value of resources, processes and quantities of production to determine the various cost alternatives available as they vary the quantity of resources, the productions processes, and quantities of output. Consumers use the relative value of goods and services to determine the priorities, budget, and quantity trade-offs they need to make to remain within their incomes both for the short term and for longer term economic/financial goals of the household. The importance of the standard of value tends to be overlooked by most consumers and many businesses because we generally do not deal in markets outside the United States where a different currency provides a completely different translation of value of the resources, goods and services. Many military personnel learn this lesson often as they get stationed in differing overseas areas where the currency used is completely different from our United States dollar. Most of the time, we Americans in an overseas environment have to translate the resources, goods, or services to dollars in order to make our evaluations of the value purchased using the foreign currency. This generally means that we have to do initial research into the value received using the foreign currency for common purchases such as food, clothing, shelter, energy, and transportation costs and prices. Gradually we get comfortable with our translation of value for these recurring expenses. But, for purchases of either rarely purchased items, or high-cost items, we often have to take more time in order to translate the values to our familiar dollar standard in order to accurately and comfortably assure ourselves of value received as well as impact on our budget priorities and affordability.

The third function that money performs in today's complex U. S. Economic system is as a store of value. As we build wealth, whether it be physical in the form of capital goods, or in the form of paper savings, money provides the common denominator and translator for the value of that wealth. That does not mean that the dollar value of those capital goods and financial debentures won't change on a daily basis. Rather, it simply means that at the end of each day, we can translate our wealth in all forms to our monetary common denominator, the U. S. dollar. Finally, the ability to place wealth in financial debentures that are merely pieces of paper is a very convenient way to build wealth because the value of the paper transactions are easy to vary and usually very fast to complete. On the other hand, capital wealth, although translated to the dollar denominator can take days, weeks—even months in some situations for the transaction to be completed, recorded, and documents distributed.

United States Money Defined

In the United States, the federal government defines money into two levels—expanding the type of money as the level numerically increases. The federal government has two levels of money that it has defined— M1 and M2.

The first level of money recognized by virtually everyone in the U. S. is called M1 (pronounced as MMMMMMM-one). It consists of four types of money—currency plus coin plus demand deposits plus time deposits. Demand deposits include checking accounts or current accounts issued by banks, credit unions, stock brokerage houses or any other financial institution that permits checks or immediate demand drafts to be drawn against a customer financial account. Currency are the "greenback" paper money issued by the Federal Reserve, and coins are all coins minted by the U. S. mint. Each type of coin issued by the U. S. Mint has a standard purchase vale associated with it. The paper money issued by the Federal Reserve, and the coins used for transactions in the U. S. are called fiat money. Fiat money is money that has no intrinsic value in the money itself representative of the purchasing value that you receive when you use it to purchase a good or service. The U. S. Mint does also mint coins that are made of 99.9999% pure precious metals that have a vastly understated value in use of purchase transactions for goods and services. The most popular coin they mint are the American silver Eagle 1 ounce pure silver coins that have a face purchase exchange value of $1.00, but, of course sell at roughly the international silver price for the calendar year. Each year the U. S. mint also makes proof mint sets which have a pure silver dime, quarter, and half dollar. The total dollar sum of M1 dollars in the U. S. Economy at the end of July 2023 was 18.447 trillion dollars. In 2019, Federal Reserve defined M1 to include a very limited amount of savings (basically called passbook savings accounts). But, in 2020, the Federal Reserve Board elected to combine the vast majority of all savings except for Federal Money Market holdings into M1. The result was an increase in M1 of $4.0 trillion in 2019 to $17.8 trillion in 2020. In July of 2023, M2 totaled $18.45 trillion

The other level of money generally used by the American public, both individuals and businesses is defined by the Federal Reserve Board as M2 (pronounced MMMMM-two). It consists of the three types of money defined in M1 plus savings accounts that consist of U. S. Federal Money Market certificates with maturities of less than 12 months. As of July 2023, the M2 Account was $20.90 trillion..

From What Does Money Acquire Usefulness/Value

To this point we have now defined the purposes of money (medium of exchange, standard of value, and store of value) and the two major functions of money (to permit quick and easy transactions for resources, goods, and services between households and businesses, and permits holding of financial assets). Additionally, we have defined the two relevant levels of money as defined by the federal government. But, an issue that every economic system faces, every day of its existence is: What is the source of the usefulness/value of money to the households and businesses in the economy? Over the history of mankind, there are three reasons that a particular monetary system and specific types of money have been seen valuable and useful for transactions by households and businesses.

The first reason that a particular type of money has been useful in an economic system is simply because a particular government entity declared it to be used by everyone in the economic system for all economic transactions. This method of making money useful for transactions by government dictate (called declaration as legal tender) has been around for as long as five thousand years. There is evidence that the ancient Egyptians used the equivalent of government minted coins and weights of gold and silver as designated units of value to be translated in the exchange of goods and services among merchants, government offices, and households as early as 3000 BC. Certainly, since before the first day that the American Revolution began, the American Continental Congress established government printed currency (paper) and government minted coins as dollars which were to be used in all transactions among the fledgling federal government, businesses, and households. However, many cities and most of the 13 colonies continued to mint their own coins and currency for transactions conducted within their colonies and cities that had no federal involvement in the transaction. After the Revolutionary War, the newly formed United States of America quickly established mints to make new U. S. coins. The first U. S. minted coins appeared in the 1792-time frame after the United States Congress passed the Coinage Act (or Mint Act) of 1792. This act declared the U. S. dollar as the country's standard unit of money, created the U. S. Mint, mandated that the U. S. coinage be regulated, dictated the U. S. coins and established the silver dollar as the standard for all other coins minted in the U. S. Notably, the Act also declared the coins to be "lawful" tender and that the coinage be based on a decimal system. The coins minted in the United States from 1792 through 1964 were, for the most part "commodity" coins which meant that the metal content of the coin was roughly equivalent to the denomination value of the coin. Silver, gold, and copper were the main metals used to mint U. S. Coins until their legislated demises at various times in the 20th Century when the value of the precious metal became far greater than the face value of the coin.

The history of currency in the U. S. is much shorter. During the Revolutionary War, the Continental Congress established the "Continental Dollar" as legal tender. However, the young "Continental" 13 colonies and their national government had no way to give the public confidence that being the recipient of this paper currency would provide them anything of true value after the exchange. The 13 colonies and the overseeing national government had no precious metals in vaults and could not issue bonds or other financial instruments to borrow funds. Thus, the paper money quickly became worthless. Hence the slogan, "Not worth a Continental," quickly into the Revolutionary War. This bad experience of a nationally mandated and printed currency kept the United States from issuing any currency. Currency existed in the United States, but generally, it was issued by individual banks, and thus currency, due to this regional acceptance (at best), was of fairly limited use throughout all but the major cities. But, in the middle of the Civil War, it became apparent to the Union States (Union) that currency was needed. The precious metals were scarce, transportation of sizable dollar amounts of precious metals was bulky, and because of the bulk made transportation secrecy difficult and slower over long distances of primitive roads. So, the United States Congress passed the Legal Tender Act of 1862 which authorized the printing of U. S. currency to be called "greenbacks" (due to its major green ink tint) and directed the paper money to be declared "legal tender" to be accepted as if U. S. minted coins. National Banking Acts of 1863 and 1864. These acts collectively established the Comptroller of the Currency as part of the Department of the Treasury with one of its major missions to establish a national currency, print the currency, and ensure that the amount of currency printed was backed either by tax revenue or Treasury Securities sufficient to cover the amount of currency printed and issued to the public. These three acts collectively established the basis for U. S. currency to be enforced by the federal government as legal tender to this day. Today, 31 U.S. Code, Section 5103 states, "United States coins and currency (including Federal reserve notes and circulating notes of Federal reserve banks and national banks) are legal tender for all debts, public charges, taxes, and dues. Foreign gold or silver coins are not legal tender for debts." Finally, each and every Federal Reserve Note (today's currency) has the statement, "This note is legal tender for all debts, public and private," on its face.

The problem with this reason for giving money value is that throughout history, in most modern economies of the past three centuries, history is replete with examples where a government's declaration of its currency and coins as legal tender proved to be baseless. We have already discussed the lesson the infant U. S. learned before it became the nation under its current Constitution where the Continental dollar became virtually worthless in terms of exchange value for goods and services. The pain of this lesson was faced to the greatest degree by our Revolutionary soldiers whose pay for food, clothing, and war materials was in in Continental dollars. Many of our wealthy patriots went broke during the Revolutionary War because they depleted their hard wealth in precious metals, land, and business capital for the goods necessary for the United States to prosecute the Revolutionary War. During the Great Depression of the World in the 1930s, many of the European countries experienced the collapse of their entire monetary system. Germany was perhaps the harshest example. They had such a collapse of their monetary system that they issued 1 million Mark notes (paper currency) that had a purchase value of around 10 cents in U. S. dollar purchasing power at the time. And, the final example is the U. S. once again. Remember that the Great Depression in the U. S. began with a severe run on the banks because people had no faith that the banks had sufficient funds to cover their personal and business checking and saving balances. Finally, we must not forget that the majority of the dollars in our M1 money stocks is composed of checking and highly liquid savings accounts. The Federal Government certainly provides no declaration that our checks are guaranteed for payment. Imagine the number of bounced checks that occur in the U. S. Economy in any single day because the Federal Government has no stake in ensuring sufficient funds to cover checks written by businesses and individuals. After all these examples and considerations, we should conclude that our money in the United States does not have value due to any Federal Government declarations of legal tender.

The second reason that money has value is because it is based on a precious metal standard. We have already discussed the fact that until various times in the 20th century, U. S. coins had a precious metal value (by content) that was roughly equivalent to the face value of the coin. But, as the price of the precious metal content became widely greater than the face value of the coin, the federal government would simply take the coins with the overstated coin content versus the face value out of circulation. The Federal Government made it illegal to hold or hoard gold coins, bullion, or certificates. This was mandated by both an executive order and federal law in 1933 and can still be enforced today. But, apparently the vast majority of the gold was turned into the Federal Government, because you can purchase U. S. minted historical gold coins and printed gold certificates in the possession of individuals through numismatic auctions without much fear of prosecution. During World War II, the Federal Government recalled silver coins (particularly silver dollars) and bullion from the public in order to melt them down for war equipment needs. This was a less successful effort because the Federal Government continued to issue high silver content coins from dimes through silver dollars through 1964. However, the Congress passed a law in 1964 that U. S. coins should no longer be made with silver content for circulation to the public for use of exchange of goods and services. Thus, in 1965 the U. S. began to coin the "sandwich" coins made of multiple low value metals, usually in alloy combinations. The U. S. Mint still makes pure silver and pure gold coins, but they have face values several hundred percent below the current market value of silver and gold. These coins are issued and sold to the public either for numismatic value or for a store of value as part of savings portfolios. However, the bottom line for today's U. S. circulating coins and currency is that it is all "fiat" money, meaning that neither are based on a precious metal standard nor issued at anywhere close to the commodity level.

Nor should we forget the definition of M1 money. It is the sum of currency, coins, demand deposits and a huge volume of liquid savings accounts in our banking system. Currently only about one-tenth of the total value of M1 money is composed of currency and coins. The other 9/10ths of the M1 money are demand deposits and liquid savings accounts. Demand deposits held by households and business have absolutely no backing of or connection to a precious metal. Thus, even if our U. S. currency and coins were backed by some precious metal standard, we would still have the majority of our monetary base that could not possibly be based on a precious metal hoard held by each American and business in a dollar value equal to its highest monthly bank balance. Thus, we must conclude that this particular reason that might be offered as what gives money value in the U. S. to simply be a non-player and falsehood.

That gets us to the final reason that money has value in our economy. That reason is simply acceptance by the public in general as a system, and acceptance by individual households and businesses as payment for individual exchanges for resources, goods, and services. I assert that, in the U. S. Economy, it is only the acceptance of our payments for resources, goods, and services among us both as households and businesses that money has value to us. As a business person, how willing are you to take payment of a check for a sale if you find that the purchaser has a recent string of rubber checks? As a household, how willing are you to accept a check in payment for your paycheck if that company recently went into receivership? And, what about the numerous times, as a customer that you have been told by a proprietor that they would accept only checks, no cash (as is often the case with apartment rentals and college business offices)? Or what about proprietors who will take only credit cards, no cash, no checks, and no debit cards. And, of course, I am sure most of us have been embarrassed by a credit card or debit card that we know has money in our account, but gets refused due to administrative mix-ups on the part of the credit/debit card company. The point here is simply that the only way a transaction can be completed financially is for the purchaser to have faith that the method of payment will indeed be accepted by the financial institution(s) involved between the buyer and the seller.

So, in conclusion to the question of what gives money value, the ultimate reason/alternative payment that will complete the transaction rests solely in the eyes and the psyche of the receiver of the payment. Whatever they are willing to accept is golden, and neither implied legal pressure from the Federal Government to force someone to accept payment by cash, nor insistence by a customer that a business accept a check in payment for their purchase can be forced upon the seller. It is only the form of payment that a particular seller is willing to accept from a customer for a particular sales transaction between them that matters. And, generally speaking that form of payment that is acceptable to the seller from the purchaser can be greatly influenced by the payment reputation of the buyer.

Missions Stated and Perceived by the Federal Reserve System

On 23 December 1913, the Federal Reserve System was created by the Federal Reserve Act. The U. S. Congress stated three objectives for "monetary policy" in the Act which were to: maximize employment, keep prices stable, and "moderate" long-term interest rates. The Federal Reserve Board of Governors, Open Market Committee, and Presidents of the 12 Federal Reserve Banks, collectively form the decision-making structure of the Federal Reserve. These decision-makers of the Federal Reserve are often simply annotated the "Fed." For the remaining part of this Treatise, the Fed will represent the Federal Reserve or Federal Reserve System as an exact and interchangeable term. According to the Board of Governors, the purpose of the Federal Reserve System, as stated on their Web-site is to: "Conduct the nation's monetary policy by influencing money and credit conditions in the economy in pursuit of full employment and stable prices; Supervise and regulate banks and other important financial institutions to ensure the safety and soundness of the nation's banking and financial system and to protect the credit rights of consumers; Maintain the stability of the financial system and contain systemic risk that may arise in financial markets; and Provide certain financial services to the U. S. government, U. S. financial institutions, and foreign official institutions, and play a major role in operating and overseeing the nation's payments systems.." These, then are the stated missions of the Fed both from its inception in 1913 and currently, today in mid-2016.

I contend that since the early 1980s, the Fed has added three perceived missions of the Fed which they can neither control, nor greatly influence. The first perceived mission has been for the Fed Chairman to loudly and persistently decry the continued deficit spending of the Congress which has resulted in a perpetual trend of increased federal debt. Paul Volker, Fed Chairman under Presidents Reagan publicly scolded the Congress every 6 months about the danger to the long-term financial solvency of the United States Government with their continued fiscal profligacy. Alan Greenspan became the Fed Chairman late in Reagan's Presidency, remained for the entire presidencies of George Bush, Sr. and Bill Clinton, and through the first 6 years of George Bush, Jr., Greenspan continued the clarion call for fiscal restraint by the

Congress and their necessary action to establish long-term annual budget surpluses to begin to pay down the burgeoning Federal Government debt. He cautioned the Congress that the Federal debt which approached $8 trillion by the end of his term (31 January 2006) was a danger to the Federal Government's future solvency. In fact, he was probably the first economist to coin the categorization that the continued Federal budget deficits and fast-growing Federal Debt were, "unsustainable."

Ben Bernanke became the Fed Chairman on 1 February 2006. On 18 January 2007, Mr. Bernanke spoke before the Senate Budget Committee and stated that he was concerned about the probable steady annual increases in future annual Federal Budget Deficits and the resulting increase in the Federal Debt. He pointed to the projected ever-increasing expenditures on entitlement spending each year as the major cause of the deficits and stated that increased Federal Debt each year necessitated larger annual interest expenses for all future budgets. Thus, Ben Bernanke continued to highlight the Fed's concern on the continued Federal Budget deficits and increased Federal debt.

However, although the two Fed Chairmen of the First Decade of the 21st Century continued to hammer Congress on the dangers of a continued growth in Federal debt, they both failed to recognize and warn of the significant growth in subprime home loans, later to be defined as "toxic" home loans. In March of 2007, the first signs of stress due to a large portfolio of these toxic home loans that had been distributed throughout the U. S. and global financial institutions including many non-banks arose. Mr. Bernanke did not feel a crisis was brewing. And, he continued to have this view until mid-September of 2008 when a number of U. S. financial institutions filed for bankruptcy. The vast majority of the large financial institutions throughout the U. S. including the largest banks, the largest insurance companies, the mega stock brokerages, and even some large industrial corporations had holdings of these toxic home loans sufficient to put them into the financial brink. As a result, the Fed established a new (the second) perceived mission of mitigating a massive U. S. and global financial meltdown through drastic and unprecedented financial measures. The Fed extended loans to troubled banks and investment firms that totaled approximately $1.5

trillion and provided financial guarantees of an additional $1.5 trillion by the endo of November 2008. However, this extraordinary and quick action by the Fed did little to help the U. S. Economy.

The U. S. fell into a grave recession quickly. The U. S. Gross Domestic Product (GDP) fell by $135 billion from the 4th quarter of 2007 to the 4th quarter of 2008 and fell by $460 billion from the 3rd quarter of 2008 to the 3rd quarter of 2009. The GDP then began a slow sluggish rise each quarter from the 4th quarter of 2009 to the 2nd quarter of 2016.

The U. S. Stock Market fared far worse. The Dow Jones Industrial (DJI) Index reached a high of 13,727 on 10 December 2007. By 9 January 2008 it fell 1,000 points. It remained above 12,000 through 19 June 2008 (closed at 12,063). 26 September 2008 was the last day the DJI topped 11,000 (closed at 11,143) until 8 October 2010 (closed at 11,006). On New Year's Eve 2008, the DJI closed at 8,776. But, the DJI continued to fall during the first quarter of 2009, hitting its low point of 6,547 on 9 March 2009. From 10 December 2007 to 9 March 2009, a matter of a mere 15 months, the U. S. Stock Market wealth had fallen by greater than 50%. Since that time the DJI has skyrocketed to just over 33,400 as of early October of 2023

The Fed decided to take another unprecedented monetary policy stance. The discount rate (the rate the Fed charges commercial banks to borrow money from the Fed) for September of 2007 averaged at just below 5%. As the subprime home loans problems began to rear their ugly heads, the Fed began to swiftly lower the discount rate. It decreased the discount rate by a full percentage point in January of 2008, another full point in February of 2008, and a third full percentage point (down to 2%) by May of 2008. The Fed continued to reduce the discount rate another percentage point in October of 2008, and by December of 2008, the Fed lowered the discount rate to an average of .16% for that month. The discount rate remained at that rate or lower through November of 2015. In December 2015, the Fed, under its new Chairwoman, Janet Yellen, raised the discount rate by roughly a quarter point to an average of the first two quarters of 2016 of around .39%. In 2017 through 2019, the Fed gradually raised the discount rate until it reaches roughly 2%.

But then in 2020 and 2021, the Fed suddenly decreased the discount rate to .38% in 2020 and almost 0% in 2021. This, then became the third perceived mission of the Fed—to provide essentially free loans for a substantial period of time to the banking institutions of the United States. These free loans to banks have, indeed provided homeowners much lower interest rates on home loans, leading to some homeowners being able to afford the loan payments. It has helped the banks by allowing homeowners to refinance at these low interest rates without having to face the market devaluation of their homes. These free loans to financial institutions have also made the purchase of high value consumer goods such as automobiles, home furnishings, and home electronics and appliances available for 0% interest over reasonably long periods of time. However, the really bad news for consumers is that it has not promoted a drastic reduction in interest rates on credit cards. What is fairly incredulous with this particular policy of long-term near 0% discount rate is that it has not resulted in a major boom in consumer spending and a major growth rate in GDP. Finally, thanks to the huge increase in the inflation rate during 2022, the Fed has reacted dramatically and swiftly to increase the discount rate.

The fourth

Fed Monetary Policy versus Mission Accomplished by the Federal Reserve System

Now, I would like to conduct a summary evaluation on how well the Fed monetary policy has accomplished their various major mission statements over the last 3 and one-half decades. The Fed for decades has stated that its major method of implementing monetary policy to influence the U. S. Economy is to attempt to control the amount of money in the U. S. Economic System at all times. Generally, if they increase the U. S. money supply, the Fed expects the U. S. Economy to expand in GDP, increase employment and wages, and increase output. But, there is a major potential down-side with increasing the money supply. The increase in the money supply increases demand in the economy which in turn can quickly result in a general rise in prices, known as inflation. Inflation, especially as the rate of inflation increases, tends to deteriorate the purchasing power of consumers and pinch the profit levels of businesses. Additionally, inflation places severe profit pressures on financial institutions because they get monthly payments on long term loans with ever-decreasing purchasing and lending value of those funds. As lending values decrease, profit opportunities decrease along with them. So, from an economic performance perspective, the implementation of monetary theory is definitely a two-edged sword.

The Fed has three theoretical methods of affecting the money supply in the U. S. Economy. First, the Fed can decide to place more or fewer federal securities for sale in the "open market." If the Fed sells securities to Americans it decreases M1 because people take money from their checking accounts to purchase the securities. If the Fed purchases securities it has the opposite effect on M1 because the money paid by the Fed to households for the securities they previously owned now increases the money in their checking accounts. However, if the Fed expands their policy effects to include savings accounts, which generally include government securities, the results of purchase or sales of securities to households is nominal. The reason--households are simply transferring money from savings to checking accounts or vice versa. Thus, the effect to M2 is really only the difference in interest earned or foregone on the dollar value of the securities. The other reason that this policy goal option is really not within the control of the Fed is that the Congress determines the purchase or sale of securities through its annual revenues and expenditures. And, as has been the situation in the vast majority of the years, the Federal Budget has run a deficit which meant that the Fed (by order of the U. S. Treasury) had to sell securities in order keep the Federal Government financially solvent.

The second method that the Fed has to influence the total money supply within the banking system is through its changes in the discount rate. As stated earlier, the discount rate is the interest rate that the Fed charges commercial banks to obtain loans from the Fed. If the Fed wants to encourage banks to borrow more funds from them, they decrease the discount rate, and if the Fed wants to decrease loans from the commercial banks they increase the discount rate. If commercial banks increase the value of their loans from the Fed, they have more money to lend to households, which increases the amount of demand from consumers in the market. If the Fed increases the discount rate, commercial banks will presumably acquire fewer loans from the Fed, lend less money to households, which leads to lower demand for goods and services by consumers. The effectiveness of this Fed policy tool depends on the willingness and ability of commercial banks and households to either increase their loans in their household portfolios, or absorb the interest increases in their monthly/annual incomes. But, currently, the Fed has destroyed the use of this tool for other than increasing the discount rate, because it is already only about 5 tenths of one percent. In other words, the only currently available policy option for the discount rate tool is for the Fed to increase the discount rate. The threat of decreasing GDP and placing the U. S. in another recession has been a major concern of the Fed. Thus, even after an advertised economic recovery measured by the annual increases in GDP over the last five years, it has been so anemic that the Fed has been hesitant to increase the discount rate because of fears of causing another economic recession. In short, the Fed really has, at best, half the discount policy tool available to it, and the current condition of the U. S. Economy seems to cause the Fed pause in increasing the discount rate to give the Fed future discount tool use flexibility.

There is one recent historical event where the Fed made an unprecedented change in the discount rate (or today called the federal funds rate). The U. S. annual average inflation rate, measured by the Consumer Price Index, rose from 5.8% in 1976 to 13.5% in 1981. The Fed, headed by its Chairman, Paul Volker was determined to take drastic immediate steps to bring the inflation rate down. The main policy action taken by the Fed was to increase the yearly average federal funds rate from 5.05% in 1976 to 11.2% in 1979, 13.35% in 1980, and 16.39% in 1981. The impacts of this policy change were both immediate and substantial. The average annual prime interest rate rose from 6.84% in 1976 to 1.67% in 1979, 15.26% in 1980, and 18.87% in 1981. The prime rate than began to diminish beginning in 1982 at 14.85%, then 12.04% in 1984, to slightly less than 10% (9.93%) in 1985. Additionally, the average mortgage interest rate rose from 8.86% in 1976 to 11.19% in 1979, to 13.77% in 1980, to 16.63% in 1981, 16.08% in 1982, and then leveling off to slightly over/under 13% for the next three years. The broad-based economic results due, at least in part, to these Fed Policy actions were two-fold. First, the annual inflation rate diminished almost immediately from the high of 13.5% in 1980 to 10.3% in 1981, 6.2% in 1982 and hovering in the 3% to 4% range from 1983 through 1988. However, the production sector of the U. S. Economy paid a heavy price in that the unemployment rate climbed from an average 5.8% in 1979 to 7.6% in 1981 to a high of 9.7% and 9.8% for 1982 and 1983 respectively until it began to fall between 7.0% and 7.5% through 1986 to around 5.5% per year from 1988 through 1990.

The third policy tool which the Fed has available for increasing or decreasing the money supply is truly direct, with immediate impact on the performance of the economy. That policy tool is to increase/decrease the required reserve rate. The Fed implements a minimum rate of M1 and M2 dollars carried on the books of each commercial bank that each bank must keep "on reserve" with the Fed at all times. The Fed monitors the dollars officially placed on reserve with the Fed each day and strictly ensures that each and every bank is in strict compliance with the minimum funds held on reserve with the Fed each day. The Fed is quite intolerant of any bank that habitually fails to keep the minimum funds on reserve with the Fed. The reason this policy tool is so powerful is that it any change in the required reserve rate immediately changes the posture of all commercial banks' ability to issue, or necessity to "recall" loans. This policy tool was changed structurally by the Congress in the Monetary Control Act of 1980. The Fed has been very reluctant to use it. Perhaps the greatest reason for the hesitancy is that fact that a change in the reserve rate has a significant change in the dollar value of the money supply and it is difficult for the Fed to accurately forecast the impact on such a drastic change in the money supply to the GDP and employment rate.

In summary there are two things that should be noted about the Fed's ability to influence/control the U. S. Economy. First, is the fact that the simple use of the policy tools creates a conflict between the two economic goals assigned to it by the Congress. Because the Fed's policy tools affect demand much more substantially than supply, the predictable overarching results to the economy will be to decrease inflation, but almost always at the expense of employment and output growth. Conversely, should the Fed implement policies to spur economic growth, it will almost assuredly do so with concurrent increases in inflation. Secondly, implementing Fed monetary policy is a very imprecise science. It is almost always like shooting into the dark. For it is virtually impossible to predict how much tweaking of a particular policy tool will provide in effect whether it be an impact on inflation or on economic output. Thus, implementation of monetary policy in the past has often tended to be by small increments with a desire to acquire some empirical data as to the results before making another increment of change. This has oftentimes led to a painfully small changes in the positive economic changes desired. This is perhaps no better shown than the rather lackluster economic recovery from the recession experienced 8 years ago (August 2008 to August 2016).

Federal Reserve Oversight of the Overarching U. S. Financial System

The Fed, as an organization has both sought more designated responsibility and deliberately inserted itself in the general oversight of the overarching U. S. Financial System. However, their greater insertion in the oversight of the Financial System has not always proven to provide the kind of benefits to the Financial System, the U. S. Economic System, and certainly, the American public as we probably had the right to expect. I will cite three specific historic situations that I believe illustrate how the Fed has been either of little help or counter-productive to the prevention of or active positive intercession of a major financial issue problem.

Let us first go to the late 1970s, early 1980s. As the home loan interest rates soared, the federal savings and loan institutions quickly began to experience a massive reduction in real estate sales due to its unaffordability to more and more American families. Additionally, the value of a greater and greater percentage of real estate properties began to diminish as people were forced to reduce the price of their properties to accommodate the higher interest rates that would make the monthly payment for their resold property affordable to potential buyers. This crunch of lower property prices/values, substantially fewer buyers who could afford to buy property, and the significantly longer times property had to be held prior to sale placed the entire federal savings and loan industry in financial receivership. As the problem continued to grow in both dollar size and savings and loan industry breadth, the Fed's response was to continue their monetary policy initiatives with no change. Ultimately, the Fed, who had for years pressured the Congress to give them oversight and monetary policy influence over more types of financial institutions in the Federal Financial System used the savings and loan crisis to successfully persuade the Congress to let them combine non-bank financial institutions with the failing savings and loan industry to create a new group of banks with broader functions and opportunities than the then current traditional banks under the Fed's control. As a result, non-bank financial institutions as diverse as insurance companies and   stock brokerage firms were brought into the definition of a bank and placed under the control and oversight of the Fed, so long as they bought the entire portfolio of one or more failing savings and loan institutions. The result was the dissolution of an entire specialized financial institution (savings and loans) and the development of conglomerate, greatly diversified financial institutions defined as banks in name only when measured against the traditional banking functions and roles. This began a revolutionary restructure of the entire U. S. Financial System that created a new, more disastrous financial setback to the U. S. Economy.

Just what was the result of the newly restructured U. S. Financial System? In just a few words, the result was the massively severe financial meltdown experienced by the United States in the 2007-2008 time frame. By the beginning of the 21st Century, the U. S. Financial System had morphed into a conglomerate set of financial institutions, all of whom had been able to expand into areas of financial services for which they had neither the capital nor the expertise. Banks had expanded heavily into home loan financing, sales of commercial and personal insurance of all types, purchase and sales of stocks and bonds and multi-specialty brokerage houses. Insurance companies were the main purchasers of savings and loan institutions and were rewarded with the capability to provide untethered full banking services to their members and new bank only customers. Even stock brokerage houses were able to venture in certain bank services such as checking and saving accounts. The only financial institutions left relatively untouched during the financial revolution of the 1990s were credit unions who essentially retained their member-oriented financial services. This diversification also helped the Federal Government implement the fair housing loan issuance laws that had been put in place during the 1980s and 1990s with greater and greater scrutiny of enforcement among all these financial institutions. This financial system restructure, accompanied by the Fed's inexperience at dealing with the larger number of financial institutions and their substantially larger diversity led to the Fed's lack of timely recognition of the full breadth and risk of the high-risk housing loans. Thus, not only did the housing bubble burst quickly with great impact affecting the entire U. S. Financial System, but it happened with no one at the Fed predicting or forewarning of the inevitability or scope of the meltdown. Furthermore, the Fed had no plan as to how to deal with the situation so that they developed a quick fix which was to simply "create" $3.0 trillion in the Federal Reserve Banks for distribution to financial organizations, private or government that needed an infusion of cash to stay afloat. The Fed also established the concept that financial institutions could be "too big to fail."

The third historic situation that the Fed has had a major role in creating is the federal budget deficits. The federal debt has more than doubled in the last 7 years over what it took the 70 plus years to reach. The first four years of the Obama administration budget deficits totaled more than $5.0 trillion. I submit that these four years of unprecedentedly large budget deficits were able to exist with little negative public fanfare because they were seen to be financially inconsequential. Why? Because the Fed had a federal funds borrowing rate of almost 0%. In other words, the federal government borrowed (and continues to borrow) that $5.0 trillion of debt as if there were no cost. When the Fed does increase the federal funds rate to a more historically reasonable 5%, the annual interest cost may finally catch the American public's attention. Although the $5.0 trillion may not be much to worry about, the annual interest cost of $250 billion could become a major area of discussion. And, if the $250 billion in annual interest charges doesn't get people's attention, perhaps the $1.0 trillion or so annual interest charges on $19 to $20 trillion in debt will wake them up.

Now that we have a pretty good picture of the Federal Reserve Banking and Monetary Policy basics, we will turn to a number of U. S. Financial System issues we face in the next chapter.

CHAPTER NINE
History And Issues of The Modern U.S. Financial System

Before I begin this chapter, I want to immediately confess that many of the details in this chapter will not meet the normal academic rigorous tests of accuracy. Nor will the details necessarily be sufficient to verify the more general statements about various conclusions on major historical conditions and events about the modern U. S. financial system. Rather, my intent is to bring the reader to an accurate picture of the modern U. S. financial system's significant modification in structure and risk over the last 30 years or so. My goal, at the end of this summary of the history of the restructure of the U. S. financial system during the last 3 plus decades, is to provide the reader a good feel for the current structure of the U. S. financial system, and the major financial issues inherent in our current financial system. Then, I will provide a brief summary of my personal assessment as to the current financial risks we face as individuals and as a nation.

A Brief History of our Modern-Day Financial System

I will begin at a baseline of the U. S. financial system circa 1975. The U. S. financial system at that time was a composite of several financial institutional industries segregated by financial services and products. First, we had the banking system in the United States, which consisted of the 12 Federal Reserve Banks, commercial banks chartered by the U. S. Comptroller of the Currency, and commercial banks chartered by a state governmental agency. In 1975 there were approximately 12,500 commercial banks in the U. S. The singular mission of the banking system for the American public in 1975 was to facilitate financial transactions throughout the economy whether exchange of goods or savings accounts. Second, we had brokerage firms whose mission was the sale of stocks and bonds to the American public. Another type of brokerage firm were commodities brokers who provided a means for the purchase and sale of commodities between commodity owners and purchasers/customers. A third industry evident in our U. S. financial system in 1975 was the insurance industry. Their singular mission was to provide general and specialized insurance to business, and insurance to households such as life, fire, auto, and personal liability. The fourth financial industry was savings and loan institutions. These institutions were chartered by the Federal Home Loan Bank Board and their major mission was to collect savings and issue home and real estate loans to households. They did have some latitude to issue a small percentage of real estate loans to organizations other than households and they could allow some draft account (similar to checking accounts) capability to the holders/owners of the savings accounts. A major structural facet of savings and loan institutions was that all their financial transactions were initiated through a savings and loan institution by only their members. Each savings and loan institution was totally member-owned. The final major financial industry in the U. S. was the credit union. Credit Unions were chartered by the National Credit Union Association. Credit Unions were formed through a petition of customers with a fairly narrow focus. Oftentimes the focus was through a business or other narrow organizational definition. Like a savings and loan, a credit union was totally owned by the members. A credit union had the capability to establish savings accounts, share draft (similar to bank checking) accounts, and make specialized singular purpose loans and lines of credit.

The wisdom and the beauty of the structure of the U. S. financial system as it existed in 1975 was that the U. S. financial system could not be brought down by a problem in on industry/sector. The reason is that whatever event might drive a crisis in one sector, could not affect any of the other sectors because they were not involved in the conditions that drove the financial difficulties of the original sector. For example, a group of major losses suffered in the insurance industry due to a season of major floods and hurricanes in one year did not affect any of the other financial industries/sectors because they had no money invested in insurance and their financial well-being and operations were not dependent on insurance industry losses. Had stock market prices reduced to half of what they were 3 months prior, people and businesses owning stock would have suffered losses, but those losses would not translate immediately into a crisis in insurance or commodities sectors. The banking industry could be impacted by a huge loss in stock prices because some of the banks' borrowers may have had trouble paying on loans for some period of time. But the losses in the stock market would not affect all stock owners in the same manner and thus, the other financial sectors would not experience nearly the financial downturn experienced by the stock market industry. The bottom line is simply that the structure of the U. S. financial system in 1975 which segregated the various financial industries/sectors from interacting with each other was a major factor that the risk of a meltdown of the entire financial system was quite low. However, all this changed with the passage of a rather innocuous piece of legislation in 1977.

In 1977, the Congress passed, and President Carter signed into law the Community Reinvestment Act of 1977. This law's purpose was to assure that financial institutions did not fail to make home and real estate loans to individuals and businesses of low and moderate incomes. The aggressive enforcement of this law drove the United States financial system to bankruptcy and the U. S. Economy into a deep recession. It also negatively affected banking and financial systems of several countries throughout the world, particularly those in Europe. The basic elements of the financial meltdown of the U. S. financial system, fully recognized in August of 2008 are discussed below.

The U. S. Financial Meltdown of the First Decade of the 21st Century

The U. S. Financial Meltdown of the First Decade of the 21st Century The cause of the financial meltdown was a singular condition—far too many people who were granted home loans with monthly payments way beyond their ability to pay because of their income levels. There were several root causes which contributed to this condition, all of which were predictable to eventually come together to create the disastrous perfect storm of the financial meltdown. The financial meltdown became generally recognized by the U. S. financial institutions and American public in August of 2008. The root causes of the financial meltdown of 2008 were all tied to a two decades long set of incentives and coercions handed to the newly formed U. S. financial structure from the savings and loan debacle in the mid-1980s. These incentives and coercions came from the desire by the Congress and presidential administrations to promote home ownership to low- and moderate-income families using the Community Reinvestment Act of 1977 as the carrot and stick to make home loans happen. In short, the financial meltdown in the U. S.

was caused by the ultimate recognition that there were far more insolvent home loans in the U. S. financial system than could be absorbed without causing most of the largest financial institutions going bankrupt. Note that the financial meltdown had not occurred in earnest where many or most of our financial institutions had suffered a sufficient number of home loan defaults that they had already lost vast sums of money. Rather, there was a simple recognition by the financial industry that they had become saturated with these home loans with a high probability of default. These home loans became segregated in the financial industry through identification as "toxic" loans or secondary market home loans. Let me annotate some of the root causes of the meltdown that took almost two decades to come to the nightmarish recognition.

1. *Private (commercial) banks were encouraged to issue loans to low- and moderate-income families by relaxing their standards of income, indebtedness, and job security necessary to grant a home loan. This resulted in a number of families being granted loans under the new standards that would never have qualified under the older, stricter standards.*

2. *Commercial banks were encouraged to issue loans to lower and moderate-income families using the relaxed home loan qualification standards because the Federal Government expanded the home loan guarantees and loan assumptions by Fannie Mae and Freddie Mac. These two quasi-federally managed, but jointly owned (private and federal) agencies became targeted almost solely to the secondary market loans. Their purpose was to consolidate secondary (toxic) loans and sell them in the commercial financial markets with higher than standard market mortgage interest rates as recognized high risk/high reward investments. Because they were presumed "backed" by the Federal Government, Fannie Mae and Freddie Mac were able to continue to increase their percentage of these marginal home loans each successive year during the twenty or so years prior to the 2008 meltdown.*

3.   *Fannie Mae and Freddie Mac were the first financial institutions forced to recognize their insolvency. By August of 2008, their stock prices per share had declined by 90% as compared to August of 2007. The recognition of the high rate of toxic loans quickly precipitated to the private financial sector of the U. S. Economy because Fannie Mae and Freddie Mac owned or guaranteed approximately 50% of the total $12 trillion home loans originated in the U. S. The assumption was that what was true for the financial health of Fannie Mae and Freddie Mac had also to be true for the commercial side of the housing market.*

4.   *Because of the restructure of the entire U. S. financial system during the late 1980s and early 1990s, virtually every institution of every sector of the industry had access to the purchase of the toxic or sub-prime home loans offered by Fannie Mae, Freddie Mac, or private home loan brokers. Additionally, the new investment bankers expanded particularly from the insurance sector were able to directly issue their own loans as well. This meant that the poison of toxic, sub-prime home loans spread throughout the entire U. S. financial system.*

5.   *Banks were coerced into making high-risk, financially unsound home loans because every home loan that the financial institution failed to grant could easily come back to haunt them as failing to comply with the stated goals and intent of the Community Reinvestment Act of 1977. Banks simply could not withstand the repercussions of significantly greater scrutiny by bank examiners and public outcry from the assignment of the label of being an unwilling home loan originator to low- and moderate-income families.*

6.   *The high demand for housing created a new home building industry that promoted profiteering by home builders in three ways. First, home builders increased the standard size of homes and a consumer desire for upgraded interiors. This increased the average price of new homes, thus increasing the risk of budget affordability of low- and moderate-income homeowners approved for their loans. In general, the number of sub-*

prime borrowers increased as time continued, because home prices increased substantially and the availability of affordable new homes diminished greatly. Second, the price of used homes increased as well because there was a general shortage of homes available to meet the high increase in demand due to the general atmosphere of lending money for home ownership to all but the worst risk home loan applicants. The general rise in used home prices certainly meant that some of these older properties became part of the number of sub-prime loans issued. Finally, given the fact that from 1992 through 2007, the demand for new homes continued to increase, there was also some degree of profiteering on the part of the home builders. It is of course, not provable, but the general nature of producers in a market of supply shortages always exhibits some incremental increases in profit rates charged by producers.

7. *The final, root cause of the financial meltdown I want to address, is perhaps the most influential of meltdown itself. Simply put, the governmental agencies having oversight of the financial system and its various financial sectors and institutions were all asleep on the job. The Federal Reserve had to know a major home loan "bubble" was being created, both from an observable data perspective and from adherence to common sense financial and banking theoretical conditions, causes, and effects. Yet, they remained silent on the impending growing crisis and, most egregiously, failed to halt the practices of lowered banking lending standards rampant throughout the banking sector of the U. S. Economy. Not far behind in the stupidly silent and inactive overseers is the U. S. Congress. The House and Senate each have committees whose charters include oversight on the conduct of the banking industry and institutions in the U. S. Here again, neither committee in the House or Senate raised any alarm to the looming financial system disaster. Furthermore, there is evidence that members of the two committees may have individually encouraged the enhancement of the coercive elements of enforcement of the Community Reinvestment Act. Certainly, there is no evidence of legislative changes to reverse the known*

trend of issuance and distribution of toxic and sub-prime home loans throughout the financial system. And finally, although the Secretary of the Treasury of the United States, during the period of 2001 through 2008 apparently had no clue of the looming crisis in the U. S. financial system before its sudden recognition in August of 2007, because there is no evidence that he either rang alarm bells or worked to prevent or repair the damage from the sub-prime home loans.

The Probable Long-Term Effects of the U. S. Financial Meltdown of 2008

The financial meltdown of 2008 and the subsequent measures taken by the Fed and the Congress have had some identifiable long-term consequences, most of which need near term correction. The summary consequence of the meltdown of 2008 is simply that today, the U. S. financial system is weak and vulnerable to any near-term misstep in that there really remain no tools to remedy another major financial mishap. Let me briefly list the major policy options used historically and a summary of our current status for each option.

1.   *The first option used substantially to "fix" the meltdown was the major infusion of cash from the U. S. Treasury to make the compendium of financial companies who became insolvent—solvent. Over the last 7 years, the U. S. federal debt increased by over $9 trillion (from $8.591 trillion at the end of 2008 to $18.120 trillion at the end of 2015). The vast majority of those additional indebted dollar expenditures were either a direct effect of the meltdown in terms of payments to or on behalf of the financial institutions to keep them from bankruptcy and provide a pathway to "wholeness," or the significant increases in federal expenditures to offset the negative effects on families and individuals resulting from the recession that followed. Should the U. S. experience any type of negative economic incident which would cause a major financial crisis and/or recession, this option of significantly increasing our debt is problematic at best. The debt load of the United States now exceeds the total annual Gross Domestic Product. The general world consensus on the credit worthiness of a country seems to be that the break*

point for being regarded credit worthy ends when a country's public debt exceeds its annual GDP. Since the U. S. will have crossed that threshold by the end of Fiscal Year 2016, we cannot have any assurance that this option of significantly increasing our debt over a short period of time will be acceptable to the rest of the world. And since as much as one-half of our indebtedness each year is purchased by foreign countries, their threshold of acceptance is a major determining factor in our ability to use this option.

2. *The second option used to reduce the cost of the financial meltdown to the U. S. Economy in general was for the Fed to quickly reduce the interest rate charged to commercial banks to borrow from the Fed (discount rate or the federal funds rate) to the unprecedented low rate of .25% (that is one-quarter of one per cent). The Fed retained this low discount rate through the first quarter of Calendar Year 2016— roughly 7 years at this sustained low rate. The Fed reduced this rate not only to help banks reduce their overabundant portfolio of bad home loans, but also to keep the recession from being any worse than it quickly became. The reduced discount rate has gradually permitted homeowners to reduce their interest rates on their home loans from 7% or higher to 3% or less. This has promoted sizably reduced monthly house payments to homeowners, making their homes more affordable and easing the number of foreclosures throughout the U. S. each year into the future for the next 20 to thirty years. The low discount rate has also allowed financial lending institutions to provide low interest or zero interest loans on large purchase items such as autos, home repairs and furnishing, and large appliances. All this has led to an increase in purchasing power on the part of working consumers and has helped pull the U. S. Economy from the scourge of recession. However, the price has been to render the Fed unable to use this policy option during any near-term economic slump because you cannot lower interest rates below 0%, and the current .5% discount rate is painfully close to 0%.*

3.   *A major negative effect of the meltdown of 2008 was a significant loss of confidence by a number of representatives and senators in the U. S. Congress. In fact, there are many members in the body politic throughout the United States at the federal and state and local levels as well who blame the financial meltdown on the institutions' leaders within the financial industry/system itself. Thus, on 21 July 2010, President Obama signed into law, the Dodd-Frank Act which made the most significant reforms to the financial sector of the U. S. Economy since post-Depression legislation in the early 1930s. It created a new regulatory authority, called the Financial Stability Oversight Council (FSOC) whose job is to oversee and monitor the financial performance of all financial institutions and create regulations by which those financial institutions will conduct business. This comprehensive act was a direct hit to the hearts of the varied financial institutions to indicate that the Congress and the President no longer trusted the financial institutions to act towards the general benefit of the American public or the U. S. Economy. The financial institutions have bitterly complained that compliance with the sometimes-competing elements of the bill make it difficult, if not impossible to meet all of the tenets of the law. Additionally, the financial institutions complain that the continual issuance of new regulations by the FSOC are costly in terms of implementation and complexity of objectives and reporting. This current culture of mistrust between the Congress and the collective institutions within the U. S. financial system is neither good nor productive for the U. S. Economy currently or in the future. This rift needs quick repair, for unless the political community can reach happy accord with the institutions in the financial system, the current and future economic engine cannot run smoothly.*

In summary, the current state of the U. S. financial system and its component industries and institutions are in a major state of disarray. As a conservative economist, I believe that we need to realign the financial system into distinct segments of products and services that do not overlap, and that we combine the roles and missions of the myriad of regulatory and administrative agencies in the financial system. This is necessary to ensure that we promote economy of effort within the federal government; ensure non-proliferation, duplication, and conflict of regulation; and prevent the future potential of finger-pointing as institutional problems flare up. Finally, the Federal Reserve System is over 100 years old. It seems to me to be ripe for comprehensive review and potential restructure. One thing that really sticks out to me is that the Fed's Board of Governors have on the one hand a tremendous amount of unchecked power and influence over the operations and performance of the U. S. Economy. The seven people of the Board of Governors have historically acted independently, with no oversight, nor personal or organizational repercussions to their actions or inactions that have greatly affected the performance of our economy and brought severe consequences to the U. S. public. I am reminded of Paul Volker's actions to reduce inflation quickly in the 1979–1984 time frame which brought the U. S. into a grave recession, and the failure of the Fed's Board of Governors to identify the housing loan bubble slightly less than a decade ago, and their failure to prevent it from bursting, or at least greatly reducing its disastrous effect when it did burst.

Now that we have completed the background on the mechanics and operations of our U. S. Capitalist Economic System, we will delve into our final Section of the book which deals with a number of our persistent economic issues starting first with the issue of economic growth and our two competing theories on how best to accomplish it.

The New Era of Banking in the United States

The U. S. Treasury Secretary, Janet Yellen on/around 1 July 2023 said that the Federal Government was immediately entering a new era of money in the United States. The new monetary tools for exchanging goods and services in the U. S. will gradually convert to a "Digital Currency." She did not, nor has the Treasury Department or Federal Reserve provided a lot of specifics of what is to come, but here are a few things I have been able to conclude from my research and reading on the topic. The formal new name of this digital currency is the U. S. Central Bank Digital Currency (CBDC). This digital currency will be controlled by the Federal Reserve System and is meant to immediately replace the recent breakout of crypto-currencies throughout the world and the United States. These crypto currencies all arose after the development and use of Bitcoin across the world markets. Rumors abide that Bitcoin was established by the Russian Mafia in order to be able to translate financial transactions throughout the world with a common "currency" that translated to the Russian Ruble. Most of the cyber attacks asking for ransom in the U. S. tend to ask that the ransom be translated from U. S. dollars into Bitcoin. Whatever the reason for the development of Bitcoin, and the use thereof, crypto currency became of great interest to the U. S. Today there are dozens of crypto currencies being bought and sold in financial trading markets. The problem with crypto currencies in general is that most still cannot be exchanged for true goods or services which is the only real reason for any currency to exist.

The U. S. had several incentives working to bring a digital currency about. First, the budget to print the dollar bills in all the various denominations (known as fiat money) for 2023 was $931 million for all denominations of U. S. paper money (also entitled Federal Reserve Notes). Additionally, the Board of Governors of the Federal Reserve System asked for an additional $787 million for a multiyear project to revolutionize the method of printing U. S. currency and making it much more difficult to counterfeit. Second, all U. S. banks who are members of the Federal Reserve System continue to complain that in this day of modern digital data transfer capability in a matter of a few seconds from Point A on the West Coast in the U. S. to Point B on the East Coast of the U. S., the Federal Reserve usually takes a couple of days to clear data payment transactions between banks in the U. S. It is, I believe a softly stated hope of the Federal Reserve that the CBDC will rectify the conditions of this complaint. Third, since all digital currency transactions are supposed to be registered almost immediately, the banking customer benefits by having an accurate, up to date, list of transactions for the day and end of day balance of dollars left in their accounts. In effect, the household and small business banking customers won't get caught by 3-day old transactions still not being subtracted from their balance. Additionally, the Federal Reserve hopes that all deposits will be made digitally so that the need for banks to hold adding money from person or small company for deposit into their customers account because of waiting for the check to clear the books of the bank of the person or small company will virtually vanish. Finally, there is no doubt that investigative agencies within the Federal Government want to limit the use of hard currency cash transactions that are rampant in so many illegal operations such as on the street drug sales, international drug sale transactions, and money laundering transactions. Additionally, there are many non-criminals in the U. S. who are afraid a Federal Government Agency may use the digital currency transaction records to "spy" on them and as a result freeze their accounts for some perceived, but erroneous suspicious illegal activity.

What is not clear to me is whether the concept of the digital currency will provide any of the aforementioned "advantage" when we pretty much get all those advantages as consumers and transaction reviews available to the Federal investigative agencies with a debit card. However, a true digital currency that promotes and truly promotes the advantages of speed to register transactions may have some of the expected benefits. Ultimately its usefulness to banks, business, and consumers in their use of money to exchange goods and services should provide the only real measure of CDBC's usefulness or lack thereof.

SECTION III

U. S. ECONOMIC ISSUES

DR. JOHN C. BREDFELDT

CHAPTER TEN
Creating Economic Growth In The United States

The Three Competing Theories on How to Achieve Economic Growth

Before we discuss the competing theories on promoting economic growth, we should briefly define what economic growth is. The Congress, as signed by President Truman on 20 February 1946, a law entitled, "The Employment Act of 1946." This law stated the public policy goals to be full employment of human and other resources so as to promote "maximum employment, production, and purchasing power." This act was and today, continues to be interpreted into two major economic policy goals of full human employment, and stable prices (low inflation or low deflation). The Employment Act of 1946 was amended on 27 October 1978 by Public Law 95-523, the Full Employment and Balanced Growth Act of 1978. This Act set the numeric goals of a maximum unemployment rate of 3 per cent per year and a maximum inflation rate of 3 per cent per year. Interestingly enough, both these laws placed the responsibility of achieving these economic growth goals squarely in the lap of the president. The Congress mentions no responsibility on their part to ensure the achievement of these goals from/via their many and varied legislative actions. But, obviously these two laws expect action on the part of the federal government to promote and ensure the achievement of the goals of low unemployment and low inflation. But how, specifically, do the combinations of economic policy and governmental public policy achieve these two goals. For the last century or so, three combined economic and governmental policies have developed world-wide towards the achievement of these goals.

The first, economic/public policy alternative to achieve economic growth was developed just prior to World War I with the establishment of the Marxist revolution in Russia. The Marxist revolution simply organized into a centrally planned and controlled economic system. The central planners and controllers were members of the Communist Party. They controlled all levels of government and all production. They collectively planned the output goals for each industry, firm, and individual business enterprise. The also collectively planned the allocation of the entire country's resources, including the education and skill levels of each human resource, their individual compensation, and specific places of employment. Carl Marx generally declared that there would be not stratification of economic or social status in a Marxist state. However, within Russia, there did develop a two-tiered economic state combined with two major levels of social status and culture. Generally, those who were members of the Communist Party were given the jobs of authority and control of the economy, and were rewarded by a much higher standard of living with many perquisites not granted to the mass public of non-communist party member employees. The economic growth, or lack thereof was completely in the hands of the elite politicians and senior level decision-makers of resource allocations and production output. In short, the entire economic system was run by the equivalent, if not declared central government. The economic system was thus a product of 100% human intervention with no external market incentives being permitted to influence or interfere with the human decision-makers. As a result, the government had complete control of the amount of all resources employed, the total output produced, and the price levels.

Capitalism was practiced to varying degrees in the western European countries, Australia, Canada, and the United States during the first 3 decades of the 20th Century. However, the Great Depression that hit the United States in 1929 and lingered stubbornly, spread quickly world-wide with the devastating effect of challenging the efficacy of the Capitalist economic system in terms of its long-term viability. Indeed, many wondered if the warning of capitalism's self-destruction had not arrived. An economist from England by the name of John Maynard Keynes proposed that capitalism had failed, not because of its inherent life-limited shortcomings as predicted by Marx, but rather from a catastrophic cataclysm of economic events natural to occur on occasion in any economic system. He proposed that, a free market economic system such as capitalism, unbridled by forced corrective mechanisms were subject to the drastic results from the aftermath of capitalism's self-induced corrective mechanisms. These corrective mechanisms in capitalism were a natural outgrowth of the ebb and flow of market interactions that he called the "business cycle." Basically, the business cycle was a continuum of periods of progressive business growth spurred by increased demand/consumption which then would peak and begin a downturn of decreased demand/consumption that would result in decreased business output, decreased employment, decreased consumer income, and decreased demand for goods and services. In short, he stated that the cause of the Great Depression in the U. S. was a massive decrease in consumption by people when they lost massive amounts of income and wealth from the stock market crash. Businesses could no longer continue to produce because they could no longer sell their goods. In order to reduce costs and minimize losses, businesses laid of a large segment of their workers, which, in turn exacerbated the drastic decrease in consumer incomes and demand. Keynes considered the Great Depression a severe trough in a business cycle.

Keynes proposed that central governments in a capitalist economic environment, needed to reverse their policies of non-interference in the economic system towards policies designed to increase demand. By increasing demand, supply and output would necessarily increase because people would have renewed income to spend on a greater quantity of goods and services. The central governments should deliberately spend more money than they raised in revenue thus incurring budget deficits. They could place more money in the hands of people by either decreasing taxes and/or providing them additional income. He recommended that incomes be increased by providing the unemployed with direct infusions of cash from the government and by developing government programs/projects designed to increase employment and output. President Franklin Roosevelt and the U. S. Congress quickly began rather modest implementation of the policy recommendations by Keynes under what President Roosevelt called, the New Deal. During the decade of the 1930's the United States gradually improved the economic lot of the American public, but the Gross Domestic Product did not reach the same level of output of 1929 until 1941. The United States federal government's economic policy from 1933 through 1980 has been decidedly a continuation of Keynesian concepts. However, there is a theoretical flaw in the exercise of Keynesian theory to meet the two major economic goals stated by the two federal employment acts stated in the first paragraph of this chapter. That flaw is the recognized results of a change in the demand for goods and services in a capitalist economy. Should the Congress and president be successful in increasing the total demand via their targeted federal policies, the theoretically predicted results would be an increase in output of goods and services, but with a general rise in prices? Should the federal government policies create an environment that would decrease total demand, prices would decrease, but total output in the U. S. Economy would decrease as well. Thus, the implementation of Keynesian policies which focus on demand management by the federal government can never result in the achievement of both U. S. economic goals. There is always a trade-off where you either achieve greater output, but with higher prices, or you can lower price levels, but only at the expense of production output. There simply is no conceivable theoretical basis where government economic policies focused on affecting demand will meet both the stated U. S. economic goals in law. By contrast to the U. S. experience of the slow 11-year recovery of the U. S. from the Great Depression, Germany got out of their depression in a matter of less than 5 years. Their climb from the recession began in 1933, and continued through the early years of World War II. The reason that Germany suffered less than five years in their Depression versus the U. S. period of 11 years is that Germany's economic policy was much different from the Keynesian policy of demand management. Rather, Germany's approach was to vastly increase the supply of war goods and services by providing significant funds to the war-making industries to prepare for the reclamation of German lands and peoples that he knew would probably precipitate war. The U. S. economic engine increased in GDP from $103 billion in 1940 to $203 billion in 1943 and $225 billion in 1944. Additionally, the unemployment rate decreased from 8.1% in 1940 to 2.7% in 1942 and 0.7% in 1944. Furthermore, the unemployment rate remained at less than 3% through 1949. The U. S. during the World War II time frame experienced the same phenomenon of huge economic growth during WWII that Germany experienced in their 6 years prior to their starting WWII—they had adopted central government economic policies that increased supply, a focus on output, rather than a focus on demand as cited by Keynes.

After WWII, the U. S. federal government economic policy reverted back to Keynesian theory. It was enthusiastically applied by President Lyndon Johnson and a democratic-controlled Congress when they established the "War on Poverty." Once again, the federal government brought about a significant increase in demand by providing cash or the equivalent of cash services to the American public. Within a decade and a half of the creation of these new programs, the U. S. experienced an inflation rate of 11.3% in 1979, 13.5% in 1980, and 10.3% in 1981. Additionally, the unemployment rate was 8.5% in 1975, averaged slightly less than 7% from 1976 through 1980, was 9.7% in 1981, 9.6% in 1982. In short, this major demand management push from the War on Poverty resulted in a major increase in inflation and a reduction in output sufficient to place millions of Americans out of work.

Largely because of the myriad of unfavorable economic indicators at the end of the 1970's, the United States public sought and received the third (new) economic policy vision for our federal government to follow. It was called supply-side economics, and it placed the entire focus of government economic policy on influencing the supply/production side of the economic equation. From an economic theory perspective, the policies would be directed at increasing supply with the result of increasing output while at the same time reducing inflation in the U. S. Economy. In summary, the implementation of supply-side theory would meet both the stated economic goals in law. This new policy initiative had a few major proponents from academia, but its implementation would be assured if the American public placed Ronald Reagan in the presidency and retained a few notable Republican Congressional leaders in office in 1980. Ronald Reagan won the presidency, the Republicans won the U. S. Senate, and key House Republicans retained their seats. As a result, the experiment in supply-side economics became implemented policy. The inflation rate went to 3.2% in 1983, and averaged 3.95% from 1984 through 1990. The unemployment rate fell from 9.6% in 1983 to 5.6% in 1990. The number of people employed in the U. S. increased from 99.3 million people in 1980 to 118.8 million people in 1990. Real Gross Domestic Product increased from $4.615 trillion in 1980 to $6.136 trillion in 1990 (in 1992 constant dollars). This represents a 10-year growth in output of 33%. By all of the economic statistics that represent the achievement of the stated economic policy goals in federal law, supply side economics was a success. The major detractor from these economic achievements were the sizable federal government deficits that occurred for the 1980 to 1990 time frame. Federal budget deficits grew from $73.8 billion in 1980 to $221 billion in 1990. These budget deficits were blamed solely on the implementation of supply-side economics, but the continued significant growth in the federal government welfare expenditures from the demand management federal policies were at least a major contributor to the deficits. And, as we have already seen, the federal budget deficits generated from the historical demand management federal government policies certainly did not always achieve the economic goals of increased output, stable prices, and low unemployment.

For the remaining discussion of government policy options to control/influence a country's economic system, we will ignore any more discussion about Marxist and total socialist political and/or economic systems. Rather, we will limit the discussion to the two major governmental policy options to influence a capitalistic economy—demand management, and supply-side.

The Implementation Methods of Government Demand Management

Demand management is a simple economic tool which the Congress can implement to increase or decrease the amount of money placed in the pockets of the American populace in general or targeted segments of the American populace. There are two major methods of the Congress placing money in the hands of the American populace. One is through a general tax decrease which, in turn leaves more annual income of each taxpayer in the taxpayers' pockets. This additional money can then be spent on additional goods and services which becomes a direct increase in the demand for those goods and services. Multiply this by the 100 million or so tax-paying households in the U. S. and the increase in demand throughout the economy can be substantial. The other way that the Congress can increase demand is by providing targeted segments of Americans with direct cash in hand or subsidies. During the last 80 plus years, the Congress has created a vast myriad of programs designed to provide money or consumer specified services to the American public. These programs collectively, totaled slightly over $1.0 trillion in Fiscal Year 1985 (in FY 2022 dollars) which ended on 30 September 1985. As you will see in much greater detail, the Payments to Individuals increased to $4.527 trillion in FY 2022 (FY 2022 dollars). This deliberate Congressional increase from Fiscal Year 1940 to Fiscal Year 2022 did not come without a price. The Federal Budget will be addressed in total in and in detail in Chapter 11. Below are a few broad reasons for both the current and historical growth in Federal Government Payments to Individuals.

First and foremost, the Keynesian demand management public policy in this long-term application instance was a miserable failure in curbing Federal Fiscal Spending for Payments to Individuals once started in 1933. The implementation of this demand-management public policy from 1940 to 2022 increased the Federal Government's indebtedness from 51.6% of GDP in 1940 to just over 100% of GDP in 2013 to 123.4% of GDP in FY 2022. This significant increase in our federal debt has placed the United States in peril in that approximately half that debt is owned by foreign governments. Some of those foreign governments are not our friends and owning significant amounts of that debt provides them a considerable amount of political leverage in that they simply have to say, "Meet our political demands, or we will demand immediate payment of our entire debt holdings." Secondly, the growth in Payments to Individuals in FY 2022 dollars has gone from $33.8 billion in 1940 to $4.527 trillion in 2022. The sizable indebtedness not only poses dire financial threats as long as it remains at this level, but, there seems to be nothing happening in the Congress to begin a significant decrease in this category of Federal Government expenditures.

There are those who state that the demand management model worked well for the U. S. since 1940. I'm not one of them. One quick example should indicate the major financial jeopardy we are in with our debt at ONLY $30.8 trillion. Every 1 percentage point increase in the U. S. interest rate, increases our annual interest payments on the Federal Debt as of the end of FY 2022 by over $300 billion per year. Because the current Federal Funds Rate established by the Federal Reserve is now at 5.5%, within a couple of years, the annual interest expense for the federal debt will quickly exceed $1.5 trillion The continued application of Keynesian economic policies since 1933 and particularly since 1957 has resulted in the Federal Government spending more than the tax

DR. JOHN C. BREDFELDT

revenue received because some segment of society needed to be "helped" or "bailed out" by the Federal Government.

One Keynesian policy element needs a review at this time. That is, how does the United States achieve a surplus or, at least a balanced Federal budget? The Keynesian approach, as has been greatly advertised by the Democratic Party is to raise taxes. In the U. S., we have two major sources of tax revenue—income taxes and payroll taxes (otherwise known as Social Security plus Medicare taxes). Setting the payroll tax increases aside, since they are not meant to be an element of annual Keynesian theory implementation, that leaves the Federal income tax as the singular source to adjust to balance the Federal budget or create a surplus Federal budget. So, for policy argument, let's say that the Democratic Party won the presidency and both houses of Congress for four years beginning in 2020 and 2022, and that they truly were determined to create a surplus Federal budget for those four years. Let us further assume that their policy goals would be to create that surplus by budgeting expenditures at a growth not to exceed the rate of inflation for each of those four years. The focus then turns towards creating a surplus budget solely through tax increases by a goal of $1.5 trillion a year for as many future years as it takes to significantly decrease the Federal Government's debt. In FY 2022 the Federal Government's revenue was $4.897 trillion. In 2022, the two direct income taxes that the Congress could implement immediate increases were personal income taxes ($2.632 trillion collected) and corporate income taxes ($424 billion collected). Suppose the democrats chose the alternative to make all income taxpayers share proportionately in the income tax increase necessary to achieve the $1.5 trillion increase. This would mean that every taxpayer (both people and businesses) would need to pay an increase in their tax burden of 50% for 2024 through all future years to meet the current established Federal Expenditure programs. It is easy for each of us taxpayers who are not in the top 5% income earners to imagine the devastation such a tax increase would have on us. But, we need to understand that a current proposal to more double the taxes on the top 5% of income earners in the U. S. would not be free of consequences either. These top 5% income earners also tend to run many of the most prosperous "small companies" that provide a sizable number of jobs throughout the United States. A substantial increase in their taxes would not simply reduce their incentive to earn income, it would destroy their ability to hire workers because their reduction in profits due to the significant increase in taxes becomes an unaffordable cost increase to their businesses. Such a large increase in their taxes would also destroy their capability to expand their company's operations, thus placing additional pressures on a diminished rate of employment and total number of people employed in the U. S.

A proposal of the democrats, liberals, and progressives is to increase corporate income taxes along with increasing taxes on individuals. Many liberals, progressives, and members of the Democratic Party believe that corporate taxes are too low. However, the current U. S. corporate tax rates have been cited as a major contributing factor to U. S. corporations sending large segments of their production to countries outside the borders of the United States. This certainly reduces the number of U. S. workers employed and the associated GDP that would go with their incomes they would spend to increase our GDP. We conservative economists believe it is great folly to increase taxes on those who provide the jobs and output of the entire U. S. Economy.

In short, solving the current sizable Federal budget deficits solely by increasing taxes would be counter-productive to achieving the economic goals of growth of economic output and low unemployment. Additionally, income tax changes are fraught with complexities that make estimating the impact to Federal tax revenues difficult and the tax change estimates themselves highly imprecise. Furthermore, every income tax increase involves the Congress having to determine which group(s) within their constituencies to gore by those tax increases, and how much to allocate to each constituency. The truth of the matter is that virtually every income tax increase passed by the Congress during the last century has affected many more groups of taxpayers than advertised at the passage of the bill. Because of the complexities of the Federal Income Tax Code, it is virtually impossible to accurately predict whether all the targeted tax law or tax rate change will affect only the targeted groups, and whether those changes will affect every taxpayer in the targeted groups. The news is filled every week with horror stories of wealthy people and mega-corporations escaping the payment of taxes, or ordinary, middle-class taxpayers paying exorbitant taxes due to inescapable oddball circumstances that place them in an unusual one-time wealthy income earner status. An example of the latter often happens with the transition of wealth and assets from parents to children due to large dollar value gifts or the major "death tax" rate of estate transfers. Finally, it is political suicide for our representatives and senators in Congress to propose, let alone, implement a general income tax increase across the board to all taxpayers. These taxpayers will always remember who increased their taxes when the next election arrives.

Thus, the Keynesian policy initiative of raising taxes during good economic times to promote budget surpluses and decreasing total demand pressures in the U. S. Economy simply rarely occur. Nor, during those same good economic times, is it reasonable to expect the Congress to reduce the government payments and subsidies to those who have been collecting them for several months or several years. These people, too, are voters and their memories of lost income from Federal government payments and subsidies will weigh heavily on their minds at election time as well. So, the truth is that the Democratic Party, because of their embrace of Keynesian demand-management public policy has placed themselves in a position of continued political ineptitude. Though it is easy and welcome politics to deliberately expand the demand of the entire U. S. population by cutting taxes and increasing payments and subsidies to individuals, it is certain political suicide to decrease the general pressures of hyper-demand by increasing taxes AND reducing government payments to the American public. The Democratic Party might be able to survive angering either the taxpaying portion of the public, or the major segment of the U. S. public collecting revenue and subsidies from the Federal government. But, angering the entire U. S. voting population by doing both at once provides an absolute certainty of being relieved of office at the next national election. So, in the final analysis, not only is demand-management public policy unfavorable because of the probable effects on the U. S. Economy, it is not viable because of its disastrous political ramifications.

The Implementation Methods of Supply-side Economic Public Policy

Keynesian economic theory became the singular major public policy instrument for the United States beginning with President Franklin

Roosevelt's New Deal in the early 1930s. It dominated academic teaching and governmental economic public policy implementation through the 1970s. The Keynesian demand management theory and public policies became the mantle of all economic activity of the Democratic Party by the end of the 1930s and has remained their singular economic thought through this day. However, in the mid-1970s, a new economic policy alternative began to take shape with beginnings both in academia and with a few "true believers" in the Republican Party. This fledgling economic policy became known as supply-side theory. This new policy got a major boost in national discussion and attention when Ronald Reagan began to run as a candidate for president of the United States prior to and during the Republican Party primary season. Supply-side theory became the base economic theory and policy of the Republican Party platform after Reagan was nominated as the presidential candidate for the Republican Party in 1980, and the economic public policy of Reagan and the Republican Party when he was inaugurated as President in 1981.

Supply-side economic theory is quite simple in its over-arching concept. The economic goal is to increase supply. This, in turn results in increased production output, increased employment of all resources with a focus on increased usage of human labor, and an increase in GDP. Not only does the implementation of Supply-side theory via public policy increase output, but it also results in low inflation and once achieved, a long-term period of low inflation. The benefits of increasing supply were easily accepted by the Republican Party. But, the policy implementation methods to achieve an increase in supply was more troublesome. Generally, the public policy implementation had to target how to get businesses to expand their production. Ronald Reagan proposed that the key was to develop policies that would greatly encourage businesses to invest in new plants and equipment and to innovate new technologies into new products. In short, public policy should target an increase in the national pools of savings dollars and accelerated depreciation on new plant and equipment. The increase in the national pool of savings would provide business the seed money needed to accomplish aquick increase in business purchase/construction in new plants and equipment, as well as significant business innovation of new technologies on the horizon.

The only way to provide a sizable pool of savings to be available for business investment was to decrease taxes. And, the best way to ensure the largest pool of savings would be to decrease taxes for the wealthiest Americans because their rate of savings was much higher than low- and middle-income Americans. Low- and middle-income American households had to spend most of their income on consumption to achieve and maintain a reasonable standard of living. But wealthy households spent much less of their annual income on consumption because homes needed to be only so large to house a family, only a car in the garage was needed for each driving-age member of the family, and people could only eat three basic meals per day. In short, opulence in consumption did have its limitations, and wealthy people had a lot of income remaining beyond their consumption levels which was placed in financial savings instruments of some type. Another way of looking at it was that the means of production were owned by the wealthy Americans and they were the ones who needed both encouragements to save more and the ability to save more. So, President Reagan and the Congress implemented a reduction in income tax rates with the greatest tax rate reductions to those in the highest tax brackets. Additionally, to encourage business boards of directors and chief executive officers to expand their business production and more quickly incorporate new technologies into new products and services, President Reagan proposed and the Congress passed legislation to greatly accelerate depreciation on newly invested plant and equipment. Buildings were to be depreciated in 10 years versus the previous time frame of 30 years or more. Major manufacturing equipment depreciation time was depreciated in 5 years, rather than 10 to 20 years. And, small equipment items' depreciation time was reduced to 2 years versus the 5-to-10-year depreciation time frame prior to the implementation of Supply-side economic policy.

The implementation of these Supply-side policies took the United States from the worst recession in the 1980-1982 time frame on a robust 8 year sustained economic growth spurt from 1980 through 1988. The Gross National Product (roughly equivalent to GDP) rose from $2.732 trillion in 1980 to $4.881 trillion in 1982. The number of employed Americans rose from 100.9 million people in 1980 to 116.7 million in 1988. Proprietors' income rose from $180.7 billion in 1980 to $327.8 billion in 1988. Corporate profits rose from $177.2 billion in 1980 to $328.6 billion in 1988. Business expenditures for new plant and equipment went from $282.8 billion in 1980 to $429.7 billion in 1988. Consumer prices fell from 13.5 % in 1980 to 3.2% in 1983 and remained and averaged less than 4% per year from 1983 through 1988. By virtually all measures of economic performance, the implementation of Supply-side economic policies brought the U. S. Economy from a major recession quickly and a very robust sustained 8-year growth.

There was one major drawback. The annual federal budget deficit grew from $73.8 billion in 1980 to $1278.0 billion in 1982 to hover around $200 billion per year from 1983 through 1986, then around $150 billion for 1987 and 1988. These deficits were blamed on everything from lost revenue due to the tax cuts implemented in 1981 to a sizable increase in annual defense spending to a failure of Supply-side economic policy to generate sustained future tax revenue as the GDP increases. In truth the deficits were not caused by a reduction in tax revenues except from 1982 to 1983 when the Federal receipts decreased by $18 billion. From 1984 through 1988 annual tax receipts increased by over $60 billion from year to year such that the revenues rose from $600.6 billion in 1983 to $909.2 billion in 1988. Thus, Supply-side economics affected the annual revenue stream to the Federal government as expected from a theoretical perspective. Defense Expenditures rose from $134.6 billion in 1980 at an annual increase of approximately $20 billion until it reached $290.9 billion in 1988. The average annual revenue increases more than offset the annual defense expenditure build-up. A major single causal factor for the growth in the annual deficits were the collective payments to individuals programs which rose from $280.4 billion in 1980 to $510.0 billion in 1988 (an average increase of almost $30 billion each year). The final major component for the increase in the annual budget deficits was the interest paid on the ever-increasing debt. The annual interest payments rose from $52.5 billion in 1980 to $214.0 billion in 1988 (and average annual increase of $20 billion).

Once the Federal budget deficits reached $200 billion a year in 1983, the two economic policy alternatives of Demand-management versus Supply-side were placed on hold because the federal indebtedness became a visible portion of the annual budget due to the size of the annual interest payments and the realization that the annual interest payments were going to increase each year as long as the debt rose. And, by 1988, the annual interest paid on the ever-increasing debt became the singular causal factor for the deficit itself because the annual interest payments began to exceed the annual deficit. For the next 20 years beyond 1988, federal budget policy focused solely on the annual deficits and accumulating debt and economic policy discussions were mostly set aside. But the financial meltdown of 2008 brought another major economic downturn in the U. S. Economy, and with the Democrats in power in the presidency, the Senate, and the House, Keynesian economic policies of severe annual deficits became the norm. The implementation of Supply-side economic policy awaits a Republican President and Republican control of both houses of Congress, because Democrats adamantly oppose Supply-side economic policies.

As a conservative economist, I certainly support Supply-side economic policy over Keynesian Demand-management policy. The more successful Demand-management policy is, the less our country will realize the achievement of our stated economic goals. But, with Supply-side economic theory implementation, economic growth should happen more quickly because it focuses on encouraging businesses to expand and innovate. And, because suppliers and producers in the economy drive expansion through hiring more resources, Supply-side policies should have a more direct and a more immediate positive impact on economic growth than with Demand-management. This is true because it takes a lot more time to convince a business to grow as a reaction to demand increases, because there are no direct incentives to produce more, especially in times where there is no assurance that aggregate demand throughout our economy will be sustained.

The Lesson of Human Participation in the Production of Goods and Services

I want to briefly mention here a Necessary concept and issue that we will need to remember on all the topics that follow in this book. Beyond remembering to talk about it, we must ALWAYS remember its immutable truth. So, what is this concept? It is simply this. Every able-bodied individual in our borders of the U. S. needs to be either be preparing to produce a necessary good or service to society, or in fact, producing a good or service in society. Any economy who permits some part of its population to refrain from being an economically productive member of our society will cause a great deal of pain on those of us who are either working towards being a producer in our economy or is actively producing something in our society. An economy that has a large number of people who are not being productive takes a necessary activity or product from the rest of us. We have two major problems in our U. S. Economy today in which this issue will be discussed in greater detail because the cost to the American public is enormous not only in terms of the dollar costs to provide them food, shelter, and clothing cast on those of us who do work, but the drastically reduced output that their production of any good or service of their choosing that we all face. Additionally, some of these enormous economic costs to our entire society are often hidden and rarely discussed.

CHAPTER ELEVEN
Federal Government Deficits, Debt, And Expenditures on Entitlement/Welfare Programs

Negative Effects of Long-Term Federal Government Deficits and Debt

I placed this U. S. Economic issue at the top of our U. S. economic troubles intentionally. The U. S. has experienced federal budget deficits for all but 12 years out of the last 82 (1940 through 2022). As an economist, outside of an all-out nuclear war, I contend that this is the most important and impactful problem the U. S. needs to solve. The major problem inhibiting solution is that the Congress of the United States is constitutionally the only assembly of Americans that can solve it. In fact, the Congresses of the last 83 years caused today's annual federal budget deficits and added to the annual end of year Federal debt. It has been solely the Congress due to their Constitutional powers of determining annual revenue and expenditures. Their power of the entire financial condition of the U. S. comes from their Constitutional authority to appropriate the annual funds that can be spent by all U. S. departments and agencies, and their singular Constitutional authority (and responsibility) to set the Federal tax rates and levies that determine the amount of revenue generated by the Federal Government each year. Simply put, the reason the U. S. Government has experienced annual Federal budget deficits for 71 out of the last 83 years is that the Congress has simply ignored taking the actions either to decrease expenditures or increase taxes to promote annual Federal Budget surpluses.

The reason for the relatively continuous Federal Budget deficits year after year results from the likely irritation of the American public to see their taxes increased and/or Federal cash benefits reduced. The political ramifications to the members of both houses of the U. S. Congress are tremendous both as political parties, but most assuredly as a member of the Congress who votes to increase taxes on either people or businesses, or decrease some Federal Government subsidy or payment received by businesses or individuals. Today, to solve the annual Federal budget deficits by creating annual Federal budget surpluses will take significant tax increases AND cuts in annual Federal expenditures. As you might imagine, either of these two actions taken by a member of Congress would usually be sufficient for enough of his/her constituents to vote them out of office in the next election. A Congressional member who votes for both tax increases and Federal expenditure cuts might even be recalled from their seat in the Congress to be replaced by someone who will go with the normal Congressional flow to simply let annual Federal Budget deficits continue, thus also increasing the indebtedness of the U. S. Government each year.

The advent of sustained implementation of Keynesian Demand-management principles of Federal Government involvement in the U. S. Economy has had disastrous effects on both the performance of the U. S. Economy and the financial health of the Federal Government. The Federal Debt has grown to over $30.0 trillion dollars at this point (end of September 2022). The Federal Government has racked up budget deficits for 71 of the last 83 years which has translated into this massive debt. The United States has a "welfare" mentality that has destroyed our cultural fiber and altered the views of millions of Americans as to what their responsibilities of adulthood are. Finally, this welfare mentality has drained the United States society of tens of trillions of dollars of lost output during the last half century as we pay more and more people to stay at home and collect welfare rather than work for their income to support themselves and their families. Just as happens in the private sector with businesses and individuals, the amount of indebtedness carried by the Federal Government matters to its creditors. And, at some point in time, the creditors of the U. S. Federal Government will, without prior warning, declare that the United States must pay down its debt substantially, if not completely before the creditors will renew purchase of our debt. Unless the United States Federal Government gets its financial house in order soon by achieving sustained annual budget surpluses and paying down its debt, we will face the same awful dilemma that businesses and households do—we will go into bankruptcy. However, unlike the U. S. legal system where businesses and individuals go into bankruptcy court for restructure and forgiveness of debt, international creditors have no similar legal system to force them into financial restructure of debt forgiveness. In short, for over 80 years, the U. S. Federal Government has been a "debtor" nation and we have become addicted to it.

Federal Government Annual Budget Deficits/Surpluses

Current Year Dollars in Billions

Fiscal Year	Total Revenue	Total Expenses	TOTAL Surplus/ Deficit (-)
2022	4,897.40	6,273.30	-1,375.90
2020	3,421.20	6,553.60	-3,132.40
2010	2,162.70	3,457.10	-1,294.40
2000	2,025.20	1,789.00	236.2
1990	1,032.00	1,252.00	-221
1980	517.1	590.9	-73.8
1970	192.8	195.6	-2.8
1960	92.5	92.2	0.3
1950	39.4	42.6	-3.2
1940	6.5	9.5	-3

Many economists and politicians have told the American public for the last 30 years that sizable annual Federal budget deficits and ever-increasing Federal debt are not alarming because our indebtedness was less than our annual GDP and because our annual deficits were "modest" compared to our annual GDP. However, over the last seven years, these two conditions were negated by the facts that our annual Federal budget deficits were as much as 10% of our annual GDP and our Federal debt now exceeds our annual GDP by over $2 trillion. Furthermore, the outlook for decreased annual deficits, though projected to stabilize around $1.5 plus trillion per year over the next 5 years are laughable. Why, because, we paid only around $540 billion in interest expenses in FY 2022. This equates to an interest rate of approximately 1.7% against an end of FY 2022 total indebtedness of approximately $32 trillion. However, the Federal Reserve, as it knows it must, has begun to ratchet interest rates upwards. The Federal Reserve has already increased the interest rate to somewhere in the more normal historically stable home borrowing interest rates of 5.5% or more as of the middle of

Calendar Year 2023. The impact of these rates to the Federal budget will be astronomical. The annual interest paid by the Federal Government will skyrocket from a mere $540 billion experienced in FY 2022 to a tidy sum of around $1.5 trillion per year by no later than 2028. The expected interest expense for the Federal Government for Fiscal Year 2024 is predicted to be around $770 billion according to the Fiscal Year 2024 President's Budget. Alas, the Federal Government's indebtedness is scheduled to increase by another $8.0 trillion plus from FY 2023 through FY 2028 which will only add to the annual interest expenses. Furthermore, these annual $1.5 trillion interest expenses will continue for decades unless the Congress takes aggressive action to significantly reduce the annual Federal budget. At this time, there appears to be no consensus in the Congress to accomplish such a feat. Truly, as I write on this topic today, continued inactivity of the Congress to bring us to a sustained Federal budget surplus soon will result in their hand being forced when, one day, the U. S. Treasury offers its debentures of debt only to have the rest of the world reject them in the market place. At that moment, the Federal Government will be placed on a cash flow basis where they can spend only as much money as they receive from taxpayers each month. At that time, the Congress will have only hours, but certainly not more than a few days to completely redesign its budget to live within our monthly cash income.

A third major negative impact of the last 83 years of welfare largess practiced by the collective Congresses during those years is the fact that, with those welfare programs, the United States society and the U. S. Economy have received no output. When the Federal Government provides cash money and or cash equivalent subsidies, yet receives no output, it is the equivalent of a business paying its laborers to stay at home for 2 six month vacations a year. No economy or society can survive when we pay people income for no output. At some point, you have an entire populace with income that outstrips the available goods and services in the economy because you have too few people in a work environment producing too few goods and services for the American populace as a whole. Even socialist and communist economic systems understand this fact. Both these systems ensure that people who collect government incomes in any fashion, provide useful products or services through employment to ensure the availability of goods and services to all in their society. People, especially economists and politicians who state that the U. S. public policy of a huge portion of our population receiving cash income from the Federal Government is necessary to offset the inhumane results of the Capitalist Economic System ignore the fact that people need to be incentivized to both prepare themselves to be productive employees and then to go through the daily grind of producing goods or services for the benefits of their fellow Americans. The negative statistics in segments of our society provide ample evidence that we have created geographic locations where people fail to do the minimally necessary actions to become and remain employable in decent paying jobs for which they provide a valuable good or service. One major example are the "inner cities" of metropolitan areas of the country. Statistically, the inner cities are where you will find high school graduation rates at or below 50%, drug usage and drug crime rates much higher, major crime in general much greater, an abnormally high rate of single parent homes (many of them fatherless), and a significantly high rate of unwed mothers, oftentimes with a larger number of children per household than the national average. All of these people struggle to make ends meet, even with welfare because they have incomes at or below the poverty level. American society either as a whole or as segmented is oftentimes named as the culprit for the woes of those in poverty in inner cities, with a hidden meaning that the ultimate cause is really the insistence of the Capitalist Economic System that people produce something of value to society in order to gain the income necessary to live a "decent" living. Yet, people who decide not to graduate from high school, do drugs, commit crimes, and have children out of wedlock, have made conscious decisions to live in poverty because these decisions, unless corrected condemn them to be unemployed or employed for life at the level of poverty income.

It is time for the United States presidents and Congresses of the immediate and long-term futures of our country to completely revamp our thinking that the Federal Government can solve poverty only by infusions of large dollars of cash to the "downtrodden" in America. Rather, we need to ensure that we bring back the economic incentives that drive Americans to work and climb the economic ladder in order to achieve a better standard of living for themselves and their families. Additionally, our politicians need to instill the sense of personal responsibility within each American individual such that each recognizes his/her accountability in providing for the economic welfare for themselves and their families. Only by achieving highly successful results from these initiatives, will the United States solve its severe Federal financial budget deficits and indebtedness crises, as well as promote a sizable increase in economic output resulting in explosive economic growth. So let us now get to this conservative economists' vision of how to revise the current U. S. welfare system to a powerful economic engine.

Three Methods of Creating a Surplus Federal Budget from Current Deficits

There are only three methods possible to move from our current habit of annual Federal budget deficits to annual Federal surpluses. The first method is to drastically reduce our annual expenditures. Since almost two-thirds of our annual expenditures are identified as payments to individuals, this is the area upon which future presidents and Congresses must focus. We will cover this topic in this chapter. The second method is to drastically increase our annual revenue to the Federal Government. Since the vast majority of our revenue to the Federal Government comes from taxes, we would need to increase taxes to at least some major segment of American business or people. We will address this topic in the next chapter. Finally, a combination of decreasing Federal expenditures and raising taxes could be used to bring about an annual Federal budget surplus. Let us now address the method of reducing our annual expenditures by drastically decreasing our annual Federal programs that provide payments to individuals.

Thoughts on Developing a True Capitalist Approach to Welfare

The first element that conservatives would apply to significantly reduce the annual amount of funds that the Federal Government spends on transfer payment and welfare programs is to make a correct distinction of the varied federal transfer programs. A popular definition used by politicians and the media for all payments to individuals programs is "entitlements." This is a significant misrepresentation of the collective sum of payments to individuals made by the Federal Government. The concept of an entitlement dictates that the individual has some "right" to something. Generally, this "right" has to be earned in some manner, as opposed to simply reside in a certain state of defined existence. There are only four major programs which the Federal Government pays to individuals for which they have "earned" a right to their benefits based on long term historic actions on the part of the individuals who receive the benefits. The three programs are Social Security and disability benefits, Medicare benefits, and Federal Government retirement. In all three of these programs, each recipient had to work a minimum number of years, reach a certain age, or meet a significant covered life event to collect those benefits. Finally, we have the veterans' benefits provided mostly through the Veterans Administration. These benefits were earned by veterans for serving in the United States armed forces. This program has been a part of the Federal budget since the days immediately following our Revolutionary War through the total history of our country.

For all other federal payments to individuals, the individual never "earned" the benefit through working. Rather, the benefit came to the individuals simply through a specified set of circumstances in which they live in their current state of existence. To be sure, one cannot collect from any of the many, varied federal benefits unless they meet certain criteria, but none of these programs require prior payments to the Federal Government through a structured system of federal collections for a long-specified period of time in order to receive benefits. I believe the myriad of these federal programs should be classified as "transfer payments," or "welfare" programs and definitely segregated from the true federal "entitlement" programs. And, as a conservative economist I submit that it is critical to any significant revision or restructuring of individual programs or collective federal programs that we consistently make and publicize these distinctions as to program type payments to individuals.

So, let us get a historic view of how the payment to individual programs have grown since their inception from FY 1940 through FY 2022. The table below provides a good summary of the growth trends of payments to individuals made by the Federal Government.

In fact, the annual increases in the Federal Budget Deficits grew significantly for so-called social programs. We will dissect the significant causes of the gradual increase in annual Federal Budget Deficits by looking at the trends of Expenditures through a historical looking glass at the beginning of each decade from 1940 through 2020 and finally 2022 as the most recent year with actual Federal financial data. These following charts will also all be translated into Fiscal Year (FY) 2022 purchasing power. All the expenditures in the following charts come from the Fiscal Year 2024 President's Budget Historical Tables document. The methodology of the translation of Current Year expenditures to FY 2022 was to take the current year actual data and multiply it by the cumulative Gross Domestic Product deflation rate for each year. The important thing to note is that the data in the following charts provide the purchasing power of Fiscal Year 2022 for each of the previous fiscal year data.

Federal Government Expenditures

FY 2022 Dollars in Billions

Fiscal Year	Operatns Expenses	Paymnts to Individs	TOTAL ANNUAL EXPEND
2022	1,746.37	4,526.96	6,273.32
2020	2,577.43	4,662.27	7,239.70
2010	1,504.59	3,018.08	4,522.67
2000	1,165.91	1,724.60	2,890.51
1990	1,310.68	1,179.70	2,490.38
1980	942.43	851.08	1,793.51
1970	734.26	368.67	1,102.93
1960	515.41	184.14	699.55
1950	279.52	129.75	409.28
1940	120.87	33.83	154.69

The chart above shows the annual total expenditures which the Federal Government spent on all operating expenses of the entire Federal Government's cabinet departments and other agencies. The operating expenses also cover the interest expense of the Federal Government's debt as well. The important thing to note here is that the percentage of the annual Federal Expenditures goes down significantly with each 10-year comparison. In FY 2000, the percentage of Payments to Individuals tips the scale to just under 60% of the annual expenditures, and slightly over 72% of total expenditures. Whereas the percentage of Payments to Individuals was at 47% of total expenditures in 1990. It is an obvious conclusion that Payments to Individuals has become a significantly more important category of Federal Expenses than the operational functions of the Federal Government in the last 30 years.

There are two general types of benefits provided to individuals by the Federal Government. The first type of benefit is a broad category called "Entitlements." Entitlements are benefits that have been earned by specific groups of Americans because of some form of payment to the American public and a financial premium in some form or another to the Federal Government for their future benefit payments. The chart below shows the Federal Government payments to individuals that are in the general category of entitlements.

Expenditures for Federal Government Entitlement Programs
FY 2022 Dollars in Billions

Fiscal Year	Social Secur	Fed Retire	Unem-ploymt	Veteran Benefits	Medicare And Resrch	Annual Total
2022	1221.87	173.1	48.04	264.67	1642.79	3350.47
2020	1215.82	174.04	521.78	236.74	1628.79	3777.18
2010	924.41	161.31	207.04	139.27	1083.63	2515.67
2000	663.56	128.7	34.15	75.67	563.07	1465.15
1990	503.49	106.22	34.8	59.63	308.27	1012.41
1980	365.23	82.75	52.02	64.2	167.85	732.05
1970	181.66	34.24	18.3	52.64	63.54	350.38
1962	108.97	15.31	25.86	41.93	3.71	195.78
1960	89.1	12.76	21.12	40.23	2.42	165.64
1950	9.86	4.79	19.34	82.73	1.34	118.07

All of the programs in this Chart, Entitled, Expenditures for Federal Government Entitlement Programs show the growth in annual expenditures every 10 years since 1940 through Fiscal Year (FY) 2022, all translated to FY 2022 equivalent purchasing power. Veterans Programs have been part of annual Federal Expenditures since the first U. S. appropriating and recording Federal Government revenue and expenses in 1792. Although military veterans pay no insurance "premium" financially, the American public has always considered the act of being a member of the U. S. military to earn the rights of care for any short term or life-long injury incurred during the time a military veteran wore the U. S. uniform. The formal system of payment of veterans for pensions and medical care first began in 1818. The concept of military retirement was formally recognized by the U. S. Congress in the mid-1800s shortly after the U. S. Civil War. The U. S. unemployment program became established in a limited form in 1910. The Federal Civil Service retirement program was established in 1920. Social Security became a formal program as part of President Roosevelt's New Deal list of programs in 1932. Finally, the Medicare program began in 1965. All the Entitlement programs require an individual to provide participatory funds on a monthly basis into each specific program in order to become eligible at a later time in their lives to collect benefits from the program. The one program that does not require individuals to pay a monthly fee for benefits received is the Federal Unemployment Insurance Program. However, American companies usually pay a monthly rate of around 2% of total payroll expenses to the Federal Government which then distributes funds to the state governments for administration and distribution of the funds.

The key factor in all of these programs is that either the individual "earns" future payment of these funds when they reach certain criteria to collect AND have participated either through direct payment of insurance-like fees, or participation in an employment of service to the U. S. Government and the American public.

The other type of monetary benefits paid to individuals come from programs that require no payment to the Federal Government or activity of service or output to receive the financial "benefit" from the Federal Government. These types of programs are generally called

"Welfare" programs because the individuals who collect these funds will be provided them when they certify that they have certain life circumstances that have forced them into poverty. They do not "earn" these funds from the standpoint of producing any output to the American Economy or to any American organization. Rather they collect the benefits from these programs having a large probability of NOT having provided much if any output.

Expenditures for Federal Government Welfare Programs
FY 2022 Dollars in Billions

Fiscal Year	Student Ed. Asst	Housing Assist	Medicaid	Food Assist	Public Assist	Other	Annual Total
2022	541.23	57	591.9	193.32	367.67	17.27	1768.39
2020	179.68	57.22	506.75	127.07	507.73	13.39	1391.84
2010	61.06	75.38	358.88	124.23	234.02	5.96	859.53
2000	14.94	46.25	190.48	52.3	138.14	7.82	449.93
1990	20.75	31.54	81.89	47.78	62.17	5.11	249.24
1980	15.45	16.93	42.49	42.29	49.16	6.69	173.01
1970	2.98	2.82	16	5.69	24.55	1	53.03
1962	0	1.22	0.74	2.04	17.26	1.79	23.06
1960	0	1.02	0	1.76	15.71	0	18.49
1950	0	-0.36	0	0.8	11.2	0	11.64
1940	0	0.31	0	0	11.07	0	11.38

The main point I want to make with the chart on Welfare payments is that they have doubled in total cost to the Federal Government and American public. They have become simply unaffordable and are the major collection of expense items that have driven much of our explosive federal budget deficits each year. That is, the Welfare programs are unaffordable IF the American public is accurately perceived as being loathe to significant tax increases.

As a conservative economist, I believe that we need to conduct a complete review of the structure, benefits received by society, and costs paid by society so that we can modify these program areas and each of the discrete programs within these program areas to ensure that we revitalize the personal economic incentives and individual responsibilities to provide output through work during the majority, if not entirety of their productive adult lives. Thus, I propose that the broad economic policy goals that future presidents and Congresses of the U. S. Federal Government should follow are as:

1.   *Restructure the Social Security and Medicare systems to increase revenue to the Federal Government and deny benefits to wealthy Americans.*

2.   *Transition our current welfare programs from transfer programs of cash and subsidies to welfare recipients to a workfare program where welfare recipients provide productive output, with a normal workweek to develop skills to transition from government welfare to real jobs.*

3.   *Ensure that welfare recipients meet the same drug, and alcohol abuse standards that all federal employees must meet to get and keep their jobs.*

4.   *Insist that people on welfare with no skills attend school to complete their high school diploma, and attend a trade school or technical college to become equipped to obtain long-term employment with wages/salaries sufficient to keep them above the poverty level for the remainder of their adult lives.*

5.   *Ensure that the Federal Government provides no welfare or transfer payments to illegal aliens.*

I will deal with a set of macro-level economic and social public policies that I believe conservatives should embrace and implement. I also expect that by implementing these policies, the United States Economy and Federal Government will achieve substantial benefits in economic growth, a major permanent reduction in the number of people out of work (otherwise defined as structural unemployment), and lead to annual federal budget surpluses as opposed to annual our current state of annual federal deficits.

Before I embark on these policies, I want to address an issue frequently levied at conservatives whenever we speak of restructuring our welfare programs, or deleting some of these programs completely. Today, we conservatives who propose that welfare is an insidious destroyer of both our American culture and our economy are usually decried as hard-hearted, people-haters. To all these liberal, progressive democrats, I pose the following statement:

"A large proportion of these unemployed and their dependents have been forced on the relief rolls. The burden on the Federal Government has grown with great rapidity. We have here a human as well as an economic problem. When humane considerations are concerned, Americans give them precedence. The lessons of history, confirmed by the evidence immediately before me, show conclusively that continued dependence upon relief induces a spiritual disintegration fundamentally destructive to the national fiber. To dole our relief in this way is to administer a narcotic, a subtle destroyer of the human spirit. It is inimical to the dictates of a sound policy. It is in violation of the traditions of America. Work must be found for able-bodied but destitute workers."

The above is a quote from Franklin D. Roosevelt's State of the Union Address in 1935. It is with these words in mind, along with the reality that our expenditures for individuals, outside those of Social Security and Medicare are out of control, that I will make the ensuing broad policy proposals.

How to Fix Social Security and Medicare

Social Security has collected more revenue than benefits paid for most of its 80 plus years' lifetime. However, beginning in FY 2021, Social Security expenses (including disability expenditures) began to exceed Social Security revenue for the first time. Medicare expenses began to exceed annual revenue beginning in FY 2009. Invested surpluses from past fiscal years have been used to pay for the excess expenses in Medicare and will be used to cover both Medicare and Social Security expenses for future years as long as the invested cumulative surpluses remain available. Should the time ever occur with the cumulative surpluses in either Medicare and/or Social Security the Federal Government will have to either raise taxes to retain benefit levels as they are, or decrease the benefits paid to beneficiaries. Fortunately, the fix for both programs is relatively simple and does not have to be painful for too many Americans.

In the case for Social Security, we can raise revenue by deleting the income ceiling currently placed on individuals and businesses paying into Social Security. In 2023, the cap on wages/salaries earned against which the 12.4% (6.2% paid by individuals and 6.2% paid by employer) Social Security tax was applied was $160,200. In 2024, the cap on wages and salaries for payment of Social Security taxes is anticipated to be around $168,000. A simple way to bring additional annual revenue into Social Security taxes would be to delete the cap and have Social Security taxes paid for the total wages and salaries earned by each employee. The Congress could further enhance this revenue by including all cash and non-cash bonuses received at the end of the year by salaried employees. My rough order of magnitude estimate of the annual increased Social Security revenues is $100 billion each year. This estimate could vary widely based on how inclusive the Congress applied the term "earned income" to annual bonuses traditionally received by salaried employees. Additionally, the Congress should pass legislation to delete the collection of Social Security benefits by individuals or couples with a total annual taxable Adjusted Gross Income of some number of dollars as shown on their Federal Income Tax Returns. For example, an individual whose income exceeds $125,000 per year excluding Social Security benefits, or a couple whose income exceeds $175,000 per year excluding Social Security benefits, could simply be ineligible to collect Social Security in future years where they met these non-Social Security income ceilings. This policy option would not only ensure substantial increased revenues, but keep Social Security benefits out of the hands of those seniors who do not need the income. In other words, this policy option both increases revenue to the Federal Government and decreases Federal expenses each year.

The Medicare tax rate has been 2.9% each year, evenly paid by the employer and employee for the total wages/salaries earned with no pay cap. However, this rate has remained at 2.9% per year since 1986. As a comparison, the annual medical expenses as a percentage of GDP have risen from 8.9% in 1980 to 18.3% 2021. In short, the burden of medical expenses has almost doubled in the last 35 years. It is time to recognize this fact and increase the annual Medicare tax rate to twice what it is today. The current President and Congress need to make this happen no later than early in the Calendar Year 2024 legislative process.

Additionally, the current President and Congress should consider indexing the Medicare tax rate to the change in the percentage of medical expenses to GDP, or change in medical expense inflation rates every four years. The benefit of tying future changes to the rate to either of these two measures is that if, and when the U. S. begins to see long term downward trends in medical expenses throughout the entire economy, those trends will be reflected in either of the two measures suggested. Legislation implementing these two policy measures should provide a long-term solution to the current, growing annual Federal deficit in Medicare funding.

The policy changes suggested for both Social Security and Medicare, if implemented in 2023-2024 would help fix these two programs for an extended period of time. The policies should be fairly benign in terms of political fallout from the American public, and future presidents and Congresses should be able to take policy discussions, deliberations, and arguments off the table for at least a couple of decades if not several decades.

Welfare to Workfare

This policy recommendation substantially works to fix two significant problems in current public policy implementation. First, this recommendation will bring back the economic concept that income goes to those who produce output rather than providing income to people without commensurate output. Second, this recommendation will reduce the cost of an infrastructure replacement cost to the U. S. Government and the American public by transferring a large number of able-bodied welfare recipients to a sizable workforce to whom we would have to make only an incremental payment above their current welfare payments to a market-based worker wage.

The policy recommendation is simply this—make all able-bodied recipients of welfare work for their income. Those who choose not to work for their welfare income will lose it. Additionally, those who transfer into the workfare program will be expected to meet the same standards of employment as all other Federal government and most other private workers. Those standards would include productivity and quality of output and work effort as well as successful passage of random drug tests and no demonstrated drug or alcohol impairment on the job site. In short, the jobs provided by the Federal Government to welfare recipients would be real jobs with normal job performance standards and expectations at the market-competitive wages provided all other Federal Government workers with like skills and experience levels. An additional element of this program would be to transfer able-bodied welfare recipients to private contractors hired by the Federal Government to accomplish infrastructure projects. Here, the Federal Government would take individuals off their welfare rolls as the former welfare recipients were hired by the contractors.

In the first case above, the Federal Government may pay more for those previously on welfare to work on infrastructure projects conducted by Federal agencies, but the incremental increase in cost would be considerably offset by the output provided by the work effort. Additionally, the social cost in the lost dignity of those being on welfare versus employed would be greatly reduced. In the second case above, the welfare cost of the individuals transferred to employment through a contractor would disappear completely and could be used as a partial offset to the cost of the infrastructure projects issued to private contractors. Again, the social cost in lost dignity for those formerly on welfare is avoided and the incrementally higher cost of the infrastructure contractor is justified by providing former welfare recipients a real job with real, useful economic output.

Require Welfare Recipients to Meet the Same Drug and Alcohol Standards as Federal Government Employees

Welfare recipients should meet the same responsibilities as the vast majority of Americans who work for a living. They should spend their days without abusing drugs and/or alcohol to the point of addiction as a matter of receiving their stipends from the Federal Government. The Federal Government receives the money to pay welfare recipients from the working people of America, who, as part of their good fortune to have a job, pay taxes to the Federal Government. A major part of the taxes paid by Americans go to people on welfare. I know of no reason why we Americans who pay taxes each year to the Federal Government should not be able to expect those who receive welfare from those taxes paid to meet the same behavior standards as we taxpayers do. The welfare system was initiated by President Franklin Roosevelt as a means to provide income to unfortunate people for a relatively short period of time until the U. S. Economy arrived at full employment levels to furnish job opportunities to virtually the entire U. S. working-age population.

The Center for Disease Control, in July 2015, estimated that approximately 53 million adults in the U. S. "live with a disability." However, most of these people still work, or are able to work. The more telling disability statistic is that the Social Security Disability Program paid slightly more than 8.9 million Americans a disability stipend. For this argument I assume that many, if not most, of these 9 million Americans could be considered as disabled severely enough to be unable to work. As a conservative economist, I support the idea that these 9 million or so severely disabled personnel should not be expected, nor asked to work by the Federal Government. Furthermore, those who are identified as disabled by the Social Security Administration should be exempt from any drug and alcohol use standards because their disabilities could easily drive them to greater than "normal" use in order to enable the disabled individual to cope with the disability and lead a more tolerable standard of living. In short the disabled individuals collecting Social Security disability pay should not be tested for overuse of drugs or alcohol in order to keep all benefits they receive from the Federal Government.

But, the remaining Americans collecting welfare stipends of any nature from the Federal Government should be expected to avoid drug and alcohol abuse or addiction in order to be capable of participating fully in the work place as an employee. There are millions of liberal Americans who will not agree with this point. Most of those critics will accuse me and like-minded Americans of being callus. But, what is good public policy for Federal Government and most private employees should be as stringently applied to those on welfare. For, just being on welfare should not be considered a reasonable excuse not to stay clean and sober and ready to immediately go to work when the opportunity presents itself. Nor, should being on welfare exempt an individual from learning new skills and improving his/her level of education to make himself/herself more employable in the near future. Which gets us to our next major public policy initiative.

Ensure That Welfare Recipients Work to Improve Their Employability

Welfare recipients should not be permitted to collect funds from the Federal Government welfare programs and just sit around the house. Welfare recipients should be expected to go to school to enhance their education and/or attend a trade school to learn a new trade. In short, all able-bodied people on welfare should have to spend the equivalent of each work day enhancing their education levels or honing new skills to make them competitive for decent paying jobs in the U. S. jobs market. This is not just conservative bloviating here. Adam Smith considered education and trade skill development a major necessity for any economic system, but especially a free market, capitalist system. He knew that no economy was static—that each generation would develop new products, services, and the processes to provide them. Thus, every economy would face the incorporation of new technology into the market place. In response, the new products and new services incorporating this new technology would, in turn, require new manufacturing processes and new means of production through new equipment and new tools used by people to produce those new goods and services. He clearly anticipated that every individual would have to hone his/her skills during his/her lifetime in order to remain productive and retain employment. Failure for and individual to continue to hone their skills would necessarily result in either a lower standard of living because he/she could no longer compete for higher wages offered to people with current skill levels, or result in outright unemployment.

Adam Smith considered education such an important factor in any economy, but especially a capitalist economy that he proposed that both secular education and religious education could be justified to be paid by society as a whole. He states, "The expence of institutions for education and religious instruction, is likewise, no doubt, beneficial to the whole society, and may, therefore, without injustice, be defrayed by the general contribution of the whole society. Should it then, not be the intent and purpose of the Federal Government to ensure that those able-bodied individuals on welfare be encouraged to seek education or trade skills that will make them employable in the not-too-distant future? Is it not more humane and in the best interest of each able-bodied adult on welfare to make themselves more employable, and at a higher wage rate than what they had prior to losing their jobs? Or, if a young adult on welfare has never had a job, should he/she not be encouraged by the Federal Government to seek and land a job? Do liberals really want to postulate that living on welfare for an extended time provides the individual and his/her family with the same dignity as having a job that meets or exceeds the standard of living experienced on welfare? Finally, do liberals fail to accept the warnings of Franklin Roosevelt about the destruction of individuals, families, and our society in general that comes with the creation of a welfare system that allows long term dependence on government financial support? As a conservative economist, I simply ask which is more heartless—creating a welfare system that promotes inter-generational dependence of families, or a welfare system that encourages people to leave it as quickly as they are able to prepare themselves for and obtain a job that pays them more than they received on welfare? My answer is the latter of these two policy options.

It is with the implementation of the last policy option above that I propose this broad-based public policy to drastically reduce the people on welfare by the end of 4 years, and then ensure that it operates at a significantly lower annual cost to the American public from the 5th year on. The policy for welfare should contain the following elements. First, every adult on welfare should be required to enroll either in a formal educational institution to achieve a level of education contracted between the adult on welfare and the Federal Government representative approving the welfare payments. The Federal Government representative should place a formal statement in the file as to what the education level to be achieved is, and why that particular education level is deemed sufficient by that government representative to ensure that the welfare recipient will successfully become employed at a wage level sufficient to exceed the total welfare income going to that individual's family. Alternatively, the adult welfare recipient could contract with the Government representative to achieve a specified skill and skill level sufficient to get a job meeting the same income standards as with education. Or, the Government representative and the adult welfare recipient could contract for a combination of education and trade school to meet the same goal. Second, the adult welfare recipient should be given a maximum of 4 years to transfer from welfare to a job that meets the contract income goal. Third, once an adult has left the Federal welfare system, neither he/she can return to the Federal welfare system for at least 10 years. This should help ensure that the individual has worked a sufficient amount of time to qualify for Social Security and Medicare. It also helps ensure that the individual has had sufficient time to learn the skills necessary to be successful in the work environment. Finally, the adult welfare recipient could choose to transfer from welfare into the workfare program where he/she will immediately have a job, collect a livable wage, and be educated and learn a trade skill as necessary. The individual would be eligible to leave the Government workfare program for a competitive private industry job at any time. The individual on a government workfare program would not be allowed to leave the workfare job to return to welfare.

The bottom-line purpose of welfare should be to provide able-bodied individuals a temporary period of time to regroup from a major lifetime event and once again become an employable, productive labor resource with long term job prospects that will provide lifetime income significantly greater than they could hope to receive on welfare.

Ensure That No Illegal Aliens Receive Federal Welfare or Transfer Payment Dollars

It should not be the goal of the Federal Government of the United States of America to provide people of other countries who live in this country illegally any financial subsidies for residing here. Purely and simply, it is theft from the American public. And, worse than that, if the Federal Government has laws or policies that provide financial subsidies to illegal aliens, it becomes coerced theft. The reality is simple and plain, the United States cannot support the world's destitute population either financially or through diversion of our scarce resources. The United States has a history of being the most generous country in the world—to include spending trillions of dollars, and our dear young men and women's lives in fighting wars throughout the world to protect, defend, and reverse the living conditions aggrieved people. For this we get little praise and great criticism from much of the world for not doing enough.

Given the large amount of money and resources we spend throughout the world to help others in dire need of economic or basic human life support, the United States as a country has the right to prevent people from coming into our country illegally to exploit our generosity for their individual economic enhancement. The Federal Government owes the American people the stewardship of our tax monies sent to them. This stewardship necessitates that the Federal Government not waste our tax dollars on expenditures for the income preservation of the millions of illegal aliens—period. Given the history of America to spend the precious blood of our young and vast resources on wars in foreign lands, the Federal Government has the constitutional and legal responsibility to ensure that the resources spent within our borders neither support, nor foster a long-term residence within those borders by illegal aliens. Nor is it heartless for the American public to insist that the Federal Government keep from harboring illegal aliens who take jobs from American citizens. To those who say that illegal aliens only fill jobs not desired by or fillable with American citizens, I say—BUNK!!! Ask construction workers if they would like the construction jobs held by illegal aliens. And what of casino workers, shelf-stockers and cashiers in the hundreds of thousands of retail facilities, and the growing number of managers and professional positions filled by illegal aliens—most of whom were educated in public universities throughout the U. S. The first travesty of our current, hugely broken immigration system is that it costs the federal, state, and local government hundreds of billions of dollars each year in direct transfer payment and welfare subsidies, and in providing access to public entities such as schools, medical, parks, and recreation activities. Additionally, there are tens of billions of dollars each year in uncollected taxes at each level of government because a significant portion of the income earned by illegal aliens is invisible to government collection agencies and thus, neither withheld nor collected at the end of the year tax filings. Also, even if illegal aliens pay taxes they tend to be on wages less than the governments' directed minimum wages, thus depressing the amount of taxes paid to each level of government. Finally, we cannot ignore the fact that many illegal aliens send substantial portions of their income earned in the U. S. to their families in their home countries. Thus, income earned in the United States, having been diverted to families in foreign countries, ends up being used to purchase foreign goods in those countries, rather than within the U. S. Economy.

None of these conditions is disputable. Only the estimates of their annual impact to our government entities at all levels or the U. S. Economy reach any level of credible dispute. But, generally, the estimates of annual increased expenditure to our government entities rarely are less than $200 billion per year. We know much less about the impact to the U. S. Economy in terms of depressed income due to lower wages paid to illegal aliens and the greatly diminished employment of American citizens. But let me pose this simple set of assumptions, and implore the reader to consider the impact in your own mind. A generally touted number of illegal aliens in the U. S. seems to be 11 million, with an upper-level estimate of 22 million people classified as illegals. Let us suppose that approximately 3 million of those 11 million illegal aliens are unemployed. According the Council of Economic Advisors, the May 2017 number of American people unemployed was 6.861 million people. Were 3 million Americans employed in place of the illegal aliens, the U. S. number of unemployed people would be only 3.8 million Americans and the unemployment rate would be less than 3%.

In summary, in order to get rid of the annual federal budget deficits and achieve annual federal budget surpluses, the Federal Government must significantly decrease its annual expenditures on welfare. Furthermore, the Federal Government must ensure that all able-bodied people who collect welfare become employed both during their time on the Federal dole through a workfare and/or skills development and enhancement program. Finally, we need to quit providing government payments and subsidies to illegal aliens as well as ensure that they do not earn incomes in the United States—especially by stealing jobs from American citizens. In short, we must redesign our welfare program towards the necessity of receiving output for federal dollars provided to non-working Americans, an prevent illegal aliens from receiving economic benefits provided U. S. citizens in every facet of life, including illegal employment.

In our next chapter, we will deal with the other financial side of governments in general, but the Federal Government specifically. That side involves the current Federal income tax system and its inherent economic and public policy attributes and consequences.

CHAPTER TWELVE
The Federal Government's Tax System and Taxes

Our Federal Tax System's Compliance to Adam Smith's Maxims of Taxation

Before we delve into the structure of a tax system as proposed by Adam Smith, we need to address a more basic issue. Just what is the purpose of taxes collected by governments from their constituents? Historically, in the United States, through World War II, tax deliberations by members of Congress and their theoreticians clearly centered on generating sufficient revenue to keep the Federal Government running. With the advent of Keynes' introduction of using taxes as a method of affecting economic behavior of people and businesses in the early 1930s, U. S. economic theoreticians began to speculate on how to structure a tax system that could and would profoundly change individual and business economic behavior. The use of public policy to influence economic behavior was placed on hold in the U. S. for almost two decades because two compelling economic problems consumed our country through the decade of the 1940s into the 1950s. The first economic problem with which the Federal Government contended was the Great Depression. The immediate economic need was to focus on generating economic activity in the U. S. Keynes supplied a ready solution of deficit spending and the creation of public funded jobs programs to put people back to work. In the 1930s, the public economic policy of the Federal Government was focused not on the tax system, but rather on establishment and expansion of Federal Government public jobs programs. When World War II (WWII) erupted in 1941, the Federal Government was singularly focused on generating as much tax revenue as possible in order to fund our war effort. Changing behavior of individual and business taxpayers was not a part of the deliberative process in establishing tax rates and tax policies.

After WWII, the Federal Government was focused on retooling American business from war production to consumer production, and in re-integrating returning war veterans into private sector employment. The progressive income tax rate had been established as a major revenue-raising policy with the goal of getting as much tax revenue for the Federal

Government as possible. Business and individual tax deductions were more a matter of practical accounting theory than being based on conscious influence of economic behavior. The Federal Government's tax laws changed almost every year in terms of tax rates and/or tax exemptions, deductions, and exclusions during the 1950s, but again the focus of the Congress seemed preeminently on collecting sufficient taxes to meet annual expenditures. The decade of the 1960s were boom years for the U. S. Economy and major tax changes were not seen as a necessity. Tax theory in terms of public policy were discussed mostly in the academic community with an eye towards trying to measure the impacts of various tax policies. But the Congress seemed little interested in making any major adjustments to our tax system. In the early 1970s, U. S. tax policy seemed firmly stabilized behind Keynesian thoughts about the effects of tax policy on U. S. economic activity.

However, in the mid-1970's a new school of economic thought called Supply-side economics renewed a discussion of the effects of federal tax policy on U. S. economic activity and performance. A key element of the Supply-side theory of economic policy was then and is still now the assertion that tax rates have a great negative effect on the savings behavior of individuals and investment in new plants and equipment on the part of business. The Supply-side economists propose a policy to reduce tax rates on all individual and business taxpayers in order to stimulate greater savings by people and significantly increase investment in new innovative technologies by business. Additionally, Supply-side economists recommend accelerating business depreciation schedules in the federal tax law to greatly encourage businesses to invest in new equipment and buildings every 10 years versus every thirty years. Ronald Reagan made Supply-side economic policy one of his pillars of his campaign for president in 1980, and after winning the Presidency, and a with the majority in the Senate, the Republicans adopted Supply-side economic theory into their tax policies. Suddenly, the United States had two competing economic theories upon which federal tax policies were based. The U. S. Federal Tax System became a major point of public policy departure between the republican and democratic parties. The tax system public policy departure became more vociferous as annual budget deficits greater than $200 billion per year began to appear in Fiscal Year 1983 and were persistent at that level for Fiscal Years 1984 and 1985. As a result, in 1986 Federal Budget deficits became a national topic of debate. The republicans wanted to retain the lower tax rates initiated in 1981, and the democrats wanted to raise the rates— particularly on the rich. Thus began the great American debate on U. S. tax policy which continues through this day.

In 1986, the Congress compromised on tax increases to the U. S. Tax System, but achieved the tax increases without changing the lower tax rates established in 1981. For the most part, the Congress tinkered with the change or elimination of tax deductions, deleted exemptions from federal taxes of certain income categories, and placed limits on existing tax deductions. During the first half of the decade of the 1980s, the Federal Government became awash with the significant revenue decreases resulting from tax policies that had been in place for decades or just since the 1981. These significant revenue decreases became known as "tax loopholes" which benefitted some taxpayers while being unavailable to other taxpayers. It became evident that Congressional tinkering with the Federal Income Tax System since the early 1920's had finally come home to roost in terms of discernable, measurable tax revenue reductions to the Federal Government. So, in 1986 the tax loophole debate began within the Congress largely along party lines. In 1986, the Congress passed major Federal Tax System Changes (via the Tax Reform Act of 1986 and other legislation) that increased the annual taxes paid by virtually every individual and business taxpayer. Just a few of those tax changes are listed below:

1.   *Whereas Social Security benefits had been previously untaxed by the Federal Government, in 1984 the Federal Government began taxing 50% of an individual's Social Security benefits. Since that time, the Congress has increased the level of taxable Social Security benefits to 85%.*

2.   *Whereas individuals could deduct interest paid on all indebtedness prior to 1986, the Congress eliminated deductions for interest paid by individuals for all but interest to purchase a home. All credit card interest, auto loan interest, and interest on any other secured or unsecured indebtedness was eliminated.*

3.   *The Congress established a cap on home loan interest that could be deducted and limited the deductible home loan interest to a single place of residence plus one place of temporary (vacation) residence.*

4.   *The Congress increased the scheduled time for business asset depreciation. Simply put, in 1986 they began to walk away from the incentive for business to invest through significantly shorter periods of time of depreciation for tax purposes which they had established in 1981.*

5.   *The Congress also raised the Social Security and Medicare Tax rates in the 1986 legislation as well as delaying the full-term eligibility age by 2 years for future Social Security beneficiaries.*

Since 1986, there has been persistent debate throughout the United States among economists, accountants, lawyers, the American public in general, and especially between the leaders of the two political parties. Terms such as unfair, inequitable, laborious, unfathomable, prohibitive, loopholes, double taxation, stupid, and incomprehensible... can be heard by individuals and any number of groups of taxpayers who feel aggrieved by our current Federal Income Tax System. The Federal Tax System has been configured to implement public policy such as redistribution of income from the rich to the poor, punish those who fail to implement specific federal regulations, punish those who pay their taxes late or not at all, promote home ownership, and discourage saving. During the election year of 2016 we heard politicians brand the current U. S. Tax Code unfair to low-income people at the advantage of higher income people, driving American production from the U. S. to foreign countries, overly generous to families of deceased individuals with large dollar estates, yet choking the life out of family farmers due to high rates of estate taxation. Finally, the Federal Tax Code, in terms of written Federal Law is only around 4,600 pages. The problem is that the litigation decisions by the Federal Tax Court and other Federal Courts have made the interpretation of the tax code in specific situations very complex for most Americans to easily and correctly pay their taxes. If you doubt this, then why is it that the democrat Congress and President passed a law in 2021 to increase the number of IRS agents of the Federal Internal Revenue Service to catch more tax "cheaters?" And, finally, (according to the National Taxpayers Union Foundation on 17 April

2023), why do United States businesses and general public pay an estimated $260 billion each year and 6.5 billion hours a year to prepare or get assistance in preparing their tax returns? Finally, I know of no one in the United States who says that they like the United States Federal Income Tax System. And, I daresay that no one in this country can state what the singular purpose of the Federal Income Tax System is.

Given this background, I believe that it is time that conservative economists propose a singular purpose for our Federal Tax System. My proposed purpose for our Federal Tax System reverts back to Adam Smith where he clearly indicates that the purpose of any (and every) government tax system is to generate sufficient funds to meet the expenditure needs of that government entity. He certainly does not indicate the use of a government tax system to promote economic or social policy. In fact, he spends much of his discussion indicating his many areas of concern about how a government tax system could impede the functioning of a capitalist economic system. Now that we have established a working purpose for the U. S. Tax System, we will compare our current Federal Income Tax System to Adam Smith's standards that a tax system should meet.

Our Federal Tax System's Compliance to Adam Smith's Maxims of Taxation

Adam Smith proposed what he termed four "maxims" to which every tax system should adhere. They are as follows:

1. *Individuals should pay taxes, as nearly as possible, in proportion to the revenue they receive due to protection of and by the state.*
2. *The tax which each individual pays should be certain and not arbitrary.*
3. *The taxes should be levied at a time and manner most convenient to the taxpayer.*
4. *The cost of tax collection should be minimal.*

If we measure today's Federal Income Tax Code, Laws, and overall System against Adam Smith's maxims, the Federal Income Tax System violates each of the maxims in significant fashion. Below is a brief summary of how, and the significance of each violation.

For the first maxim, the philosophical intent of the designers of the Federal Income Tax system in the early 1900s directly violated the principle of proportional tax rates by instituting a Federal Income Tax System that incorporated progressive tax rates. These progressive tax rates meant that the tax rate increased as income levels received by taxpayers increased. In fact, the Founding Fathers placed the concept of a proportional tax within the U. S. Constitution when, in Article I, Section 9 they ratified that, "No Capitation, or other direct, Tax shall be laid, unless in Proportion to the Census or Enumeration herein before directed to be taken." In 1894 the Federal Government imposed a federal income tax of 2% on those whose income exceeded $4,000 a year. The U. S. Supreme Court ruled against the 1894 income tax law both not just specifically for the tax law itself, but also against a progressive tax in principle. Not to be deterred, the Congress passed a proposed Amendment to the U. S. Constitution which stated, "The Congress shall have power to lay and collect taxes on incomes, from whatever source derived, without apportionment among the several states, and without regard to any census or enumeration." This became the 16th Amendment to the U. S. Constitution, ratified on 3 February 1913. The concept of a proportional tax, implemented by the Federal Government, thus became a mandate of the past, being replaced by a progressive tax system. The first maxim of proportional taxation became meaningful in historical reference only and Adam Smith made his first quarter turn in his grave.

The second maxim is that the tax should be certain and not arbitrary. The Federal Income Tax System violates these two concepts swiftly and egregiously. First, as to certainty, I will ask to questions and let you insert your personal answers. As of the 31st of any year in which you have paid income taxes to the Federal Government, was the amount of money withheld exactly the amount of taxes you owed to the Federal Government when you submitted your final income tax forms? Did you ever feel you got a nasty surprise of an amount of taxes that you owed the Federal Government versus the amount withheld or the amount of taxes you anticipated you would owe? A "yes" answer to either question validates that the Federal Income Tax System violates the concept of certainty. As to the concept of our Federal Income Tax System being arbitrary, a few observations of its century-long history should be sufficient. Let us first deal with income tax rates. The truth is, the income tax rates have changed frequently during its 100 years plus life. Additionally, the income tax rate brackets have also changed frequently during its 100 years plus life. Finally, the new President-elect, Donald Trump, and the Republican majorities of both houses of Congress have vowed to change the tax rates and tax rate brackets early in 2017. So, what, you might ask. So, by what scientific method and to what purposes have previous presidents and Congresses used to revise tax rates and tax brackets in the past? What were the specific economic goals in dollar terms and specific federal revenue goals that the rate and/or bracket changes intended to achieve? Were the tax rate and bracket changes designed to achieve a federal budget surplus, balanced budget, or deficit? If so, by how much? If economic goals were a major component of the reason for changing the income tax rates or brackets, what were the dollar changes desired? And, did we reach the goals dollar changes desired? My point here is simple. More often than not, the changes in tax rates and tax brackets have at least a major element of being arbitrary in that the effects of the dollar changes for individuals and for the Federal Government in total can be calibrated about as accurately as you can determine how many pennies you will collect and spend during the next year. And, my friends, I propose that when you commit an act that has virtually a zero chance of accurately predicting its outcome, it is, indeed, arbitrary. Of course, not only have Congresses historically changed the income tax rate and brackets, they have tinkered with the Federal Income Tax Code almost annually by changing what is or is not taxed, the types, dollar values, and allowability of tax exemptions and deductions, and the lengths of time for particular taxes, exemptions, and deductions to apply to an individual or a specific group of individuals. Again, the financial impact to the taxpayers, the federal budget, and to the U. S. Economy as a whole oftentimes are neither estimated nor accurately determined. If you doubt the absence of accurate forecasting of tax change impacts, I suggest you spend time looking at the actual financial impacts of tax changes versus any original estimates made by the Congressional Budget

Office (CBO) for specific tax changes. I suggest that you will find the actual financial impacts of these non-rate tax changes significantly different from the CBO predictions. I am not disparaging the forecasting capabilities of the CBO. Rather, I am simply pointing to the fact that virtually every change to the Federal Tax Code by any Congress will be so inaccurate as to be declared a shot in the dark resulting into unknown and arbitrary outcomes.

The third maxim of taxes relates directly to the ease of the taxpayer in paying the tax. In short, Adam Smith clearly wanted the burden of collecting the taxes to be placed on the state, not the taxpayer. This is clearly not so for the Federal Income Tax System. It is the responsibility of the individual, and the individual's employer to ensure that sufficient funds are withheld to meet the annual income tax liability for each taxpayer. It costs employers money to withhold money from every employee's pay and send it to the Federal Government every month. Although the Internal Revenue Service (IRS) provides tax tables that match the amount of money to be withheld each month to the pay period income, number of exemptions, and marriage status of each taxpayer, these withholding tables are virtually useless to households with two working adults. The reason for this is that the withholding tables are based on the assumption that each taxpayer stands alone. Yet, with two major income earners in the same household, the combined income of the two places one of those two taxpayers in a much higher tax bracket than the IRS tax tables. At this point, the IRS is no help and the family must try to determine the correct tax withholding on their own, or seek professional help. The bottom line is simple. The Federal Income Tax System begins to greatly inconvenience the taxpayer and all our businesses right at the front end of the tax process to begin to get tax revenue to the Federal Government. Then, at the end of the year, each taxpayer gets to the tail end of the tax process—that of filing our federal taxes. In the previous paragraph I asserted that at the end of the year virtually every taxpayer has to make adjustments to his withheld taxes in order to balance it with his/her/their documented tax liability determined by filling out the requisite tax form(s) required by the IRS by 15 April of the following year. Finally, paying federal income taxes is a coercive system in that the IRS is always breathing down the necks of even the most modest taxpayers. I cannot tell you the number of modest taxpayers I know who have been questioned and/or harassed about tax filings they have made. For those of us who have received letters from the IRS, I suspect most of us experience an immediate increase in blood pressure. For, seldom does and unexpected letter from the IRS contain good news. So, is there any federal income taxpayer in America that you know who considers the Federal Income Tax System non-intrusive, easy, and convenient? I have not met one in my half century of paying taxes.

The fourth and final maxim is that the cost to collect the tax should be minimal. The process of filling out annual Federal Income Tax Forms costs Americans and business as much as $350 billion per year. Additionally, the expense on the front end and year-long activities of businesses collecting taxes from their employees, determining their estimated taxes that they owe from their own business operations, and ensuring they (the businesses) send the correct employee withholding and their estimated taxes to the U. S. Treasury on a timely basis cost an estimated $150 billion. Of course, we have the added expense of the IRS charged with guaranteeing compliance by all taxpayers each year. For Fiscal Year 2016, the IRS requested $12.9 billion. A generally accepted cost of the Federal Income Tax System to the American taxpaying individuals and businesses thus exceeds $500 billion per year. The total annual taxpayer expenses in complying with the Federal Income Tax System and Laws each year is somewhat arguable. But, whether the cost of compliance is a mere $300 billion per year or as much as $700 billion per year, the cost of compliance is horrendously high and should be considered absolutely unacceptable to every American, president, and congressional member.

The Bredfeldt Principles of Taxation

At this point, I want to add two additional principles or maxim of taxation as it should pertain to the U. S. Federal Tax System. I believe that both of these principles are necessary elements of our Federal Tax System in order to promote and preserve our democratic form of national government. The first principle is that the entire tax structure should neither promote nor demote economic behavior of individuals or business. The second principle is that every American citizen needs to pay federal taxes.

Let me briefly discuss the first principle which is that no part of our federal tax system should influence economic behavior either by intent or by accident. The entire structure of the Capitalistic Economic System proposed by Adam Smith is meant to exert the natural balances of power between consumers and sellers, employees and employers, business versus business, and employee versus employee. Every time the Federal Government develops an element of tax that emphasizes or distorts any of the built-in structural balances provided in the Capitalist Economic System, we buy trouble. First, any imbalance introduced into the economic system's structure will result in outcomes that are unpredictable in terms of their voracity, breadth, and depth. Additionally, every introduced imbalance in our economic structure will most assuredly also in unanticipated outcomes. The natural long-term effect is to add more and more changes to the structural elements of our economic system via the tax code which will knowingly further distort its self-correcting and self-policing equilibriums. After decades of these changes, we reach the point where we currently exist. The taxpayers of the general American public consider the tax system onerous, non-beneficial to our individual economic pursuits, and fraught with unfairness. People begin to spend more and more of their time making economic decisions based on how to save taxes, rather than what makes the best economic sense to their particular situations. The major reason we had the financial meltdown in 2008 was that we told millions of Americans that it made sense to disregard their personal financial and economic situation and purchase the highest price home for which they could qualify. The result was that millions of Americans purchased homes at prices and the co-incident monthly payments at dollar values beyond their capability to make for the next few years, let alone a 30-year commitment. Why? Because the Federal Government provides tax subsidies to homeowners (deductions for home interest and real estate taxes), and because the congresses of the 1980s, 1990s, and first decade of the 21st Century decided that it made good public policy to encourage all Americans to be homeowners with little regard to the potential homeowner's ability to make the sustained house payments given the state of their personal finances and economic conditions. This public policy definitely helped keep the overall U. S. economic engine running for the almost thirty years that this singular public policy was law and was stringently and widely enforced by the presidential administrations during those thirty years or so. As a result, the Federal Government made a wide availability of home loan dollars, most of which were guaranteed against financial penalties to the loan finance issuers by the Federal Government. The consequence of this public policy was an avalanche of "toxic" loans that overburdened both the private lenders and the Federal Government's home lending agencies' ability to withstand to devastating losses from a large number of defaulted home loans. This singular public policy to enhance more wide-spread home purchases, further acerbated by tax policy favorable to home purchases caused the greatest financial crisis in U. S. history. If one public policy can do this much damage to the U. S. Economy, albeit after almost 3 decades of executing it, imagine the damage that the hundreds of various tax laws that promote or demote economic behavior must be doing.

The second principle where I believe our current Federal Income Tax System is greatly deficient has to do with who pays income taxes to the Federal Government. It is my belief that a part of citizenship in the United States should be to share in the sting of paying income taxes. Roughly half the income receivers in the U. S. pay no income taxes. The half that does not pay federal income taxes either earn less than the minimum amount to pay any income taxes, or receive most of their income from programs and sources exempted from federal income taxes. I submit that part of understanding the importance of being and American is experiencing the entire spectrum of our responsibilities as American citizens. For those who argue that the wealthy Americans pay too few taxes because they have benefitted most from all that the U. S. Economic System has to provide, I can agree with those thoughts. But, I look to the other side of the equation and say that those who pay no taxes, do not feel the sting of the Federal Government's enforcement of tax laws like those of us who pay taxes. Having part of your earned income taken from you and sent to Uncle Sam every time you get a pay check; having to contend with the paperwork and deadlines of filing your taxes each year; having to pay more taxes at filing when you find you have under withheld your taxes, and trying to determine how you are going to find those additional unanticipated tax dollars; and having to deal with unanticipated inquiries from the IRS are experiences that all U. S. adult citizens should face. I reject any argument that says low-income earners are below the poverty level and should not pay taxes because they are impoverished. Why? Because there are tremendous benefits to U. S. citizenship for every American no matter their economic status. As a citizen who lives under those benefits daily, payment of a small amount of taxes should help them understand and realize that those benefits outweigh the taxes they pay, just as the 50% of Americans who currently pay taxes. As for Americans receiving Federal Government subsidies (welfare) recipients, they should have to pay taxes just as all federal workers, federal retirees, and Social Security recipients pay federal income taxes. Why should receiving federal subsidies have a greater basis for exemption from federal income taxes than federal employees, federal retirees, and Social Security recipients? I cannot think of a valid economic reason, nor have I been convinced by any of the social reasons I have heard in the past. In short, having all adult Americans pay federal income taxes makes good economic sense as well as good social sense to ensure that all Americans understand the responsibility and sting of paying federal income taxes. Of course, should the U. S. do away with the federal income tax and adopt a national sales tax, this issue would probably go away.

If Not Our Current Federal Income Tax, What Do Conservatives Recommend

By now, I hope it is absolutely clear that our current Federal Income Tax System is in a shambles. It is a hodge-podge of 100 years of changes with each change making it more unfair by creating more winners and losers. It gets an F- grade when compared to Adam Smith's tax maxims. And the revenue collected each year is difficult to estimate because the estimate must take in dozens of major variants, each of which can change enough during a 12-month period to seriously degrade the accuracy of the estimate. The current Congress, in concert with the current President need to make unprecedented changes to the U. S. Federal Tax System. The first action is to scrap the current Federal Income Tax System/Law/Code in its entirety by a certain future date. Then, the current Congress and President need to establish a completely new Federal Tax System that meets the 4 maxims of Adam Smith and my two principles as well. Let me propose a couple of alternatives for a new Federal General Tax System.

The first alternative is a national sales tax. Under this tax, everyone would pay a federal sales tax at the time of purchase. Most of the States in the U. S. have a sales tax and thus the mechanics and the principles for implementing a sales tax are known, tested in time, and easily implemented and auditable. A national sales tax is fair in that everyone pays the same rate on all items purchased which also makes it a proportional tax, in line with the vision of our Founding Fathers. For those who would accuse a national sales tax of being regressive (people in lower incomes would pay a slightly higher tax rate than wealthy taxpayers as a percentage of total annual income), two adjustments could be made to essentially eliminate the regressivity. Purchases for food, shelter, and medical expenditures could be excluded from the tax. Or a standard tax rebate for all Americans could be paid quarterly by the Federal Government to cover the sales taxes paid for these three essential items. Finally, the national sales tax meets all of Adam Smith's tax maxims, and my two principles as well. The only adjustments the Congress would need to make would be the tax rate itself to achieve the annual target surplus budget amounts for the U. S. Government.

Another alternative new tax proposed by a number of economists and politicians is the establishment of a flat rate income tax. This plan would tax the total annual income for everyone who receives income from any and every income source. There would be no income excluded, nor deductions or tax credits. The form would be a simple one-page form that shows all income from all sources, and then simply applies the single federal income tax rate against that year's total income. All taxpayers pay the same tax rate, no matter their income levels or sources. This too would be a simple tax to administer and for taxpayers to pay. It is less desirable than a national sales tax, because withholding would be difficult to assess and collect for many forms of unearned income. Thus, some people would still get "surprise" unanticipated tax liabilities when they filed their final tax returns for the year. And, many taxpayers might still have tax liability adjustments during the end of year filing process, but those adjustments should be much less in degree and absolute value each year because the rate is the predictable, singular rate for all income levels.

The final alternative would be to initiate a new progressive income tax system. This new system would be devoid of all the 100 plus years of changes and garbage hanging on our current income tax system. Like the flat tax, taxes would be paid on all income from all sources with no exemptions, deductions, or tax credits. The tax liability would be determined by applying differing tax rates to different income brackets and then adding the taxes owed in each bracket to reach the tax liability, just as we do in our current income tax system. This annual form would be filed each year just as we do in our current tax system. However, its only complexity is determining the total tax liability by determining the taxes owed in some number of tax brackets. This tax system would probably require 2 pages. And, it suffers the uncertainty of the annual final tax liability that any income tax system imposes. But, its simplicity makes it attractive because it meets 2 of 4 of Adam Smith's maxims and, if properly structured could meet both of my principles.

I am sure there are myriads of other proposed alternatives to the current Federal Income Tax System. However, I believe the three above cover the major alternatives currently most seriously being discussed. The Congress and the American public do need to determine and definitively ascertain whether or not a progressive tax rate is to the liking of the American public as opposed to a simple proportional, single rate tax applied across the board against all income or expenditures. Secondly, the Congress and the American public need to determine whether a tax against consumption via a sales tax or a tax against income is preferred. As a conservative economist, I prefer a consumption tax because it does not affect the behavior of individuals beyond their need to determine whether or not the expenditure for a purchased item or service is affordable. This is a decision that Americans make on a daily basis.

How to Make the Egregiously Unfair Social Security Tax System Fair

Just another quick discussion about the current Social Security Tax System. Our current Social Security Tax System is egregiously regressive and unfair. Our regressive Social Security Tax System forces lower income level Americans to pay a higher tax rate than low- and middle-income class wage-earners. The reason for this is that the Social Security

Tax is paid only up to a ceiling dollar value of wages or salary earned each year. For 2023 the Social Security tax rate is 6.2% each for the employer and employee (12.4% for self-employed) up to a ceiling of salary/wages earned of $160,200. All wages/salary earned above $160,200 are exempt from Social Security taxes. This means that the high income, mostly salaried employees escape Social Security taxes on some portion of their annual earned income. In turn this means that the Social Security tax rate paid by higher income salaried employees is less than those who earn $160,200 per year or less. This results in a condition known to economists as a regressive tax. This condition where the high wage earners pay a lower tax rate than their lower-paid co-workers (regressive tax) is considered both unfair and immoral. Immoral because those lesser able to pay the tax are paying a higher rate than those who can afford to pay at the same rate, but pay a lower tax rate. Unfair, for the same reason of immorality, but unfair also, because the benefits paid to the lower income people will be less than for the higher income people who paid into Social Security. The higher income people should need less Social Security benefits upon retirement because they should have a substantially higher base retirement income from other sources than those who retire with lower lifetime incomes.

An immediate fix to this regressive tax system is easy. Congress should simply take the ceiling for paying Social Security taxes off the books. Thus, the tax rate becomes proportional and significantly less regressive. In order to solve the fairness issue, the Congress should put a ceiling of income earned from other sources in place to assure that those whose income from other sources do not collect Social Security benefits unneeded for a comfortable retirement.

Implementing these two changes in the Social Security Tax System and benefits received has one other significant bonus. It would go a long way to solving the future financial crisis currently forecast for the Social Security System.

In summary, the current Federal Income Tax System needs to be completely scrapped and a new Federal Tax System put in its place. Our current income tax system simply cannot be fixed. It is too complex, and any amount of mere tinkering will generate more unanticipated results than anticipated results. The replacement federal tax system should be structured in such a fashion that it is neutral in terms of modifying economic behavior of either individuals or businesses. Finally, the replacement federal tax system should be measured against the four taxation maxims of Adam Smith, and it should be structured to comply significantly with those maxims.

Now that we have dealt with our Federal Government tax systems, let us move to another area of Federal Government intervention in the U. S. Economy—that of regulating monopolies.

CHAPTER THIRTEEN
Government Regulation of Monopolies

Monopoly Defined and the Sins of the Monopolist

We have already discussed the economic impact of Federal Government regulations in general throughout the U. S. Economy. I believe it is necessary to focus on a specific type of regulation by the Federal Government—that of monopolies. We will first discuss the definition and concepts of a monopolist and then address the negative economic effects of monopolies.

A pure monopoly is a market condition where there is a single seller or provider of a specific good or service. The customer base may be only one or a few people or organizations, or a large number of people and/or organizations. In today's modern U. S. Economy, the definition of a monopoly has been modified to meet legal and/or U. S. cultural situations. The legal definition of a monopoly was implemented in July of 1890 under the title of the Sherman Anti-Trust Act. Section 1 of the law defines the following illegal:

"Every contract, combination in the form of trust or otherwise, or conspiracy, in restraint of trade or commerce among the several States, or with foreign nations, is hereby declared to be illegal."

Thus, under the Sherman Anti-Trust Act, the legal definition of a monopolist is not the evidence of a single seller of a product or service in a given market, but rather focuses on the result defined as a restraint of trade. Interestingly enough, the Sherman Anti-Trust Law places the definition of and enforcement against "restraint of trade" under the jurisdiction of the circuit courts of the United States.

In 1914, the Congress passed the Clayton Act. The Clayton Act was a comprehensive expansion of legal doctrine about monopolies. It contained several provisions which expanded the Federal Government's concept of a monopoly and the agencies and methods of monopoly prevention enforcement. Among the most major provisions on monopolies were the following:

Section 2 which prohibits price discrimination by a firm to different buyers if the price discrimination results in lesser competition with competitive firms.

Section 3 which prohibits a producer/seller from selling a good or service whereby the buyer cannot purchase identical or similar products from other firms (who are presumed to be competitors). Nor, can a producer/seller enter force the buyer to purchase other goods or services from that producer/seller in order to purchase the desired good or service from that producer/seller.

Section 7a which prohibits a firm to merge with or acquire other firms in the same industry or product/service market which results in "substantially" lessened competition.

Section 8 which prevents an individual from serving as a director on more than one board of a firm in a particular market or industry.

Section 11 which establishes the authority of enforcement of Sections 2, 3, 7, and 8 "be placed in the hands of the Interstate Commerce Commission for cases applicable to common carriers, the Federal Reserve Board for cases applicable to banks, banking associations, and trust companies, and the Federal Trade Commission for all other characters of commerce." Enforcement in this instance means the responsibility to bring about adjudication in the Federal Court System through the office of the Federal Attorney General.

The second definition of a monopoly in the United States has to do more with process than any legal definition of a monopoly. This definition results from the final major legislation on monopolies in the United States which came from the "Hart-Scott-Rodino Antitrust Improvements Act of 1976. This law established the responsibility of administrative review of proposed mergers by the Federal Trade Commission (FTC) and the Assistant Attorney General, Antitrust Division (AG/AD). This review is to determine whether or not the merger will violate the antitrust provisions of the Clayton or Sherman Acts. It is the responsibility of the firms who propose to merger to submit the request to merger with the FTC and AG/AD. The FTC and

AG/AD have 30 days to make a determination of whether or not the proposed merger violates anti-monopoly statutes. This process has been used extensively since its inception with a number of large mergers being proposed and accepted by the Federal Government via this administrative process without adjudication. I consider this process and the results of this process an administrative monopoly in that it is allowed by administrative review rather than through judicial review.

A third definition of a monopoly in the United States is that of a "natural monopoly." A natural monopoly is the establishment of a firm to provide services to a geographically defined customer base in order to permit the services to be provided at an economically acceptable price to the customers. Natural monopolies exist where there are huge infrastructure costs necessary to provide the service. These natural monopolies, once created are then monitored for price stability and service quality by a regulatory agency formed usually by the state government.

The fourth definition of a monopoly is generally not recognized in many government or economic textbooks, yet certainly fits the definition of a monopoly. The fourth entities that meet the general definition of a monopoly are government entities at all levels, federal, state, and local. The justification of declaring government entities as monopolies is quite simple. Governments have the ability to control both price in the form of taxes or fees, and output in the form of quantity and quality. We will discuss this at more length later in this chapter.

What then are the economic sins of a monopolist? The sins come in the form of harm done to the buyer or customer of a monopolist. There are two major negative economic outcomes of monopolistic firms should they choose to exercise those negative outcomes. The first outcome is the ability to increase prices for the mere reason of bringing significantly larger profits to the monopolistic entity. The second is to restrict either product/service quantity or quality to their customers. Usually, monopolists deliberately restrict product/service quantity or quality in order to convince the customer to pay a higher price to acquire either more of the product/service or a higher quality of product/service. In both instances, the economic effect is that all customers pay higher prices for lower quantity or quality of the goods or services.

U. S. Historic Examples of Pure Monopolies

Few examples of pure monopolies exist in the history of the United States. This is because the anti-trust laws have generally broken them after a firm demonstrated they were monopolists by clearly exercising their capacity to generate undeserved higher prices and restrict product or service quantity or quality.

There are a few major company breakups that resulted from Federal Government suits brought against monopolies.

Perhaps the first major Federal Case against monopolies occurred in 1903. In the case of Northern Securities Company versus the United States, two very wealthy gentlemen, J. P. Morgan and James J. Hill created the Great Northern Securities holding company to purchase majority ownership in each of three railroads—the Great Northern Railway, The Chicago, Burlington and Quincy Railroad, and the Northern Pacific Railway. The holding company eventually was able to compile a majority of shares in each of the three railroads. In a 5 to 4 decision, the Supreme Court found the combination of the three railroads to be a monopoly and directed a dissolution of the Northern Securities Company, thereby dissolving the single majority ownership of the three railroads.

Soon to follow was perhaps the most famous monopoly breakup in U. S. history—that of the Standard Oil Company of New Jersey in 1910. Standard Oil, over a period of several years purchased the vast majority of oil refineries in the United States allowing them to fix the price of all refined oil products throughout the entire geographic area of the United States. The Supreme Court determined that Standard Oil had conducted "restraint of trade" as a result of its vast geographic holdings of refineries and price fixing opportunities. Standard Oil was broken into regional refinery holdings in order to promote price competition and eliminate "restraint of trade."

Two more recent Federal cases against monopolies occurred against modern technology companies. The first was the United States versus AT&T in 1974. In this case, the United States Justice Department observed that AT&T was using profits from its Western Electric subsidiary, a monopoly, to reduce (subsidize) the costs of its retail telephone network which covered a substantial portion of the United States. The Justice Department considered this action on the part of AT&T a violation of anti-trust laws. The case was fought by the two parties (U. S. and AT&T) for 8 years until the two parties came to an out of court settlement in 1982. The settlement was simply to break AT&T into seven regional operating companies which became known as the "Baby Bells." The most damning results of this breakup were that consumer monthly local phone ownership, and telephone line access rates increased substantially. Additionally, long distance access rates were established and further increased the telephone rates for each phone line. In short, breaking up AT&T provided decreased service and substantially increased fees of service by the "Baby Bells." To this day, I have never understood how breaking up the AT&T "monopoly" helped the American public.

The second case arose with Microsoft. Microsoft quickly grew as the major producer of personal computer (PC) operating systems. As it matured, it created a suite of application software to compete with application software products already in existence by other software companies. Eventually, in the early 1990s Microsoft found a way to integrate the operating/system software and application software into a blended suite that provided the personal computer user with all the tools necessary to complete virtually all home and business tasks. In fact, except for the Mac PC (which had its own self-contained, complete suite of integrated operating/system and application software), Microsoft became the world-wide industry standard PC software suite. In 1994, the Justice Department and Microsoft reached agreement whereby Microsoft would not tie their applications software to Windows. In 1998 the U. S. Justice Department and attorneys general of 20 states brought suit against Microsoft for illegal monopolistic practices that prevented competition. In June 1999, 240 economists issued a statement on "Antitrust Protectionism." They made the following observations, "…Consumers of high technology have enjoyed falling prices, expanding outputs, and a breathtaking array of new products and innovations...." Where antitrust authorities respond to these protectionist demands, the working of markets are short-circuited. Antitrust protectionism means that market decisions about how to compete for consumers' favor are displaced by bureaucratic and political decisions." In April 2000, the judge decided to mandate that Microsoft break into two entities—one to produce the operating system, and the other to produce other software components. The U. S. District Court judge's rulings were overturned by the D. C. Circuit Court of Appeals, yet upheld his findings of fact. In September 2001 the Department of Justice stated that they no longer sought to break up Microsoft, but would search for a lesser antitrust penalty. At this point, Microsoft decided to attempt an out of court settlement. In November of 2001, Microsoft agreed to share its operating/system software integration points to third parties upon request. The legal process and determinations are not particularly important here. However, what is important is that both the Microsoft and AT&T cases brought to question whether the modern-day implementation and application of anti-trust laws is coherent with the times. In both these high-profile cases, the consumer had in fact benefitted in both reduced prices and higher quality and quantity of products and services under a monopolistic scenario. And, in both these cases, the benefits to the consumers were disregarded by giving precedence towards enforcing the antitrust laws.

It is with this background that we move to the second type of monopoly in the United States—that of administrative monopoly.

U. S. Implementation of Administrative Monopolies

I suspect the purpose of the Hart-Scott-Rodino Act was to significantly increase the number of company mergers, acquisitions, and combinations reviewed by the Federal Government in order to prevent monopolies and monopolistic behavior before the monopoly was formed. The previous anti-trust acts were reactive in that the monopoly and monopolistic behavior occurred before the Federal Government became involved. The Hart-Scott-Rodino Act greatly succeeded in involving the Justice Department in the preview of company mergers that might become monopolists. In 1978 and 1979, the first two years after the Act became law, the Justice Department received just over 1,000 pre-merger notifications. During the decade of the 1980s, the Justice Department received almost 17,200 pre-merger notifications. During the decade of the 1990s, the Justice Department received right at 28,500 pre-merger notifications. During the first decade of the 21st Century, the Justice Department received slightly over 19,000 pre-merger notifications. Finally, during the last ten years (2012 through 2021), the Justice Department handled 19,460 pre-merger notifications.

There is no doubt that the Federal Government has tremendously increased its intervention in the determination of the creation of monopolies. In three decades, they have made decisions of tens of thousands of proposed mergers. But the major development in anti-trust determinations has changed significantly from a legal review to a much more administrative review. Additionally, the Federal Trade Commission and Department of Justice announced "sweeping proposed changes to the U. S.-premerger notification filing process" on 27 June 2023. To me, the key change in anti-trust and prevention of monopolies in the U. S. has been the switch of the majority of the data collection and analysis from a legal definition of a monopoly to an administrative determination of a monopoly in the U. S. On the one hand, the premerger process promotes the Federal Government's capability to prevent mergers that create monopolistic power in an industry or a part of an industry. However, my observation of the premerger process is that it has had some major failures. The U. S. now has some megalith companies in some industries that have definitely stifled competition in the U. S. Some of these mergers have hurt the U. S. military by limiting competition for major weapon systems—particularly aircraft and ships, as well as electronic subsystems. We also have a large smattering of electronic and airway communication platforms that all have developed major niches of customers who have to modify equipment use, learn a new platform, and generate whole new personal communication techniques and./or languages in order to use each specific platform. As such, communication in the U. S. and the world has at once become more possible, but at the same time more limited because the cost of the individual equipment for each of the platforms can become extremely expensive. Finally, as more companies merge in the U. S. and more companies ship their production to foreign countries, the U. S. quickly becomes endangered with another loss of an entire production of another major project line. The truth of the matter is that merged companies can soon learn that the expected reduction in the cost of production can indeed disappear because the merged companies have incompatible cultures, production techniques, and product characteristics. Some of the largest mergers that did not work out were the AT&T mergers and/or buyouts by AT&T and NCR, Chrysler and Daimler-Benz, AOL and Time-Warner, K-mart and Sears, Microsoft and Nokia, and Nextel and Sprint just to name a few. All of these mergers were approved by the Federal Government hierarchy, and all definitely promoted significantly larger companies that would probably have had major impact on the American public via major economic perturbations. As it was, the breakup of these companies left at least one and sometimes both of the companies more broken after the breakup than before.

What have been the economic results of these mega-mergers? My sense of the results based on observations of the price and output trends is that in four of the five industries mentioned above, we have less competition among the companies remaining in the industry that have produced higher prices to the consumer and some notable restricted quantity and/or quality of product/service output. The only industry mergers that seem to have kept prices and product output unaffected were in the oil industry. On the other hand, we certainly see at least pockets of consumer dissatisfaction of high price levels and quality of product/service in the communications industry. In fact, in a lot of rural areas of the country, "natural monopolies" in the communication industry prevail and the concentration of mega-communication corporations has, if anything, made the capability of competition in these more limited markets even more difficult to achieve than before.

In the pharmaceutical industry, prescription drug prices continue to climb well above the annual rate of inflation. For certain prescription drugs, mergers allowed by the Justice Department created drug monopolists who raised prices severely, not because their costs of production increased, but simply because, as a monopolist they could. One prime example is the Mylan EpiPen whose prices rose from $100 for a two-pen pack in 2009 to over $500 in August of 2016 according to the Business Insider (who quotes the website GoodRx). Several business articles have indicated that monopolist suppliers of prescription drugs oftentimes raise prices significantly as they catch wind of producers of generic equivalents coming to market soon. With the pharmaceutical industry becoming more and more consolidated with fewer manufacturers, drug prices seem destined to continue their high inflation. The problem with this situation is twofold. First, many consumers of these numerous high-priced drugs simply cannot afford them either individually or collectively with or without insurance. Additionally, as drugs become more expensive, they consume a larger share of the annual Gross Domestic Product which requires a general rearrangement of societal priorities of goods and services consumed.

In the banking/finance industry (alias, Wall Street), consolidation of banking services and loanable funds creates an environment ripe for fleecing the American public. This has already happened to a large degree in the United States when you cite what has happened in the credit card portion of the industry. Even though annual interest rates charged the banks and financial institutions has been below 1%, they "lend" that money via "consumer" credit cards for annual interest rates oftentimes between 18% and 24%. You cannot call the profits these financial institutions make off these cards anything other than "usurious." There simply is no general competition among banking companies or individual institutions for these types of cards, which allows them all to charge these exorbitant rates. The cost to the economy as a whole diverts tens of billions of dollars each year from the purchase of a greater volume of goods and services for the sake of monopoly profits on the part of the financial institutions. Additionally, many families and individuals are unnecessarily placed in financial turmoil because they cannot afford to pay those rates based on their limited incomes.

The final industry that has greatly benefitted from this Antitrust Division pre-merger administrative process is the defense industry. The consolidations in the aircraft industry and shipbuilding industry have already proven to be disastrous to the Department of Defense (DOD). For the aviation arms of the military services, competition has been virtually reduced to nonexistence. When you look at the structure of the aircraft industry in the United States today, we have three main manufacturers—two of which are almost, if not completely, dependent on DOD sales for survival. Each of the three manufacturers has become specialized, through formal recognition by the DOD via contract awards during the last couple of decades. Northrop Grumman manufactured the B-2 aircraft because Northrop designed the flying wing concept upon which the B-2 design was based. Lockheed captured both the F-22 and F-35 fighter aircraft programs because they had experience in stealth technology for fighters through the F-117 program. Boeing captured the C-17 program by merging with McDonnell-Douglas and by capturing the new KC-46, a Boeing 767 airframe modified to a tanker similar to the way the KC-135 tanker was modified from a Boeing 707. Although competitions for the B-2, F-22, F-35, C-17, and KC-46 programs were held, they were held only with paper submissions from the competitors and each of these aircraft had only two true competitors. It seems to me that, because of the differing, yet specific technologies incorporated in each of the types of aircraft, true competition for stealth bombers, stealth fighters, and large wide-body commercial technology airlifters, the DOD aircraft industry has really morphed into three monopolists. Certainly, the results for the F-35 and KC-46 have shown to have significantly higher prices, fail to meet schedule, and have yet to completely meet their operational specifications. On the one hand, the F-35 and KC-46 have experienced a "typical" history for brand new, high technology DOD weapon systems. However, the DOD recently had to direct a previously-negotiated price with Lockheed for the F-35 because Lockheed wanted to increase the price to cover projected higher costs.

The Navy has a similar problem with shipbuilding contractors that the military faces with aircraft. The Navy has four major corporate contractors for shipbuilding. However, each of those corporations has specialized in certain types of ships they make, oftentimes creating a monopolist. General Dynamics builds the DDG-51 class destroyer, the new large DDG 1000 class destroyer, the Virginia Class submarine, and an assortment of sealift support and cargo ships. Huntington Ingalls Industries builds the New Ford class aircraft carrier, Virginia class submarines, the DDG 51 class destroyer, the LPD 17 class amphibious support ship, and the LHA amphibious assault ship. Austal and Fincantieri Marine Group each build versions of the Littoral combat ship. As you can see, under the current shipbuilders' industry structure, they compete only in the DDG-51 class destroyer, the Virginia class submarine, and the Littoral combat ship. All other ships procured by the U. S. Navy are under a monopolistic condition. And, competition between the two corporations for the three ships is probably not significant in that the opportunity for cost reduction is limited due to the small quantities produced.

The absolute or near monopolistic conditions that exist in the aircraft industry and shipbuilding industry present the DOD and U. S. military with major problems. For the military air arms, the first major problem is that the limited producers of fighter aircraft have limited the aircraft configuration available for the current inventory to a single new technology fighter for the Navy and the Air Force—the F-35. For the Navy and Marines, the F-35 is slated to replace the F-14 and F/A-18. For the Air Force, the F-35 is to replace the A-10, the F-16, and the F-15E. Technologically, it is virtually impossible for one aircraft configuration/platform to fully satisfy the broad spectrum of missions previously met by a fairly wide array of platforms with more specialized capabilities. The second problem is that major cost reduction opportunities generally exist in large quantity production aircraft manufacturing. But, without the threat of a military service being able to substitute an alternative platform to meet many of the mission requirements satisfied two or more platforms, the monopolist of the single aircraft is significantly less incentivized to seek methods of achieving major cost savings. The third problem revolves around the future. When things are this limited for this generation of aircraft, what might that mean for the next generation of aircraft? At least the DOD had the capability to conduct a paper aircraft competition for the F-35. But, will there even be two or more credible fighter aircraft producers for the next generation if this generation has only a single producer? These same questions exist for cargo/tanker and bomber aircraft. Finally, with only a single producer for each type of aircraft, how is the DOD to ensure a robust development and incorporation of new technology into the next generation of aircraft. With only one experienced producer of each type of aircraft, and with no competitor, what will drive the development and introduction of new technology? Competition is a major impetus for technology advancement both in terms of new products and new production processes. How does DOD expect to secure the technology advancement without competitive products made by separate competing companies? I know of no realistic way to assure the re-establishment of a competitive environment through government that has been lost through the allowance of monopolies.

The same questions that exist for the military aircraft industry also exist for the shipbuilding industry. But the negative economic effects have created great stress for the Navy in the near term as well as the long term. The cost growth in the DDG 1000 class has been so significant that the Navy has made the decision to truncate the program by reducing the production quantity of DDG 1000 class ships from 32 to 3. An additional problem with this particular ship class is that the first ship has serious operating problems that have yet to be worked out. This certainly places the Navy in a perilous near-term predicament. The threat(s) against which this class of ship was designed certainly have not gone away either in quality or quantity. The Navy apparently has a new plan of warship configurations and deployments to meet the threats, but one wonders if the new plan will meet and beat the threats as well as the DDH 1000 ships would have done. The Navy faces another challenge of cost control with the new Ford class aircraft carrier. The Congress has imposed a cost ceiling on the four Ford class aircraft carriers currently planned by the Navy. The Navy has indicated that they will need to make production process changes and slow technology innovation in the three remaining follow-on carriers. The Navy faces the typical problem with a monopolist which is to try to incentivize the producer to determine ways to significantly reduce costs without impeding timely incorporation of new technology. The Navy may need to design a new, smaller aircraft carrier to meet future affordability/cost goals.

The major conclusion which I draw from the evidence cited above is that the administrative process used by the Justice Department to be proactive and try to prevent monopolistic power from developing through mergers has not been particularly successful. Indeed, in four of the five industries permitted to experience greater monopoly power, the two economic behavior ills of monopolists—artificially raising prices and/or diminishing the quality/quantity of product or service have occurred to the detriment of millions of consumers and our U. S. economic society as a whole. Furthermore, once these monopolistic companies clear the Justice Department's administrative process with an approval, they are no longer regularly monitored to ensure that they do not practice monopolistic behavior. Finally, the monopolists seem to continue to practice these monopolistic behaviors in spite of Congressional pressures or Federal Government executive departments' arm twisting (such as the F-35 price impasse with DOD).

We now transition from the Federal Government's attempt to prevent monopolistic power to governments' establishment of "natural" monopolies with the intent to regulate their behavior.

U. S. Implementation of "Natural" (Regulated) Monopolies

Governments at all levels allow the establishment of monopolies to provide services to geographically defined locations. These monopolies are established in order to provide services that otherwise would not be available to the general populace. Generally, these monopolist suppliers provide the services usually to all customers in a specified geographic area. The need for a monopoly arises from the fact that the service provider must invest a large sum of money to acquire the capital infrastructure necessary to provide the service to all customers in the defined geographic area. Finally, most natural monopolies provide a service rather than a product. The monopolies are defined as "natural" because the business structure for a monopolist occurs due to a set of economic circumstances that demand substantially large capital expenditures prior to the delivery of the service. Once the necessity of a natural monopolist has been established, at least one government entity at a governmental level (federal, state, local) is given the legal responsibility to regulate the behavior of the monopolist created. The government regulation authority approves the prices the monopolist can charge, the distribution of those services, and quality/quantity of output standards to be supplied to the consumers within the monopolist's geographical service area.

There are thousands of regulated natural monopolies throughout the United States. Most providers of telephone, electricity, television cable, and internet services are monopolists. Each service is provided by a single company for all business and household customers within the geographic area. No other company can provide the same service within the geographic area. The natural monopolist trades its decision sovereignty on prices and output quantity and quality via a regulatory authority for the guarantee of no competition for a long period of time. Customer satisfaction of the prices and output become a joint responsibility of the supplier and the regulatory commission who oversees the monopolist. The monopolist has the responsibility to satisfy its customer base in service quantity demanded and quality desired for the rates approved by the governmental agency. The governmental agency accepts the enforcement role to ensure that the majority of customers of each monopolist under their oversight are satisfied with the quality and quantity of the service for the price paid to the monopolist. Whenever the customer base is dissatisfied with either the price paid to the monopolist or the output quantity/quality, the monopolist supplier will usually be the first to feel the heat from the customer base. However, if a large segment of the customer base remains dissatisfied with the monopolist supplier's price levels (usually accused of being too high) and/or output quantity/quality (usually being declared inadequate), the government entity regulating the monopolist becomes the focus of the public outcry.

The problem with the allowance of any government regulated "natural monopoly" is that the monopolist being regulated will always act like a monopolist. That is a monopolist will always seek ways to decrease output quantity or quality in order to force an increase in prices allowed for their services. Most government regulatory authorities feel pinched by the public outcry of price and/or or output dissatisfaction, and the possible real economic needs for the monopolist to increase prices in order to upgrade their infrastructure to improve output quality or quantity driven by technological invention. The regulatory entity has a lot of power in terms of directing the price structure of the monopolist, but little capability to influence the output quality/quantity provided the public by the monopolist. The monopolist may have to live with the dictated rate structure, but how does the regulatory agency prove output quality or quantity deterioration? Or, more importantly, how can the regulatory agency dictate improved output quality or quantity without allowing the monopolist a rate increase to invest in the infrastructure to meet the expanding customer base or incorporate rapidly expanding technology. The communications industry arenas in land line telephone service, cable television, internet services, radio wave services, and satellite services have all seen massive explosions in technological growth and capability. The major mergers and consolidations of the communications industry in the last 20 years or so have created new structural business models whereby current regulated monopolies no longer even apply. Companies like AT&T are no longer tied to land lines to provide telephone services. They now provide world-wide telephone services through radio wave and satellite services. Additionally, several single service communications companies have combined to create megalith companies that provide a complete spectrum of internet, television cable or satellite service, and land-line or radio wave and satellite telephone services all under the same company. These companies now offer "bundled" services, oftentimes giving their customer base the option of either upgraded land-line technology such as fiber optics versus metal core, or over-air radio wave or satellite services. But, many rural areas throughout the United States do not yet have upgraded land line technology like the urban areas of the country have received. In urban areas, the concentration of the potential customer base is dense and thus easily justifies the infrastructure cost of incorporating the new land lines because the cost is spread over thousands of customers per square mile. Additionally, because the customer base is concentrated in a small geographical area, the cost per customer is a small fraction of the cost of laying new land lines in rural America. In rural America, there are hundreds of miles of land lines that must be laid, with only a few thousand customers to share that large infrastructure cost. As a result, within the U. S., we now see a growing disparity of quality of communication capabilities offered to urban customers versus rural customers. And, rural areas receive limited and stagnant communication services that fail to meet even the minimum standards of customer output levels experienced by urban Americans. The Congress of the United States understands the current disparate levels of communications industry output quantity and quality between urban and rural America and is trying to bring communication land-line infrastructure enhancements to the rural areas, but it is slow going because the federal, state, and local governments have been unwilling and unable to provide direct government funding for these upgrades. Rather, they are trying to provide financial inducements to private companies, but without ensuring a reasonable long-term investment, few companies if any have taken the bait. This recapitalization of rural America with current land-line technology has started to occur under the newly proclaimed national infrastructure upgrades and repair laws passed by recent Congresses.

Some of the natural monopolistic business structures have benefitted from innovative thinking. One example is that in the State of Georgia, many rural areas have Georgia Electric Membership Cooperatives (or Corporations). These are private corporations, chartered by the State of Georgia to provide electricity to a defined geographical rural area. They are owned by the customers they serve, earn a rate of return whose dividends are then usually placed in escrow for current or planned future infrastructure needs. The rates are set by a board composed of elected customers. The cooperative is run by the board and a CEO and other professional managers hired by the board. These cooperatives have proven to be much more responsive to their customer base. Because the customer base has a direct impact on the actions of the board, the prices, and output of the EMC and because the entire board is elected by the customer base, there is a much closer relationship between the business entity as producer/provider and the customers. In general, the customer/supplier relationships have been significantly more harmonious because the customers ARE the supplier.

In the end, natural monopolies, unless able to be structured as a business in a very uncommon fashion such as the EMCs in the previous paragraph are destined to run into the same difficult relationships between the supplier and customer. Customers, rightly so, will always be suspicious of monopolies, natural or not, simply because monopolies will at least at times in their relationship to their customers, desire to achieve large profits at the expense of their customers. Additionally, those same monopolists, in order to retain those large profits for longer times will be hesitant to incorporate new technology into their production infrastructure and/or deliberately limit their product or service quality and/or quantity to extort even higher prices and profits from their customer base. Such is the behavior of monopolists, and the vast majority of monopolists, as business enterprises are not steeped in Christian theology or values.

U. S. Levels of Government (Entities) Defined as Monopolies

As an economist in general, I believe it necessary to look at government organizations at all levels and as all entities as a business unit. Why? Simply because every government organization/entity at every level of government meets the basic elements of a business unit. It has a stated purpose and scope of effort. It has an organization targeted to achieve the stated purpose and scope of effort. It is composed of resources placed together in processes to provide a service or product. It has a customer base. It changes resources and processes, incurs costs for the expenditure of resources, and changes output quality and quantity. It has a source of revenue through taxes, fees, and fines, and presumably modifies its purpose and scope of effort to match its projected revenue/budgets. In short, it acts like a business enterprise. What makes it a monopoly are two aspects. First, it is in total control of its revenue, so much so that it is confiscatory to the point that it is coercive in nature. If you do not pay the total revenue that it states you owe it, the government entity will extract it from you--forcibly. Additionally, it forces you to pay for services which you do not need or want, but forces you to pay for services to other people. The second aspect is that each government entity is the only provider of a broad spectrum of services. Oftentimes, you are not a recipient of some of these services while other people you do not know are. And, thanks to Obamacare, you have no choice of the content of the medical services you must purchase. Thus, the government for this particular element of your life has dictated the sum total of medical services for which you must insure—leaving you no determination of the content or type of medical care that you wish to receive.

These government entities are the most insidious monopolists in existence. Because we are a democracy with some supposed powers as groups of individuals to choose our champions in various levels of administrative leaders and legislative organizations lessens the level of vileness as a monopolist only a small amount. It is this recognition of the structural nature of government that Adam Smith adamantly insists on a very limited government intrusion in our Capitalist Economic System. As long as government accomplishes the limited roles proposed by Adam Smith, it provides a set of standard services to all participants in our society. No one gains economic advantage over another and everyone receives the same services to aid us individually and collectively to maximize our personal fortunes, and quality and quantity of output. Once we expanded beyond Adam Smith's specified level of government's influence in our society and economic activity, we have come to realize the colossal economic, cultural, and societal folly that has resulted. Let's examine the largest negative impacts of the monopoly powers that our various levels of government have achieved to this point in the history of the United States.

First, we have the simple fact that whereas prior to the inception of our welfare state begun in 1933, governments at all levels provided services that benefitted all participants in our economy and society. However, with the advent of the numerous welfare programs begun in 1933 and ever-expanded since, we have a significant number of programs which today total over $1.0 trillion per year (just at the federal level). These programs target specific groups of people to receive benefits literally at the expense of taxpayers with no economic benefit either to the U. S. Economy in toto or to the taxpayers individually or collectively, who are coerced to pay the bill. Additionally, the United States Congress for the vast majority of the last 83 years have failed to pay for these welfare benefits, and have increased our federal indebtedness to the alarming level of over $30 trillion. Finally, consecutive Congresses and presidents since 1933 have expanded the number of and amounts of payments to individuals such that in real terms, payments to individuals have grown from a mere 19% of the total federal budget in 1940 to almost 72% of the total federal budget in 2022. And of course, the percentage of payments to individuals of the total federal budget prior to 1933 was virtually 0% (small amounts were paid to veterans).

As discussed in prior chapters, when governments pay individuals income without receiving output, it significantly decreases the total output of the U. S. Economy. When output of the total economy is diminished by any form of government intervention, all Americans are harmed because decreased output reduces individual choice in terms of employment opportunities and in terms of types, quantities, and varieties of consumer goods and services. Worse yet, the economy now has more income chasing after more limited goods and services which eventually will lead to high inflation.

Another effect is that the longer people are out of work, their employability diminishes over time due to natural loss of skill from nonuse, and also because skills that would have been learned on the job are foregone and the individual becomes less and less competitive for future employment when compared to individuals currently employed or recently unemployed. The longer a person does not work becomes an ever-greater handicap to future employment. At some point, the individual will need to get retrained to a new set of skills for a new line of work. Couple this downward spiral in job skill loss with the psychological impact of feeling of less worth and value as a person, and society now has and individual who may need counselling as well as new training to make himself/herself suitable for employment.

The financial toll to the United States has now placed us in a dangerous position of an accumulated debt that is no longer manageable. This debt has accrued over 83 years because the presidents and Congresses were unwilling to confront the American public with the bill to make the annual payments to individuals. Congress especially had the very real concern that the significant sustained annual increase in taxes necessary to merely balance the annual Federal Budget, let alone generate annual surpluses would infuriate the voting taxpayers so universally that mass expulsions of Congressional members would occur. The ploy generated by the various Congresses and presidents from the early 1980s through this Fiscal Year (2022) has been to place promises to reach balanced and surplus budgets a few years into the future into law. Then, as those future years came to fruition, the Congress would eventually revise the promised years further into the future, or ignore the promise altogether. The most recent rash of "reduced" Federal Budgets began on 1 January 2013 when the Congress levied the "sequestration" process. The Congress did, indeed reduce expenditures in some areas of the Federal Budget during the years from Fiscal Year 2013 through Fiscal

Year 2017. However, they excluded most (if not all) of the payments to individuals during these recent years, thus excluding almost three-fourths of the Federal Budget from reductions. In this way, taxpayers were supposedly appeased, while ensuring that none of the tens of millions of individuals receiving benefits from the Federal Government would vote congressional members or the president out of office. Only for a brief period of time in the last 3 decades has the political leadership in Washington DC managed to balance the Federal Budget. It happened in the late 1990s after President Clinton and the Democrat-controlled Congress passed a massive tax increase bill/law that cut the Federal Budget Deficit in half beginning in 1996. Then, in 1997 after the Republicans took over the Congress from the 1996 elections (I wonder why?), the Republican Congress achieved real welfare reform which placed a maximum number of years an individual could collect welfare. Welfare expenses decreased dramatically from 1998 through 2001, and the Federal Government achieved a cash flow budget surplus for those 4 fiscal years. The most recent deficit reduction measure came as part of the 45-day temporary funding bill for Fiscal Year 2024. This bill sets a date for all 12 separate appropriations bills to be enacted by the Congress by 31 December 2023. If any are not passed, an automatic reduction of 1% will occur in all appropriations for FY 2024.

The final major negative effect that I want to mention is certainly more psychological than economic. However, I believe the economic effect will become quite resolute during this brief discussion. As a senior citizen, now retired for a couple of years, I have had the opportunity to observe the tenor of the citizenry with some modicum of understanding for well over a half century—roughly from 1960 into the today of 2023. What I say here is neither unique nor unspoken recently. The simple truth of the matter is that the population of the United States has become more vitriolic, divided and uncompromising in our viewpoints and speaking, and the chasm between liberals and conservatives is wider than the Grand Canyon today. The American public is unsettled and nervous. I believe most Americans understand that the Federal Debt is close to its breach of tolerance by both the American public, but more importantly, to our creditors who have historically purchased our debt. Yet, taxpayers feel that government already takes too much of their earnings and are unwilling to sacrifice beyond what they already have to pay their total tax liabilities for all government sources each year. On the other side of the equation, those individuals who are collecting money from all government sources are equally unwilling to give up their current welfare lifestyle and standard of living without some guarantee from government that they and their families will be provided for economically in some substitute fashion. Governments in general, with the Federal Government being the major culprit, have placed themselves in a quandary where, from and economic standpoint, there appears to be no win-win set of solutions. In the last half of the 20th Century, the traditional Federal Government congressional debate was how much to spend on guns (the military) versus butter (payments to individuals and programs that benefitted segments of American society). Those trade-offs were then determined through ever-more difficult and bitter compromises even through the first decade of the 21st Century as we fought the War on Terror while trying to keep our welfare system stable. But, as we came into the 2nd decade of this century, the political wheels came off in Washington DC. First, the Democrats in the Congress passed Obamacare with absolutely no votes from the Republicans. Secondly, the housing financial market collapsed, taking the entire U. S. financial industry with it. Suddenly, the need for significant increases for Federal Government payment to individuals arose—but agreement could not be reached as to the balance of payments to individuals and our military without absolute last minute budget brinksmanship at least twice each year. The Federal Debt grew at an unprecedented and alarming rate. The U. S. Economy went into a deep recession in 2009 and we have seen slow growth from that condition. The political discussions in the Congress, between the two political parties, and among the states and the Federal Government became more and more bitter and irreconcilable. Then, the result of the national elections of 2016 and 2020 continued to separate the country even more between liberals and conservatives and Democrats and Republicans. There is unrest in our streets and many institutions the like of which I have not seen since the 1960's Civil Rights riots.

The dysfunction of this monopoly—our Federal Government, if it continues much longer will destroy our economic system. To get this country back on track economically, the Federal Government MUST quickly balance our Federal Budget and develop policies designed to put a massive number of Americans back to work. This is going to require current and near-term future Congresses and presidents to set tough priorities of Federal Government expenses among its large myriad of programs, departments, and agencies. The Federal Government must balance its budget soon, otherwise outsiders who used to buy our debt will quit buying it and we will get to a balanced budget overnight, by fiat, with no plan of priorities of who will get paid and who will not. The Federal Government must set policies that get the Federal Government out of the way of the U. S. economic engine, and that will promote significant growth in economic activity. This is going to take cooperating and compromise among members of both political parties in the Congress. If the Congress cannot get its act together, demonstrate bipartisanship, and agree on the many significant fiscal, budget, and program decisions before it, the members of our current Congress could well find themselves watching the entire U. S. Economy collapse beneath them. At that time, none of them will need to worry about retaining their jobs. For, not only will they all be fired, but they may each individually and collectively be recognized as the Congress that almost brought the downfall of the United States as a country, a culture, and a society. This may be their last chance. But, of critical importance is for the Congress to get spending on individuals under control to generate a surplus Federal Budget by no later than Fiscal Year 2026

Another area in which the Congress must act, and that is to significantly raise the federal income tax rates for higher income people in the U. S. I recently looked at the history of the U. S. Federal Income Tax Rates through the entire history since its inception in 1913. From 1913 to 1917 the rates were mostly below 10% for most taxpayers with the highest rate at 15%. Then in 1917 when World War II broke out the tax rates ranged from 4% to 67% for high income earners. In 1918 the rates ranged from 12% to 77%. During the idle 1920s the rates fell to a range of 3% to 25%, and remained there until 1932 when they rose significantly again to a range of 8% to 63%. In 1935 the highest rate was 79% applied against high income individuals/families. The high rate remained the same until 1941 when it quickly grew to a high rate of 91% where it stayed until 1964 when the highest rate was lowered to 77% and then 70% in 1965. The range of rates from 1965 to 1981 were from a low of 14% to a high of 70%. The high rate went to 50% from 1982 through 1986, and then to 38.5% in 1987. The highest income tax rate since 1986 has hovered around 36% to 40% to this day in 2023. Here's my first point. The United States had tremendous economic and cultural growth during the entire 1950, 1960, and 1970 decades with maximum income tax rates that were at least double the highest income tax rates of the 1980s through this year 2023. And yes, the U. S. had mostly low to very modest annual budget deficits during those years where our national indebtedness was not particularly a bother either as a financial threat for ultimate repayment or a threat of international blackmail. Yet, after almost 40 years of the greatly understated highest tax rate, our country has become so concerned about our fiscal condition that the U. S. Congress and U. S. politicians fight about it publicly and have become so hamstrung on meeting their annual Constitutional financial responsibilities that they put the American public through an annual public display of dysfunctionality every year for at least 6 months, and do great harm to the efficient administration of the Federal Government on behalf of its people it is supposed to serve. I'm a conservative economist. But that doesn't mean I cannot spot a significant cause of fiscal irresponsibility and source of our Federal Governments major dysfunctionality. Folks, we have got to tell our Congressional representatives to raise income taxes on the highest income people in our country. The United States in the last 30 years has created a huge number of exceedingly wealthy individuals and families. These people are multi-billionaires, and multiples of 10s and 100s millionaires. Many of them got their money from clever investments of money over the years, but no real honest work as a producer or laborer. They all owe our country and all its people for their success and they bear a substantially greater burden of taxes to pay because of their good fortune. A tax rate on their earnings at 70% or 80% is not only consistent with the long history of our very productive years of our country, but is just as well. When I see what my generation of ultra-wealthy people have done and are doing with their vast wealth, I cannot consider that their philanthropy is anywhere close to the lifestyle they live or assumed status that they think society owes them. Many complain that they, the top 5% income earners pay 50% of the federal income taxes. I used to be swayed by that argument of "fairness" of our income tax system--but no longer. They goth their wealth because the United States is the world's best crucible for people to make billions of dollars during their lifetimes.

They didn't get there by their own deeds alone, they lived in the only country in the world that provides vast financial rewards for unique people who succeed in unique circumstances that allow them to bring many Americans under their wings to create products or financial situations that benefit those who work for them, but who also helped them make those vast millions or billions of dollars. The economic history of this country shows that they have a far greater responsibility to pay for the costs of running this country than they have paid in the last 40 years.

While I am bashing the current U. S. Federal Government Income Tax System, let me make one final point. Just as I firmly believe it is morally right for wealthy Americans to pay much higher income taxes, I believe it is just as morally imperative that everyone in this country pay some small amount of their income in taxes to the Federal Government that provides the legal system that protects and enhances their civil liberties, protects their homeland, property, and families, and provides them the opportunity to grow and become aa productive member of our society with the associated financial rewards. I simply believe this, again as both and economist and an American: Every American should feel the sting of paying federal taxes in order to understand at least a bit of what our American culture and government-protections via the U. S. Constitution are all about.

The final area of taxes controlled by the Federal Government are corporate/business taxes. In these taxes, the Federal Government has much less flexibility than with taxes on people. The reason is that the U. S. Government and U. S. Economy have a world of governmental competitors, many of whom understand that price competition for each country's produced goods and services have competitors somewhere in the world and that the price and quality competition is brutal. The means that if a national government places a higher tax is its goods and services for export, the price increase could quickly result in those goods and services being bought from another country whose government has levied lower export taxes on their goods and services for sale internationally. Smart consumers from other countries constantly switch their purchases of imported goods and services to the lower price, usually not considering the country of production. The U. S. Government can also increase import taxes to the products that come into the U. S. from other countries to discourage Americans from purchasing them. This too is a very touchy policy move because other countries throughout the world can increase the import taxes they charge on all U. S. goods and services imported into their countries. In the next chapter I will discuss economic policies that our U. S. Government might take to encourage U. S. companies to produce their goods and services in the U. S. and to help the U. S. sell more goods overseas.

The bottom line about raising taxes is quite simple. We will never come close to a balanced or surplus budget in the future if we don't bring a significant additional amount of revenue into the Federal Government's coffers. I'm not a big fan of the Federal Government's income tax system. I would like to see major changes to it in order to have it meet Adam Smith's standards. More to my liking would be a national sales tax because it ensures that everyone contributes to our U. S. Government's expenses. But if income taxes are what our Congress both today and, in the future, want to continue, they must bite the bullet and at least double the highest tax rate and fit incremental rates against incremental incomes to match.

A Final Summary on Monopolies

There is no doubt that monopolies who exercise their economic power of restricting output quality/quantity in order to increase prices to bring them excess profits are an anathema to the concept of an efficiently and fairly operated capitalistic economic system. The evidence of the Federal Government's ability to limit the power of monopolistic behavior by a plethora of monopolistic companies in the United States for the last 25 years or more has simply been dismal. In some instances, the issues are thorny because market conditions have forced the need for monopolists onto the economic scene to provide certain types of products or services. Yet, in recent years where the Federal Government has intervened either administratively or through formal adjudication processes, several decisions to permit industry consolidation of large firms to create less industry competition has certainly led to higher prices to the customer (including the Federal Government) and lower product or service quality/quantity. Granted, industry consolidation seems to be a trend in our mature capitalistic economic system. However, the Federal Government needs to go beyond simply making a determination of allowing or disallowing a consolidation of companies in an industry towards monopolization which becomes deemed as acceptable versus non-acceptable in our current economic system. The Federal Government needs to monitor the performance of consolidated or outright monopolies in industries once approved administratively to ensure that those companies do not establish price and output schemes that result in monopoly power when provided the American consumers.

CHAPTER FOURTEEN
International Trade Policies

A Proposed New Conservative View on International Trade Concepts and Goals

Oftentimes the data/information perspective given the United States populace on international trade involves simply providing the net trade deficit for a month or a year. For Calendar Year 2022, the U. S. Council of Economic Advisers reported that the U. S. had a net import (negative trade balance) of $857.1 billion. This negative trade balance equates to a mere 3.28% of the 2022 GDP. However, when we take the total trade between the United States and all other countries for the year—both exports and imports, the impact of the trade activity to our GDP becomes much greater. In 2022 the U. S. exported $2.988 trillion dollars and imported $3.845 trillion against our total GDP for 2022 of $26.138 trillion. Thus, the impact of our total trade on the U. S. GDP equated to 26.5% of our economic activity in 2016 with imports being 26.14% of our economic activity and exports being 11.43% of our economic activity.

Conventional wisdom among most conservative economists, based on Adam Smith's stated concepts about trade has held two major tenets. The first tenet is that countries should produce products and services where they develop a "comparative advantage." Comparative advantage is the situation where a country can produce a market basket of goods or services at the lowest cost of all competitor countries. This, then gives them the price advantage to sell this market basket of goods and services to all countries. When each country produces their products and services of comparative advantage internationally, the world's populace wins because everyone gets the best price on all products they produce. Additionally, each country maximizes its standard of living and economic well-being because their specialization in the production of those "advantaged" products and services lets them maximize employment of resources, income to those resources, general economic standard of living, and GDP.

The second tenet of international trade generally accepted by conservative economists has traditionally been the concept of "free trade." Free trade generally means that each country will neither generate internal economic policies that create false comparative advantage for any products or services they generate for international sale, nor will they place economic restrictions on products or services which they import from other countries. Generally, governmental policies established to enhance sales of home-grown goods or services which would otherwise not have comparative advantage are called subsidies. Simply put, the government provides companies tax rate reductions, low transportation rates, or lower resource costs to promote exports of companies under their jurisdiction that otherwise would be unable to meet legitimate comparative advantage of other countries in the international market. Alternatively, governments may lay import taxes or other restrictions on imported goods or services from other countries in order to increase the domestic sales of home-grown competitive products or services rather than the imported goods and services which otherwise meet the comparative advantage economic equation.

Today, it seems that these two tenets have been combined by most economic policy-makers into the single definition of "free trade." However, in the last three decades or so, two major international trade situations have been introduced that make the traditional arguments of comparative advantage and free trade greatly inconsequential in the reality of engaging in international trade. The first situation is that thirty years ago, companies conducted virtually all of the production of their goods and services in the country where they were corporately chartered and headquartered. This is no longer the case, particularly in the United States. Today, many companies chartered in the U. S. retain their headquarters that now are international (as opposed to national) within the safe haven of the United States, yet have no dedication to the United States to produce their goods or services within the confines of the U. S. Rather many of these megalith U. S. companies produce large segments of their products or services outside U. S. borders and regulatory reach.

The second major situation that has developed in international trade in the last 3 decades or so is that product and service quality has become a major issue as the international price wars for international trade sales have expanded. The free trade/comparative advantage discussions of yesteryear assumed that product/service quality would not be an issue because companies who produced inferior quality output would not survive any better in an international market than they do in a competitive domestic market. Unfortunately, this simply is no longer true. The United States is replete in its last 30-year history of significant quality of product and service failures that have caused great harm to many thousands of U. S. customers and even their pets. And, U. S. companies have paid severe financial penalties at least in terms of lost sales due to the discovery of tens of thousands of unsafe products made in foreign countries for import and distribution to consumers into the United States.

I contend that these two "new" conditions that have become generally evident in international trade, particularly in the United States drive a significant shift in conservative public economic policy for U. S. international trade. We will begin the discussion by an expansion of the two new conditions evident in international trade.

An Expose' on Charters of U. S. Corporations Who Conduct Production Operations in Foreign Countries

Corporations chartered in the United States receive great benefits from that corporate charter. In fact, that charter is more valuable and more advantageous than a corporate charter granted by any other country in the world. One of the most important of those unique and extraordinary advantages include first and foremost, the physical safety of production facilities and their workers from war and terrorist attack. Additionally, the local police forces generally provide a safety net of the physical plants of production and the workers unmatched in any country in the world. Corporations have the best legal protections from foreign encroachment in their business operations or business organization in the United States than they could receive in any other country. And, generally, corporations in the United States face the most business-friendly environment than any other country in the world. The legal culture in America promotes and enforces high standards of worker safety, environmental protection, and consumer product/service safety. Granted this legal posture, through governmental regulation establishment and enforcement causes corporations substantial costs, but it also generally prevents major errors in business operations that result in inferior resources or production processes leading to harmful or seriously degraded product or service output quality.

These unparalleled advantages of corporate, government, and consumer collaboration in our U. S. business culture within our national boundaries promote a relatively positive climate for a company to conduct business—especially as compared to all other countries. As proof of this assertion, I simply ask any critic to show a rash of U. S. companies giving up their U. S. corporate charter and international/national headquarters organizations residing in the U. S. for transplant to other countries in the last 10 years, let alone the last 30. Rather, U. S. companies have built numerous facilities in foreign countries in which they produce some types or models of their products for shipment to the U. S. for sale to hundreds of thousands or millions of American consumers. Much of the time, the reason these corporations have conducted production of those goods and services in foreign countries has to do with cheap labor, little or no government regulation of labor usage, little government environment oversight, and few regulations on production processes and output quality. Oftentimes, the products/services produced in these foreign plants result in increased costs because of a broad band-width of product quality created by poor production tolerances and significantly lower skilled labor than available in the United States. On far too many occasions with far too many product types, production processes of foreign plants using foreign workers has resulted in large quantities of highly unsafe products being sold to U. S. consumers necessitating recalls of entire product lines produced by foreign manufacturers with a prominent U. S. corporate name stamped on them.

During the last 30 years, many U. S. corporations have built numerous production facilities in foreign countries to take advantage of the loose production regulations and cheap labor. Many of these U. S. corporations have apparently found it easier to ship production to foreign countries rather than do the harder work of determining technologically innovative techniques which could be introduced in the United States which would bring the production cost down to the levels being experienced in foreign countries. Yet, these corporations had to have experienced high production output rejection rates due to poor quality output that makes it to inspection stations on the production lines. The production line output rejection rates have to be higher in these foreign countries with low-cost labor. It makes no sense that low-cost labor in foreign countries can produce a higher percentage of quality output than Americans when most production processes require higher levels of computer automation knowledge and production workers' greater attention to higher production tolerances. As a result, over the last 30 years American consumers have been beset with a seriously consequential number of products dangerous to consumers to the point of being life-threatening. Additionally, foreign-made products with American manufacturer names have consistently and persistently demonstrated poor quality befitting the low prices paid by the consumer. The production quality issue will be addressed in greater detail below.

The final issue I want to address involving corporate residence in the United States while doing international business has to do with current U. S. tax policy. Businesses in the United States have decried the high rates of income and business taxes in the U. S. as an impediment for production of goods and services planned for international sale. There seems to be sufficient factual information to show that the current U. S. income and business tax rates are among the highest, if not the highest of the economically developed countries of the world. High business tax rates discourage U. S. corporations from producing goods in the U. S. because the business taxes make their goods and services uncompetitive with foreign producers. The high-income tax rates in the U. S. encourage U. S. companies to produce in foreign countries to avoid paying U. S. income taxes and then direct sell them in the international market. Furthermore, there is an estimated $2 trillion resting in foreign banks, owned by U. S. Corporations that will not flow into America because those funds would be reduced by U. S. income taxes before the remaining funds could then be used to invest in new production facilities and equipment in the U. S. American corporations have made it clear to both economists and politicians that current U. S. income and business tax rates must be significantly reduced in order to encourage or induce our corporations to bring production of U. S. branded goods from foreign countries back home.

There is certainly a balance that must be struck and then maintained between U. S. corporations and the Federal Government between the unique and unprecedented national security, legal, and economic freedoms that corporations experience in the United States versus the seemingly sizable prohibitive regulations and tax policies that drive production of U. S. corporate-branded products and services from within our borders. I believe that public policy needs to contain a carrot and stick approach to U. S. corporations when it comes to production of U. S. corporate-branded products and services in foreign countries. I will address my policy proposals at the end of this chapter.

An Expose' on the Public Risks Associated with Foreign-Produced Output Quality

As U. S. corporations have shifted more and more production to foreign countries, product quality has become a greater and greater concern of both the Federal Government and the 300 million odd American consumers. The history of the last 30 years of U. S. consumers and U. S. corporate branded products and services produced in foreign countries has seriously stained many corporations' reputations towards production of high quality, or at least acceptable quality goods and services. The history over the last thirty years is replete with examples of products that were structurally unsafe, products composed of ingredients banned in the U. S., products that poisoned Americans and their pets, and products whose production processes introduced harmful elements into those products. Many of these quality issues arose to the surprise of the U. S. corporate owner of the foreign facility. Oftentimes, U. S. corporate owners claim the inability to influence production processes in foreign countries due to foreign governments' intervention in labor relations, production process monitoring and regulation, or allowance of substances in the final product that are banned in the U. S. Many of the cases of product quality failures in the U. S. have occurred because the corporation was unaware of the product safety issues until American consumers began to fall victim to the product issues.

The American public is grievously harmed by U. S. corporations who fail to exercise adequate oversight or reasoned judgment of foreign production in at least three ways. First, the social cost to customers harmed by these unsafe products is rarely fully recognized or fully paid in financial terms. Furthermore, it is difficult to place a financial compensation amount for the suffering of individual family members who had a loved one killed or permanently disabled by an unsafe product.

Second, consumers lose confidence in specific U. S. corporations due to a single major product failure of safety. But what of the loss of an entire industry of U. S. brands when a product line fails by many of them. And what of the quality of goods produced within a country that has several product line quality failures.

Third, what happens when a major incident bankrupts a U. S. corporation making many product lines by that company unavailable forever? US corporations say that America only wants cheap products and services, and cannot afford the higher prices of goods and services made in America. However, America is substantially weakened culturally, economically, and as a society whenever products and services formerly produced in the United States are transferred to foreign countries for production. Let us examine these three detriments to shifting production of U. S. goods and services from our homeland to a foreign country.

The social cost to American consumers from unsafe products is enormous. Every time a product line made in a foreign country is defective, the United States inevitably loses lives of some number of our population as the determinant of discovering that defect. The defect, once detected, is then tested for confirmation of deficient safety, and then the U. S. company who brought that foreign-made product to market usually goes through litigation to be fined for endangering American consumers, and after court findings or negotiated out-of-court settlements, some amount of money is set aside to mitigate the damages to those injured (or killed) by the product. The problem with people killed or permanently harmed by a shoddy product or service is that the true life-time cost to the immediate family can never be fully compensated, because the potential benefits of the individuals harmed by the product cannot accurately predict the financial loss in the future since we do not know what their successes and impacts to society may have been. Neither, do we ever adequately compensate the family members' permanent loss through death of a loved one, nor realistically determine the life-time cost of a family member permanently maimed and in need of constant care. Finally, society suffers a loss every time one of our people loses his/her life or is permanently maimed in some manner that alters that individual's capability to perform or meet his/her life potential. No one ever tries to calculate these "social costs," or collect the damage to society from these U. S. companies whose products were made in foreign lands. In short, the true social costs of defective products made in foreign countries on behalf of American corporations are not known, but I submit, when calculated and predicted, are always substantially less than reality.

An additional social cost to the United States population as a whole has to do with all the public expenses that are incurred by American citizens who are unemployed and out of work. The annual expenditures that we pay to unemployed people is staggering. In 2022 we paid $48.0 billion for unemployment. If you add just 5% of the remaining welfare bills to that figure for unemployed individuals and their families you would get an additional $69.1 billion or so. Thus, the total social cost of unemployment in the U. S. just for the Federal Government approached $117 billion. None of these expenses are paid by the U. S. corporations who produce their American consumed goods and services off-shore. If the American consumer paid the higher prices of producing products and services in America, we would see these annual costs to the Federal Government diminish significantly.

Another esoteric, relatively uncalculatable cost has to do with the U. S. corporations who experience substandard/unsafe production made in foreign countries, yet sold to American consumers and potentially consumers in the international market as well. Every time a U. S. corporation puts a harmful product or provides inadequate service to American consumers, the reputation of that company gets tainted. Where the number of consumers harmed and exposed is large, the company's reputation will likely be significantly damaged, especially if the output defect receives wide-spread coverage in the press. Also, a company that compiles some number of different harmful products/services over time, will most certainly lose future buyers because they gain a notoriety of unwillingness or inability to provide safe output. And, if that company is one of a few producing a particular product or service, that bad reputation may rub off on other U. S. companies, especially if their output is made in the same foreign country. The cost of having to trash a few or several hundred thousand products deemed unsafe, is substantially large—often in the hundreds of millions, if not few billions of dollars. But, companies in most cases will suffer a future reduction of sales of similar products or services to those in their history that caused harm to American consumers. Additionally, any company who has more than one incident of poor-quality products/services and/or harmful products/services brought to the U. S. from foreign production facilities/sources expose themselves to future sales losses sufficient to force them out of business. Unfortunately, loss of future sales tends to be highly unpredictable. A company who suffers a spate of product/service quality lapses and/or output liability incidents won't know the disastrous consequences of poor production quality of their foreign-made products and services until the output hits the market, the production quantities are significant, and the press has given the bad output a lot of exposure. Next, we go to the broader topic of cultural modification and destruction resultant from U. S. corporations making products in foreign countries.

How is the U. S. weakened culturally by shipping U. S. production of goods and services to foreign countries? Well, the obvious loss of jobs takes place rather immediately and abruptly. Most people focus on the loss of economic prowess within our economy as people lose jobs, unemployment increases, and U. S. GDP stagnates or decreases. But, where people suffer permanent loss of jobs due to a decrease of their industry's economic footprint in the U. S., the impacts are more insidious than mere economic loss. Entire communities become impacted whether they be a small town that loses its largest, and oftentimes, single employer or a large city that loses much of its production from a long-term mainstay product line. A strong culture comes from a population thriving with economic activity. The economic activity provides the incentive and ability of families and neighborhoods to integrate, celebrate, and create a multiplicity of community events that involve large segments of that population. Interest in the arts, fund raising events, and community outreach are robust in number and participation. Oftentimes, infrastructure to promote community gatherings in the arts, and public outreach events become established, maintained, and frequently used to expand the depth and breadth of cultural development and expression. But, when a community suffers permanent loss of major businesses or industries, the economic support of cultural events and societies often is the first loss in community activities. As loss of cultural focus within the community dwindles, the financial ability to maintain the infrastructure vanishes, and the cultural development, creativity, and sustainment disappears with it. Finally, entire neighborhoods that once had bustling activity with homes that were well maintained and inhabited by families that were culturally prosperous literally become deserted "ghost hoods." A person can try to imagine the impacts on communities hit hard by their loss of industry and infrastructure, but seeing the reality of the decay of closed factories, public and private infrastructure, and consummate degradation and human desertion of neighborhoods with once-proud, finely constructed homes is so depressing that on people with the hardest of hearts can observe unaffected. In communities such as this, culture is not diminished, it simply no longer exists because there are few or no residents, and those who remain live dismal lives with little hope.

Why did I discuss the concept of social costs of off-shore production of goods and services by U. S. companies? Because social costs are never included in the price of the good or service sold, including within our U. S. borders. Thus, the prices of goods and services made off-shore, but sold in the United States, are understated by a huge amount. And, when the prices of these goods and services produced off-shore ignore these large social costs, the comparison of prices of those goods and services made in the United States versus off-shore always give the foreign-made product or service the appearance of a lower price. Certainly, the cost and price of the product made in the U. S. at the register would be higher than the price of the product made off-shore. However, when you take the social costs into account, I submit that the cost to the American public would be substantially less because we would decrease the Federal Government Expenditures for Unemployment and related Welfare accounts. Additionally, the U. S. consumer would get a consistently higher quality good or service than we have experienced from some of the off-shore countries who now make U. S. corporation output.

Proposed Economic Policy Solutions to Bring Production Back to American Soil

As a free market economist at heart, I propose that the United States Government develop economic incentives for U. S. corporations to return production of their goods and services within the borders of the U. S. A. These economic incentives are a "carrot and stick" approach in that we provide lower income taxes on products and services made within our borders to be more in line with the vast majority of our western economy competitors. We should also provide U. S. companies who have large hordes of dollars off-shore a tax incentive to bring those funds into the U. S. to build new plants throughout America to increase our on-shore production which in turn, would significantly increase permanent jobs to American citizens. These are the carrots. The sticks are punitive in nature—intentionally. First, U. S. companies who bring harmful or deficient foreign-made products into the U. S. under their corporate umbrella, should face a new U. S. mandate to prevent that company from ever importing foreign-made products in that product line from the time of discovery forward. Second, U. S. corporations whose foreign-made goods' sales exceed 50% of their total sales for three years in a row, will lose their corporate charter and cease to exist as a U. S. business enterprise. Additionally, any U. S. corporation who moves any part of their corporate management to foreign soil, will lose their U. S. corporate charter. Finally, a new corporate import tax should be levied on any and all products and services produced off-shore. This tax would be paid by the corporation, but could be levied as a price increase only on products and services produced off-shore and imported within the borders of the U. S. A.

Proposed Economic Policy Solutions to Make Prices of Foreign Goods Equivalent to Prices of U. S. Goods for U. S. Consumers

U. S. producers oftentimes face inequivalent price competition due to intentional foreign governments' public policies designed to provide their home companies a price advantage in foreign markets. The first public policy used is direct subsidies from the foreign government to their home company designed to permit the foreign home company to charge a lower price internationally, thus making their home company more price competitive in the world market. To counter foreign government subsidies allowing foreign companies to lower their prices in U. S. markets, the U. S. government can levy import taxes equivalent to the foreign subsidies. Then, the price competition within the U. S. becomes truer among foreign competitors and U. S. producers.

Products of foreign counties may be produced by companies that have egregious labor policies. For example, the foreign companies may use child labor. Or, the foreign companies' work facilities and production processes may be radically unsafe by U. S. standards or even international standards. The United States cannot force its labor work force and work area standards on a foreign country. However, we can reject their products for import—and we should. So, U. S. economic policy in this area should be simple. Where a foreign company sends products (or provides services) that come from production facilities where labor work force and work area standards instituted are significantly outside the standards of the U. S., the Federal Government should ensure that those foreign products or services are unavailable to the American public or American businesses. By the way, U. S. companies whose foreign facilities violate U. S. labor force and work process standards, should not be allowed to introduce those products or services into the U. S. The United States Federal Government sets labor work force and work place standards, not only to protect our work force, but also to ensure the standardized production of safe goods and services for American public consumption.

Products or services produced by a foreign company for import into the U. S. should meet the same quality standards that all U. S. produced items and services must meet. Where a good or service made by a foreign company imported into the U. S. fails to meet the same standards imposed on U. S. producers of like or similar products or services, the foreign manufactured products or services must not be allowed to be sold in the United States. Furthermore, a foreign company who once fails U. S. quality standards should be disbanded from ever submitting a like or similar good or service for import into the U. S. in the future. The U. S. Federal Government establishes product and service standards in order to protect Americans from the purchase and use of products or services that harm American consumers. As a society, we can ill afford to allow foreign products or services to be purchased within our borders which pose a danger to those who use or consume those products or services.

The ultimate goals of our Federal Government should be to protect the American public from harmful products and services, to ensure that labor practices in foreign countries do not egregiously violate human decency and safety standards, and that imported goods and services into the U. S. are equitably priced to promote fair price competition between U. S. producers and foreign producers. The United States Government not only has the right to ensure that these three goals with foreign importers/competitors are achieved, it has the responsibility to ensure the enforcement of these goals on behalf of American producers and consumers.

CHAPTER FIFTEEN
Immigration Economics

A Brief Historical Context Which Formed the Current Immigration Debate

World War II was all about national borders, land space within those borders, and which country laid claim to those borders and the land space therein. The armistice of World War I created much of the friction of land space ownership during post WWI because it took bits of land space formerly held by Germany and handed it to a couple of Germany's neighboring countries. Additionally, land space became more important in Europe, Southeast Asia, and Middle East because important resources were discovered (oil being one major common denominator) in various specific regions of each of those three large land masses. It was apparent to the political and military leaders of the countries within each of those three large land masses that whoever owned and controlled those important resources would be the recipients of great wealth. Political unrest accompanied the fragile peace from WWI because several countries within each of the three land masses had major violent competitions among strong political factions to determine which political faction was going to control the economic future of the country. Indeed, much of the unrest in the Middle East continues to be the desire to expand one country's land space at the expense of another. And, prior to the official beginning of WWII in Europe, Japan invaded China in July of 1937. During December of 1941, Japan attacked Pearl Harbor and the Philippine Islands, and took control of many of the islands in between. Japan was oil poor and needed the oil fields located in China and some of the Southeast Asia islands to continue to exist—at least in the (Japan's) minds of its political and military leaders.

After World War II, Russia retained its control over the "Eastern Block" countries which they invaded as part of their march to Berlin. Again, the reason was to retain the capability to pillage and plunder the resources of those Eastern Bloc countries to the economic advantage of Russia. The lines drawn to allocate Middle East land space after WWI survived the Second World War essentially intact. However, both the Eastern Bloc countries of Europe have been in intermittent strife with

Russia since 1989 when Russia permitted Eastern Bloc countries to declare themselves independent of Russia. Yet, Russia, on occasion since the Eastern Block breakup has intervened in the political and economic affairs of some of those countries. The political and economic unrest in the Middle East has been volatile since the end of WWII with land space and resource ownership (particularly oil) being a major destabilizing factor. However, religious preference and dictatorial leadership takeovers have also been a significant factor in the constant Middle East unrest. The political, religious, and economic instability in the Mideast have transitioned into Western Europe due to the large migrations of millions of Mideastern refugees.

However, Western Europe and Japan after WWII had different experiences of land mass definition. Essentially, Japan was allowed to keep its pre-WWII land mass and gave up all land won during WWII. Western Europe, with the exception of Germany returned to their pre-WWII nation boundaries. Germany was divided into West versus East Germany boundaries with West Germany aligning itself politically and economically with Western Europe and East Germany being forced to align with Russia as an Eastern Bloc country. Japan developed as a major world economic power by the beginning of the 1980s decade by transforming a vast array of imported resources into high quality products sold to world-wide markets. In essence, Japan has practiced the art and science of free trade since WWII and has achieved economic success to be envied by all other countries.

Western Europe developed from their WWII heavily war torn, severely war damaged position after WWII using a different model. Western Europe countries retained their boundaries for political decision-making, but gradually matured to a more regional interaction of economic trade and policy. In 1957, six European countries signed the Treaty of Rome forming the European Economic Community (EEC). Those six countries were: France, Belgium, Italy, Luxembourg, the Netherlands, and West Germany. This became the beginning of formalized economic cooperative relations among all Western European countries because more countries joined as time passed. In the mid-1960's there became a hint of political cooperation among the member EEC countries, and in 1979 the member EEC countries elected members to the first European Parliament. In 1985, much of Western Europe and a few non-EEC members signed the Schengen Agreement which promoted movement of member nation citizens among all the signatory nations without passports. Thus, the concept of "open borders" was formally established by the EEC, now more commonly known as the European Union (EU).

The EU model of open borders has been adopted by a significant segment of American society so as to blunt the focus on true economic, political, and cultural impacts to the United States. Rather, the focus of those who support open borders has been on one-sided moral grounds—the rights of illegal immigrants to remain in the U. S. once they arrive because it is cruel to return them home. The open borders proponents make a case that the illegal immigrants make a positive economic impact on our U. S. Economy, an argument to be discussed soon in this chapter. We who support public policies meant to deter, thwart, and rectify illegal immigration into the U. S. believe that U. S. public policy should focus support first on American citizens, and second on legal aliens. For, no sufficient case can be made that illegal aliens have a greater or equal moral right to reside and partake of the benefits of our American society than American citizens and legal aliens already within our borders. In fact, there are laws meant to prevent the presence of illegal aliens in order to protect the rights of citizenship of American citizens and legal rights granted legal aliens.

But, the concept of open borders has a much more sinister impact on the United States. The sovereignty of the United States is defined by its borders. We cannot implement or enforce any law or public policy outside our legally defined, worldly-accepted borders. And when we have geographical patches of real estate in the United States that declare themselves as "sanctuary political zones" and large numbers of organizations, both business and cultural, who defy our public policies, whether in the forms of laws or stated governmental rules, regulations, and processes, we harm all people in the U. S. who follow those laws and government administrative procedures. Illegal aliens are not a net positive effect on the U. S. culture. Rather, illegal aliens are a cancerous sore that does not heal and will eventually metastasize into a raging body-killing disease. Illegal aliens who come to America, knowing they must disrespect and violate our laws to achieve personal gain, will grow in their disrespect of our laws and our culture the longer they succeed. And that disrespect will not translate just to their lives, but will also become a cultural expectation for their children and grandchildren. Thus, with each generation, the number of people who expect to succeed in life while trampling our culture will increase exponentially. A larger and larger percentage of our population will no longer honor, respect, and further our culture. America will change radically, and there is every reason to believe that the cultural change will be much for the worse. For, if you live your life breaking our country's laws for personal gain, where can you find the moral compass to care for others or your new country? As an American, I thank God daily for having been born in the United States of America. As a retired Air Force officer, and an individual who spent my entire adult working life in an employment relationship in or with the Air Force, I hope that I have repaid part of the debt I owe to God and this country for being born a citizen of the USA. I certainly understand the desire for people from many nations in the hundreds of millions to want to come to the USA. But the cultural realities are that a large portion of those hundreds of millions who would come to the USA would undercut our culture and our values because we are simply too significantly divergent from their culture and values for them to either desire or be psychologically able to assimilate to our values and culture. We know that already, and yet, as of this date, we have let hundreds of thousands of illegal aliens into the United States that have shown us by harmful deeds against Americans, their unwillingness to respect our laws and assimilate into our values and culture. We spend a lot of time and money to vet aliens we permit into our country legally. Yet, the millions of illegal aliens residing in our country today have not been vetted at all, except for negative behaviors that cause harm to Americans and catch our attention. It is unbridled stupidity and folly to think that ignoring illegal aliens until their bad behavior catches our attention is good or even acceptable public policy. For the reality is, that all illegal aliens have one undeniable, common trait—they are dishonest. I, for one conservative, consider this fact sufficient to rid this country of every illegal alien that we can find. And as to the argument that WE would be breaking up families, I vehemently disagree. Illegal aliens that have children born in the United States have brought another element of dishonesty into their relationship with our U. S. citizens. They deliberately had the child on U. S. soil in order to place our consciences in a position of "moral" conflict. Yet, as with any other criminal, the American legal system should separate illegal immigrants from their children just as we separate criminals who go to jail from their spouses and children. In fact, neither the legal system of the U. S., nor the American public separate illegal aliens from their children born in America. No, the illegal aliens, by their act of birthing their child on American soil cause their separation from their children.

Many proponents of the concept of open borders and simply accepting the existence of a large number of illegal aliens advertise that illegal aliens are a net economic benefit to the U. S. Economy. We will discuss that issue next.

One final point for those who think borders are internationally considered unimportant, I simply point to the current war between the country of Ukraine versus Russia. Russia invaded Ukraine for one reason only—to grab more of the fertile land that produced an abundant surplus of food, has rich deposits of ore and fossil fuels below ground, and at least one significant port to promote trade. Any U. S. citizen who thinks that the large illegal migration from many other countries of the world into the U. S. via our open southern border is a good idea or beneficial, simply refuses to face facts.

The Debate of the Economic Effects of Illegal Immigration

There has been a bitter on-going debate on the economic effects of illegal immigration in the United States of America for almost four decades. Those who support the current state of illegal immigrants into the U. S. tend to emphasize several negative effects to the U. S. Economy, should these illegal aliens not be let into the U. S. with open arms. They propose that some industries within the U. S. would diminish in size, if not disappear from our economy. Further they propose that, absent these illegal immigrants, prices to consumers would increase, probably substantially, in certain industries within the U. S. Finally, proponents of illegal immigrants, state that the illegal immigrants add a significant amount of demand which increases production, total people employed, and annual GDP. Although the supporters of illegal immigrants admit that there are some significant additional public expenditures for illegal immigrants, particularly for education, the defenders of illegal immigrants conclude that the economic benefits to the U. S. as a whole, exceed the economic costs.

There have been dozens of studies conducted by many dozens of "experts" which have assessed the net economic benefit or cost to the U. S. Economy from having illegal aliens within our borders participating in our economy through employment, expenditure of earned income, and collection and expenditure of government benefits. I contend that roughly half the studies and experts claim that illegal aliens have a net benefit to the U. S. GDP, while the other half contend that illegal aliens are a net drain on the U. S. GDP each year. I will not cite any of these studies or experts, because I find major flaws in all of the combined studies which greatly diminish the credibility of them all. From here on, I will discuss economic conditions, some theory that should tie some of the conditions together, and use some contrasts of possibilities of outcomes to attempt to draw a reasoned conclusion of the summary effect of illegal aliens on the U. S. Economy. Let me say at the outset that I do not criticize any of the economic impact studies I have researched and read. Rather, I simply state here that a credible estimate of the economic impact of illegal aliens on the U. S. Economy is impossible to date because we simply have insufficient data to develop and document a credible estimate. Many of these data deficiencies will be identified as we go through the elements of the discussion. The format will be to identify a data element and give a brief discussion of economic relevancy and contrast of estimated economic or other relevant data impacts.

The Number of Illegal Aliens: Analysis of the economic effects of illegal immigration starts here. We must have a credible, accurate number of illegal aliens that reside in the United States. Additionally, we need data that shows characteristics of segments of the illegal alien population. How many are employed? How many pay Federal and/or state taxes? How many are not employed and how many do not pay taxes? How many are male and how many are female? How many have families with them in the U. S. and what is the age and gender of each family member? Were any of the children in the household born in America? If so, how many? How many have expired VISAs? To my knowledge, no credible count of illegal aliens exists. The Federal Government needs to collect this data on the population of illegal aliens. Perhaps the most credible estimates of both the number of illegal aliens in the U. S as of the end of Calendar Year 2022 comes from the Federation for American Immigration Reform (FAIR). Their estimated total number of illegal aliens at the end of 2022 is 16.8 million. This is an increase of approximately 2.3 million since the end of 2020. These totals for 2020 and 2022 are undoubtedly understated by the "got-away" aliens who entered the U. S. by avoiding capture by U. S. or state immigration enforcement officials, or, like most, then immediately turning themselves into enforcement officials to be processed as people entering int the U. S. We can never develop a credible economic impact analysis until we have a credible estimate of total illegal immigrants and the myriad of subdivisions and characteristics of the illegal alien population in the U. S. The general lack of credible data on the number of illegal aliens (and all the necessary segments), from my perspective tend to invalidate all studies that have attempted to determine the net economic impact to the U. S.

The two Major Economic Elements That Define the Total Cost of Any Economic Policy

Economists believe that there are two types of costs that need to be considered in all economic decisions. The first type of cost is called an explicit cost. These are costs that are known and fairly exact because they are recorded in some place and in some manner where they can be reviewed and scrutinized. Such costs fit in the terms of historical, estimated, operational, and incremental. These are the costs visible to anyone who takes the time to find them because they are recorded or calculated and the source of the data depends on provable documentation. The second general type of cost are known as implicit costs. These are costs that we know are occurring or will occur, but they are generally virtually impossible to obtain through historical documents or accurate estimates. They are simply costs we know exist, but society cannot develop a generally accepted value of implicit costs. Implicit costs are generally divided into two categories—entrepreneur and social.

In the case of discussing the costs of illegal aliens within the U. S. Economy, the second type of implicit cost (social) are the most relevant here.

The Cost of Illegal Immigrants to Government: There are many costs to all levels of illegal immigration to all levels of government in the United States.

Let us first explore the most recent estimated total cost of illegal aliens in Fiscal Year 2022 for the Federal and state governments. Once again, we turn to the Federation for American Immigration Reform (FAIR) who published an annual report for Fiscal Year 2022 on the net costs to both the federal and state and local governments. The report is entitled, "Fiscal Burden of Illegal Immigration on United States Taxpayers—2023 Cost Study," dated 8 March 2023. The net costs to the American public as taxpayers was estimated to be $150.7 billion for Fiscal Year 2022 for all government levels (federal, state, and local). Fair published a second report entitled, "How Many Illegal Aliens Are in the United States? They state that the number of illegal aliens that resided in the U. S. as of the end of Calendar Year 2022 was 16.8 million people. Their estimated costs to the Federal Government were 66.5 billion dollars and for state and local governments were $115.6 billion dollars for a total cost of $182.1 billion dollars. The total spent by all levels of government were partially offset by the taxes collected by those same governments from illegal aliens. The Fiscal Year 2022 tax collection offsets for the Federal government was $15.2 billion dollars while the offset of tax collections by state and local governments was $16.2 billion dollars totaling $31.4 billion in Fiscal Year 2022 tax receipts by all governments. Subtracting the total tax collections by all levels of government in Fiscal Year 2022 ($31.4 billion) from the total expenses of all governments in Fiscal Year 2022 ($182.1 billion) results in the net cost to governments in Fiscal Year 2022 of 150.7 billion dollars.

As of June 2023, the Department of labor indicated that we had 5.957 million Americans unemployed and that the U. S. unemployment rate was only 3.6%. What the monthly employment rate does not measure is the significant interruption of production output because of severely high employee turnover rates. I have personally noticed this severe labor turnover in the lower skilled, lower education jobs throughout our local economy. Examples are fast food restaurants, sit-down restaurants, and a lot of retail store sales personnel. Additionally, the hard labor jobs of stocking shelves and loading and unloading trucks. Finally, many retail sales shops have help wanted signs at their entrances all the time. A high labor turnover rate is just as damaging to a business as it is for them to have a high unemployment rate. The problem I have with the current published U. S. unemployment rate is that there are some few millions of illegal aliens not part of the unemployment calculation because some few millions of illegal aliens don't have green cards (work permits) and thus cannot seek work through the U. S. and state departments of labor. Thus, they are not counted as part of the total civilian labor force. Nor, are they part of the calculation of persons seeking work. With so many illegal aliens in the U. S., our current unemployment rate is certainly not a bona fide rate because both the total civilian work force and the number of people who seek but cannot find work are understated. This means that the current U. S. unemployment rate through June 2023 of 3.6% is not just invalid, but most probably somewhat higher. How much cannot be realistically or credibly calculated, but if only 3 million of the illegal aliens in the U. S. really need or want work, but cannot formally seek it and thus remain unemployed or are not reported as employed, the unemployment rate would be close to 5.5%.

In the case of migrant workers who pick fruits and vegetables, it may be true, but only because the hourly wage is below what it would take to entice unemployed Americans to take the job. Additionally, the many jobs of "domestic" workers are touted as done by legal immigrants or illegal) aliens, again because American workers are unwilling to accept the jobs at the low wages provided to the immigrants. This situation could be reversed if the wages were increased to a competitive level sufficient to attract unemployed American workers. Finally, a significant number of illegal aliens and legal immigrants do take jobs in many of the low and high skilled trades. Landscape jobs, construction jobs, and food production jobs are among the broad-based trade jobs that are captured by legal immigrants and illegal aliens alike. Labor unions throughout the United States have decried that the labor rates in their particular trades are artificially depressed due to legal immigrants and illegal aliens working for wages below those negotiated with unions representing those trades. This situation is definitely harmful to the United States because we have American and legal immigrants who might be willing to work for a higher wage of say $14 or $15 per hour, but will not (or simply cannot afford to work) for say $10 per hour like illegal aliens will work. There are many low skilled jobs in the U. S. where U. S. employers hire illegal aliens because they know the illegal aliens cannot complain to anyone of their low pay (because their illegal status would become immediately known) and that the illegal aliens have better work conditions than they probably experienced in their native country.

Let us suppose that the illegal aliens were simply no longer available in the U. S. labor pool to take the millions of jobs suggested in the paragraph above? And let us suppose that those jobs became available to U. S. citizens. Finally, let us suppose that the number of unemployed American citizens goes down by another 3.2 million Americans. The positive economic impact on the Federal Government and the entire U. S Economy would be tremendous. First, the Federal Government would spend less than half the amount of unemployment compensation it spent in 2023 (approximately $48 billion). Additional savings to Federal expenditures on unemployment should accrue in the welfare accounts such as food stamps, aid to dependent children, and Medicaid. Second, Federal Income Tax revenues should increase because all the revenue of the newly employed Americans would be reported and collected versus some portion of the income of illegal aliens having been previously unreported and collected. Furthermore, any Federal Government welfare support expenditures to the previously unemployed Americans would be discontinued due to their change to employed status. Finally, since we should reasonably assume that the general wages discussed in the previous sectors of the U. S. Economy would rise because of the entry and employment of American citizens in these previously wage-depressed sectors, the Federal Government would receive greater revenue from the increased wages and salaries earned by these newly employed American citizens. In short, we could expect greater revenue to and less expenditure from the U. S. Treasury as more and more American citizens acquire jobs previously held by illegal aliens. Another cost to the Federal Government is the outlays for medical care of illegal aliens via Medicaid. These costs are probably very significant, although I have seen no credible estimate of these costs incurred annually by the Federal Government. But to assume that illegal aliens (and their families) do not routinely receive medical care ultimately paid by Medicaid is an assumption invalidated by any sense of reality.

Recently under President Biden, the cost of illegal aliens to the American public has arguably increased at the federal level. The federal government reportedly provides each adult illegal alien a phone, a cash credit card, and free transportation to the city of their choice. The communities to which these illegal aliens are sent become responsible for finding the illegal aliens suitable housing and food allowances—as a minimum. At some point, they will also incur the costs of educating not just the children, but the adult illegal aliens to speak English and learn a marketable skill. And of course, children under the age of 18 will have to be sent to local schools which will each require more 2nd language teachers.

The federal, state, and local governments should segregate the costs to support illegal aliens whose presence and residence they know. They should be able to track all food, housing, clothing, education, and medical costs associated with each of the known illegal aliens. But, as we know, we have a number of illegal aliens who either escape notice when they cross our southern border, or manage to quickly get lost in the city to which they are sent—usually by their desires. At this point, we have a situation where, due to insufficient data, we simply have no ability to credibly debate the net cost or net benefit of illegal aliens to our governmental finances.

The Undeniable Increase in Crime and American Deaths from Illegal Aliens

We now come to the significant, but literally unknown and incalculable major social costs to the United States in total. Some number of illegal aliens come into the United States owing cartels with pure, unadulterated bondage to criminal organizations within the U. S. Additionally, we have a number of illegal aliens who enter the U. S. as mules or carriers of illegal drugs. These illegals, through their deeds of illegal bondage or helpful supply and sales of illegal drugs in the U. S. cost the U. S. dearly each year in the deaths of American citizens. Young girls come to the U. S. to be prostitutes and are treated with as little respect and as much cruelty as they would have had or had experienced from the country which they came. Some number of young men end up joining gangs, or come to the U. S. as an extension of a gang that originated in another country and has found its way into the U. S. We had an estimated 100,000 Americans killed by fentanyl in 2022, and this year the estimated count of fentanyl deaths is expected to exceed last year's count. And finally, the foreign-born cartels that used to work mostly outside our borders are now establishing roots here in the U. S. The social costs in these cases are not particularly relevant in terms of dollars. But they are very relevant in terms of the resulting social degradations and many lives that are ruined and lost each year.

The Case of Outlived VISAs: The United States grants scores of limited period work and education VISAs each year. However, it has become more and more publicized in recent years that large numbers of these VISAs expire, yet the foreign visitors stay in our country, thereby becoming illegal aliens. It has also been publicized that the Federal Government has been lax in following up on this brand of illegal aliens to round them up and send them home. We need to collect the data on this particular instance of creating illegal aliens, because it should be the most preventable transition from legal residence to illegal residence in our country. We have documentation on when (and hopefully, where) these workers or students enter our country, the purpose for their stay, and the approved length of their stay (presumably with a certain date for departure from the U. S.) The Federal Government certainly should establish an office within Homeland Security dedicated to tracking these migrant aliens and ensuring that they depart the U. S. by the expiration date of their VISA. This would ensure that a segment of potential illegal aliens would not become invisible in order to become a more permanent fixture in our population and work force. Migrant workers are an important element to the U. S. agriculture segment of production. They provide the mass labor necessary to harvest many of our agriculture crops in a timely fashion to ensure that fresh fruits and vegetables hit our food marts and homes while still fresh with maximum nourishment. Migrant workers also provide a valuable service to this industry's workforce in that the mass migrant workers ensure fair wages to the worker and a dependable collection of federal, state, and local government taxes on those wages. As long as there are a sufficient number of documented migrant farm workers with current VISAs, all producers pay fair wages, have competitive costs, and can sell at competitive prices. When, the VISA program breaks down and there becomes a source of cheaper, illegal alien labor, the competition in this vital industry can quickly become unequal and unfair. When this happens, price wars among the individual producers destabilize the market for the goods of the entire industry, a number of producers are forced to quit producing and we create a market situation where a few producers have substantial control over output quantities and drive higher prices for consumers. This, again is an artificial negative economic situation created by unenforced immigration laws and policy. Where students are able to remain beyond their VISA expiration date, and they are not apprehended, they can become a competitor for high-skilled, high paying positions held for educated individuals. Here, the people harmed are educated American citizens who may be displaced from a job because it was taken by an illegal alien, educated in the U. S., and either seen as a better candidate in terms of outright resume', or simply a more desirable candidate because of his/her willingness to accept a lower salary than the market for a new hire, due to being an illegal alien. In this case, the economic impact to educated U. S. citizens both on an individual basis and on a collective basis is quite negative. We need to gather data on overstayed VISAs for both migrant workers and students to try to get a credible estimate of the economic impacts experienced in both general market force areas to determine just how pervasive these two conditions have been for the last 2 decades with an emphasis on the last eight years or so.

A Summary to the Debate on Illegal Immigration

Implicit in the discussion of legal immigration and legal versus illegal aliens is the desire of a group of people to declare themselves and their culture sovereign, separate and distinct from all others. The only way to provide assurance of this sovereignty is through the establishment of geographical boundaries which are both enforceable and immutable. The concept of "open boundaries" and/or open immigration destroys the capability of a collective culture of individuals to retain sovereignty.

The progressives in the United States have joined a world-wide effort, especially in the western cultures, to do away with national borders and boundaries. This concept is known as Globalization. As a conservative American, I desire that the culture declared by the U. S. Constitution, its drafters, and the representatives of the United States who adopted it, remains intact, adhering to the basic philosophic cultural elements which they stated in the Declaration of Independence, the U. S. Constitution, and the supporting documents thereof. If we, the people of the United States of America, continue to ignore the necessity of limiting the number of people who legally immigrate into this country, and if we continue to experience the high level of cultural upheaval and discord, the United States of America will cease to exist. For, a country without enforced borders and a stated set of universally accepted cultural values is no longer a country. In the history of mankind, no country or empire has remained on this Earth when they lost the desire or capability to enforce their borders and retain a universal sense of cultural belonging among their citizenry. So, I believe that the United States needs to reawaken is sense of common culture among its citizenry in order to reaffirm just what that culture is. Those who propose open borders, sanctuary cities, and acceptance of virtually any and all cultural values within our borders place the very continued existence of the United States of America in great peril.

A major economic point I want to make here is simply this. To my knowledge, no level of government (Federal, State, or Local) treats any of the public money spent on illegal aliens as an explicit cost. Rather, the cost of illegal aliens is probably not captured and certainly, if captured is not provided in any public forum. Yet, to me the actual costs paid to or in support of illegal aliens by each level of government should be collected and reported to the American public on an annual basis in order for the U. S. to determine whether or not bringing all these illegals into the U.S. is a financial benefit and/or cultural benefit to the U. S. A. Another way to put it is for legislators in these three levels of government to declare the payments made to or on behalf of illegal aliens is now an explicit cost that must be segregated from all other government expenses, recorded, and published on no longer than an annual period. None of the costs that government spends on illegal aliens should be a silent, unknown cost. They can be either collected as direct charges to a single person, or as a cost to a group or cadre of illegal aliens.

Insofar as the economic impact of the current large number of illegal aliens in the United States is concerned, I believe the consequences have been much greater than advertised by those advocating a broad "rebranding" of current illegal aliens to legal immigrants. We have millions of American citizens unemployed. We are paying those able-bodied, unemployed Americans to sit at home and collect compensation from governments at all levels with no productive output. Yet, illegal aliens work, usually at wages lower than market value paid to American citizens which ultimately depresses the wages for all workers in that output category. Additionally, governments at all levels pay substantial costs to support illegal aliens and their families. Illegal aliens who work do provide goods and services at lower costs to companies who hire them who then charge lower prices to American consumers in general. I grant this point. However, I know of no credible economic or financial comparison of what the sum of price increases would be to the American public, or the total associated costs American taxpayers pay to illegal aliens and their families to receive these lower prices. As a conservative economist, I am extremely skeptical at economic analyses to date that conclude that the economic benefits of illegal aliens exceed the economic costs of illegal aliens in financial terms. And, until we generate the required credible data that segregates the public sector cost of illegal aliens and the credible depressed prices we pay for their output, the economic arguments are neither instructive nor useful for public policy decisions. Opinions, including mine, are not facts—just supposition based on a set of circumstances and a sense of their economic impacts. But from a public policy perspective, I can state the following unequivocally—It is imperative that we ensure that all able-bodied Americans are employed before we entertain, let alone employ illegal aliens or legal immigrants. The United States of America must ensure that we provide full benefits of citizenship to all our citizens before we provide anything but minimal support to non-citizens residing in this country. In the United States, our Capitalist Economic system is based on the right of Americans to work in order to earn income and provide sustenance and support to themselves and their families. When we permit, if not encourage companies to hire illegal aliens, we are denying

American citizens their birthright to fully participate in our economy and society as a whole. And, if wages in certain sectors of society must increase in order to encourage American citizens to take jobs away from illegal aliens, so be it. As a U. S. citizen and as an economist, I want American citizens employed first. I am willing to pay price increases for those goods and services where displacing alien workers for American workers occurs. After all, as an American consumer, I can still choose what goods and services to purchase as those not to purchase. If some items become "priced out of the market," because the wages paid American workers make a certain good or service more than Americans are willing to pay, then at least we have permitted the U. S. Economic system to perform its function without false influence or interference.

CHAPTER SIXTEEN

Suggested Economic Policies for U. S. Health Care

The U. S. Health Care Crisis as It Currently Exists

As I complete the writing of this Treatise, the U. S. Health Care System appears to be in a crisis. As many as 20 million or more Americans now have health care insurance than prior to the passage of the Affordable Health Care Act (ACA). In 2010, the United States had 48 million Americans uninsured and 84% of Americans insured. In 2015, the U. S. had 29.2 million Americans uninsured and 90% of Americans insured, and in 2020 28 million people or 8.6% of the U. S. population had no health insurance. The medical insurance coverage is robust in (2020 information from 2020 U. S. Census) that it covers most health issues and because it covers everyone with previous health conditions. These benefits of additional Americans covered with a robust insurance plan came at a major annual cost to a large portion of those Americans who had health insurance prior to ACA. For example, millions of people have lost access to their personally preferred medical professional and/or healthcare facility. Tens of millions of Americans have seen significant premium and deductible increases in their health care insurance plans provided through their employers. Private insurers who were to provide insurance to low- and moderate-income Americans at subsidized premiums and deductibles have lost substantial sums since ACA was implemented. As a result, some states no longer have private insurers for their subsidized health care customers. Most other states have only one subsidized health insurance provider which has killed any prospect of competitive rates for their subsidized health care customers. Proponents of the ACA laud the preliminary data that indicates health care expenditures are growing at a much slower annual rate of inflation than the trends for many years prior to ACA implementation. However, I have seen no credible data that suggest that the quantity of patients and quality of patient care has shown any growth, or that perceived growth in quantity and quality of health care dispensed shows a rate of productivity greater than productivity growth prior to ACA. Finally, we do know that the number of young Americans willing to purchase medical insurance prior to ACA has not increased substantially, if at all, as desired and anticipated with the passage of ACA and since its implementation.

According to the Centers for Medicare and Medicaid Services, the percentage of annual health care expenses compared to annual GDP for the U. S. remained stable from 2009 and 2014 at between 17.2% and 17.4%. For 2022, the percentage of health care expenses decreased to 17.3% of the GDP. So, from a national trend view, the percentage of GDP spent for health care has pretty much stabilized. However, what continues to rise are the copays and annual insurance premiums that each individual has to pay. As a conservative economist I believe that the health care system in the U. S. has serious structural flaws from an economic system perspective which prevent it from providing long term cost containment, let alone long-term trending cost reductions in the cost of U. S. healthcare. I shall address those flaws next.

A Discussion of Market Forces Needed in U. S. Health Care

The only way to ensure that we reduce total U S. health care expenditures for an extended, sustained number of years is to increase the supply of U. S. health care services throughout the entire geographical area of the U. S. One can achieve an increase in supply by bringing greater efficiencies into the production of health care services, increasing the number of resources in health care, reducing the relative costs of resources, or changing the legal/institutional environment. The Affordable Care Act targeted none of these factors for increasing supply directly. They did make two indirect references to greater efficiency. The first was that ACA directed that medical records were to be digitalized and stored on computers and computer-accessible data bases. Administrative cost reductions were assumed to be an implicit cost reduction because paper handling theoretically takes more time than information retrieved from computerized digital means. The medical profession has undoubtedly achieved some administrative efficiencies to date, but the digitalization of medical records data has been inconsistently achieved throughout the geographical U. S. I suspect that smaller medical provider organizations have found it more difficult to digitalize due to limited talented computer specialist resources present in rural areas as opposed to urban areas. The other assumed cost reduction in ACA was that with more people being able to go to medical professionals when they first became ill, rather than wait until medical problems became a crisis handled by hospital emergency rooms, health care costs would be drastically reduced. The reason was that emergency room medical care costs are several times the cost of a normal doctor's office visit. Additionally, catching illness early in its cycle generally is greatly less expensive to treat and cure, than catching an illness much later in the cycle when more intensive and complex medical procedures, hospitalization, and drug therapies come into play. This is very true both in theory and in practice. But, these cost reductions have apparently not yet been realized such that the cost of health care in the U. S. has substantially decreased since the ACA was implemented. Yes, the costs of health care stabilized from 2010 through 2014, but they did not go down.

A second set of circumstances were ignored by the ACA. Those circumstances had to do with the demand side of the equation of health care in the U. S. Simply put, the ACA placed tremendous price pressures on the health care delivery system in the U. S. in two ways. First, the goal of the ACA was to assimilate the 48 million uninsured Americans into the health care system as insured customers. In essence, this could only be done through a recognition in the health care market place that suddenly there was an increase in demand for health care by placing those 48 million individuals in the standard health care system through expanding the availability and cost of insurance. This sounds easy, but the market forces that kept most of those 48 million Americans from obtaining insurance in the first place brought a tremendous burden of unpaid and unrecognized health care costs. The first major group of uninsured Americans were those who were uninsurable due to high cost of health care for major illnesses. Once a person became a high-cost patient, insurance companies discontinued coverage for that person and his/her illness at the quickest point in health care service possible. These people became the cadre of millions of Americans uninsurable due to pre-existing conditions. By creating this cadre of uninsured Americans whose medical expense liabilities were expected to be in the millions of dollars each, the cost of healthcare for this cadre became either unaffordable (and therefore no treatment was received) or paid by the individual's family, whereby the family became paupers. These catastrophic costs, if insured, had to be borne by someone. Either the price of health care private insurance would have to skyrocket to pay these catastrophic costs, or the federal government would have to pay these costs. The choice made by the Congress and President Obama in the ACA law was that private insurance was going to bear the cost by declaring that no individual could be denied insurance due to being a member of the cadre of high-expense pre-existing medical conditions. In the ACA, the Federal Government assumed the role to subsidize only a select group of low- and middle-income Americans, and to shift a large part of those higher costs on employer-paid insurance. This meant that the private insurers (known as "exchange" insurers) directly subsidized by the Federal Government had to depend on the Federal Government to pay all the costs of catastrophic costs of this cadre of high expense patients. Unfortunately, the Federal Government has not paid the full catastrophic costs paid by the insurers in the exchanges. Because of these major losses suffered by the exchange insurers over the last three or four years, many of those exchange insurers have left the Federal Government's subsidy market and the exchange small number of exchange insurers left face an astronomically large health care cost that will probably make them unaffordable by either the people to be insured or the Federal Government. In fact, the proof of the unaffordability of the Federal subsidy exchange insurance portion of the ACA has already been proven inoperable or the Federal Government would have paid the entire subsidy necessary to keep the exchange insurers financially viable in previous years.

The second fallacy of the expectations of the ACA upon its passage was that young Americans would purchase health care insurance to make sure their health care expense risks were covered. However, the insidious assumption made by the ACA was that the health care insurance industry would structure their fee schedule for the low risk, low health care expense young Americans in such a way that the insurance companies would create their own subsidy for high risk, high expense customers by charging premiums to American youth significantly above what the actual actuarial value of the premiums versus expenses for the youth would be. If you have any doubt, I simply offer the evidence that most democrats in the Congress today, and the democrats who created the economic concepts in the ACA have claimed that the reason the exchanges have not worked is because the young Americans have not taken the bait to purchase health care insurance rather than pay tax penalties. They state unequivocally that they anticipated that the premiums paid by a large contingent of young people was going to pay for the subsidized high-cost health care expenses of the Federally subsidized low- and medium-income people and the high-cost patients with formerly pre-existing health conditions. In short, not only were the exchange insurer costs and subsidies greater than anticipated by the authors of the ACA, but they greatly over-predicted the coercive power of the Federal Government with America's youth by threatening them with tax penalties if the youth failed to purchase insurance.

The third unanticipated reaction of the American public by the authors of the ACA was their arrogance in taking away all choice from the majority of the American public in their health care decisions. First, the ACA dictated a robust minimum health care insurance package. Once again, this was designed to ensure that virtually all conceivable medical illnesses and risks were covered. Yet, the broad-based medical illness package included risks that simply could not be associated with large groups of the American public. Geriatrics, for example had no need for birth control or pregnancy, yet it was included in their premiums. The youth had no need to pay premiums for the many medical maladies that affect people over 65. Religious and other ethnic and cultural groups were forced to purchase medical protection in this robust standard coverage that violated their centuries-old moral or ethical standards, or family practices and traditions. For the economic grief of getting significantly higher premiums and copays, individuals and families received significantly more restricted choices for doctors and facilities. Thus, some percentage of American patients lost access to their preferred doctors and/or their preferred medical facilities. The middle-class Americans who had health care insurance provided by their employers often saw the greatest negative impact of financial loss and medical provider turmoil from their pre-ACA days to their current post ACA implementation. To many in this group, ACA has now made them the part of American society who can no longer afford their health care costs of high premiums and high out of pocket expenses due to high deductibles. And, given the fact that the Federal Government through the Internal Revenue Service as its enforcement agency now formally coerces Americans to comply with the purchase of insurance "acceptable" to the Federal Government's ACA mandates, consumer choice of insurance content has been totally stripped away. And, because the U. S. Supreme Court upheld the ACA and all its inherent economic policies, the basic economic concept of individual freedom of choice no longer applies in the United States of America. It is the utter destruction of the concept of individual freedom of choice by the passage of ACA and its upholding by the Supreme Court that most alarms me. For if the Congress can successfully challenge freedom of choice by the American public on 18% of our annual GDP, where else will individual freedom of choice be eliminated? And, since individual economic freedom of choice is no longer sacrosanct in our country, how soon might our entire Capitalistic Economic (free enterprise) system be dismantled?

What are the results of the ACA's unbridled increase in demand for health care in the United States? Undeniably, it has been, and will in the not-too-distant future be shown to be the results of any major unchecked increase in demand in a society. The prices will continue to spiral, probably at a more uncontrolled rate than before the ACA was passed as law and implemented. Secondly, given the fact that a large sector of the American public and American taxpayers will simply not be able to afford their health care premiums and out of pocket expenses, the Federal Government will find some way to insert its way into the economic structure of health care such that the Federal Government will completely direct and manage the entire health care system in the U. S. And for any liberal, or progressive who applauds this occurrence, perhaps they should think about 340 million or more angry Americans who receive the same health care access and quality provided our veterans, active military members and their families, and military retirees and their spouses today. Perhaps as a test of such a structure, we should place all government employees including members of Congress, the entire Congressional staff, the entire federal court judges including the Supreme Court Justices and all their employees, and the entire group of federal employees in the executive branch of our government up to and including the president of the United States into the VA, and active military health care systems to test the effects on those forced into a government owned and operated health care system. And then when costs quickly become too unaffordable, let's see the government employees' reaction when their health care quality and access deteriorate quickly and precipitously. Or, we can now simply recognize the fact that we really do not want to go there—to a truly communist based economic and political structure managing a non-responsive, under-providing health care system for and to the American public.

Finally, I want to address the current structural changes to our U. S. health care system for the last half century or so. In 1960, health care costs in the U. S. were 5.0% of GDP. In 1970, they were 6.9% of GDP, in 1980 they were 8.9% of GDP, in 1984 they were 10.0% of GDP, and in 2000 they reached 13.3% of GDP. By 2015 health care costs were 17.8% of GDP and have remained fairly stable around 18% since. Health care costs from 1960 to 2020 (slightly over a half century) grew approximately 3 ½ times the 1960 percentage of GDP. Herein is a partial list of major changes in the economic structure of the health care suppliers in the last 45 years of my life.

First, medical professionals and medical facilities have vacated rural locations at a relatively steady rate. At my age of 5 in 1952, there were two doctors in our small town in central Kansas. By 1960 we had only one part time doctor who split his time between our town and another located 7 miles away. By 1970 the closest doctor was 20 miles away, and my parent's family doctor was 40 miles away. The nearest hospital was a county hospital 20 miles from my parent's home (where I also grew up). In the late 1980s, a few years after retirement, my parents moved 20 miles to the county seat where there was an active full-time hospital, with a small staff of full-time doctors, and an emergency room. By 2005, the hospital in my parent's town (the county seat remember) was mostly a nursing station with a visiting part time doctor from the next-door county seat. My parent's doctors (both primary physician and specialists) were approximately 40 miles away in the next-door county seat. What has happened all over the United States is that rural America has lost convenient and quick access to general medical care and specialized medical care has deteriorated to access often in excess of a 100 mile or longer one way drive? In many rural areas of the U. S., medical facilities are more than 60 miles away. Many states in the U. S. who have vast geographical sections that are highly rural areas can no longer meet what used to be a common goal of at least one general medical facility for each county. ACA did not address this issue and thus, millions of Americans find access to medical care a larger problem than cost.

Second, since the early 1950s, there has been a general consolidation of doctors to work in partnership clinics as limited liability corporations to blunt malpractice suits from bankrupting them all rather than the adjudicated medical profession in their midst. The economic goal of these clinics is to maximize revenue with the assumption of the doctors within that clinic that they have neither the time nor the business acumen to understand and control costs. Larger or multi-location clinics may hire a professional medical administrator to monitor and control costs, but most medical administrators feel that the operating costs are mostly fixed costs in nature. Thus, they tend to spend more of their time trying to keep their revenue rates ahead of their actual and predicted costs. Many hospitals that used to be at a single location, usually in an urban area have expanded to other locations in one or more exterior suburbs to form a sizable regional hospital with the goal of that facility becoming profitable. Additionally, since ACA many urban and suburban hospitals have purchased many of the doctors' partnership clinics. Also, the urban and suburban regional hospitals have set up urgent care clinics with extended hours 24 hours per day to make hospital staffed medical care available to more people. The advantage to the hospitals is that their associated clinics and urgent care facilities often can negotiate higher rates of service with insurance providers while paying resident doctors and staffs about the same salaries that they earned by owning the clinics outright. So, the sum conclusion of this second point is that, under ACA, the medical profession has restructured to promote a general rate increase in many geographic areas of or near a central site facility. And in my limited observations, the strategy is working.

Finally, the medical profession with the aid and help of the insurance industry and the Federal Government have made visibility into pricing by patients impossible. Every time a patient gets a billing directly from the medical provider, the patient knows one thing—the bill and the rates shown therein have absolutely no basis in, for, or to reality. We patients (customers) know that our insurer, whether private or government, has a separate negotiated rate with the medical provider for each service or product on the billing. Additionally, we patients know that it will oftentimes take several months for the medical provider and insurer to reach agreement on the specific line items on the bill. What has evolved in the structure of medical providers over the last half century is that there is no cost and price visibility provided to the patient either before or after medical procedure(s) or doctor's visit is complete. The insurer and the medical provider eventually agree on a unit price by detailed service and total price of the medical provider with neither the insurer or medical provider involving the patient (customer) unless a major disagreement erupts and cannot be resolved by the two parties. Ultimately, the patient gets a bill, which is always a surprise because neither the medical provider nor the insurance company has provided the patient with any idea as to the probable copay and/or deductible that will be applied. In our U. S. Economy, this deliberate hidden fee schedule by both the insurer and the medical provider from the patient (customer) is an abomination to our capitalist, free enterprise economic system. And the Congress has perpetuated, if not encouraged this highly egregious practice for the last half decade. The ACA, passed by only the democrats in both houses of the Congress and signed by a democrat president, greatly exacerbated this situation. Stated as succinctly and simply as I can, "You cannot influence cost if you cannot get a firm handle on the price such that you can truly understand how the insurer and the medical provider arrived at that price. Furthermore, the customer (patient) cannot give any value to the medical benefits received without knowing the specific calculations behind the negotiated price. The politicians complain mightily about patients not caring about the price of the medical care they receive. Well, personally, I care a lot about the price. But the conspiracy among the Federal Government members of Congress and Executive administrators, the insurers, and medical providers to exclude we patients (customers) from the visibility in the prices, and perhaps the negotiation table is what has made the U. S. health care system such a morass of economic absurdity. Cost control is simply not part of the current U. S. health care system, because no one in the market knows what the cost of medical service delivery is. The entire financial system in the U. S. health care system is a sham and a dishonorable representation of our Capitalist, free market system of operation. The United States Government had best ensure that we bring our health care system into the disciplines of financial visibility and economic scrutiny, or our health care system will become an unrecoverable failure of epic proportions.

As of the date of writing this manuscript, the House of Representatives of the U. S. Congress has passed their version of a new Health Care System Blueprint. I confess that I have not thoroughly read, absorbed, and understood how their new Blueprint works. But, I am sure that it falls far short of what the U. S. health care system should emulate. Thus, I provide my basic structure for the U. S. health care system that I feel will address all the issues I have identified in this section of the chapter with an economic structure that will provide great improvements to the current health care system observed, operated, and administered under the ACA.

A Proposed Economic Structure for a Vastly New U. S. Health Care System

The first goal of the new U. S. Health Care System (USHCS) should be to develop a structure that will achieve realistic expectations of reduced cost. A major element of cost reduction is to increase supply. Increasing supply of the USHCS will promote competition among health care producers, reduce the cost of resources in health care productions processes, and encourage innovation of new technologies to enhance health care quality and quantity of production. Below are my proposals to increase supply in the USHCS.

1. *First, and most importantly, the Federal Government must increase the total number of medical professionals in our USHCS. We need an immediate major influx in the quantity of our health care human providers in all areas of the profession, but particularly doctors, nurses, and physicians' assistants. Simply stated, the number of health care professionals has not kept up with the demand. Urban areas have increased their quantity of health care profession human resources over the last half century, but the growth in the number of health care profession human resources in urban areas has come at a price. Many rural areas have lost their health care profession human resources to the urban areas. Thus, although urban areas oftentimes have sufficient health care human resources to meet their population's needs, many rural*

areas have lost all their health care human resources or have seen them diminish greatly below the needs of their populations. Additionally, the educational cost associated with becoming a health care professional human resource has increased substantially, such that many potential health care professional human resources are discouraged from entering the health care profession. Finally, the current educational system that provides health care professional human resources appears too limited to provide the increased number of human resources necessary to meet the total demand for health care throughout all geographic regions, particularly rural areas in the U. S. We cannot reduce the cost of health care substantially without accomplishing a substantial increase in the supply of health care professional human resources. Furthermore, because of the high cost of education borne by health care profession students, many graduate from their studies with an unreasonably high debt load which they must recapture through substantially higher salaries to allow them to pay off their financial education debt in a reasonably short period of time.

Therefore, I propose that the following public policy initiatives be implemented through Federal law. First, the Federal Government should establish a Federal Health Care Professionals' Academy. This Academy would provide free health care education to doctors, nurses, and physicians' assistants and would be patterned from the military, Coast Guard, and Merchant Marine academies. For doctors and physicians' assistants, the Academy would accept college graduates who graduated with pre-med or medical compatible college degrees. The Academy should ensure that their graduates meet or exceed the current American Medical Association (AMA) requirements for immediate insertion into post medical professional intern and residency programs. Additionally, graduates from the Academy would have to serve mandatory placement to designated geographical area(s) within the U. S. for 10 years following successful completion of intern or residency programs. The Academy health care professional students would be a permanent addition to the annual health care professional students graduated each year within the current private/public health care colleges and universities. Additionally, the Federal Government should substantially reduce or eliminate the cost of health care education to all students attending AMA professional health care at private/public colleges and universities. The Feds need to decide what the projected average number of medical professional shortages are for the next 30 years and provide a standard number of inductees and graduates in each of the three major professional fields of doctors, nurses, and physicians' assistants. The advantages to the U. S. healthcare system are many. First, we get a relatively significant increase in medical professional providers into our healthcare system. Next, we decrease the cost of health care provider education which can reduce the cost of health care within the system because healthcare professionals no longer need to receive salaries inflated to let them repay their substantial medical school loans. Also, we can allocate medical professional graduates after they complete their residencies to rural areas who now have great difficulty recruiting healthcare professionals.

2.   *Another significantly high cost of the USHCS is the cost of malpractice insurance. Virtually every medical professional and organization of medical professionals must carry malpractice insurance in order to protect against complete bankruptcy from a successful suit brought against them from patients and/or patients' families. Additionally, hospital, urgent care, and clinical organizations must protect themselves from malpractice suits lest they be sued out of financial existence. I propose two policy initiatives to help drastically reduce the high cost of malpractice insurance for both medical professionals and medical organizations. First, the Federal Government needs to pass tort laws for medical professionals and organizations that provide reasonable financial ceilings for all medical malpractice suits. Additionally, the Federal Government should provide legal definitional guidelines as to what constitutes legal malpractice. I contend that the concept of "pain and suffering" needs to*

be eliminated as a financially reimbursable concept under malpractice. Also, I would eliminate the concept of punitive financial reimbursement to patients. If truly there was a proven controllable, known "wrong" done to a patient by a health care professional or a health care institution that injured a patient for a short period of time or for a lifetime. And, if that "wrong" came from an errant moral, ethical, or standard process/procedure decision(s), perhaps the basic "wrong" itself should be considered a criminal fault, rather than civil. In short, the goal of malpractice law, from an economic perspective should be to financially reimburse a patient for any and all short term or lifelong expenses not covered by personal, employer, or Federal Government insurance. Any moral or ethical "wrongs" should be addressed as a criminal offense and not be reimbursable through civil (tort) law.

As to medical process and/or procedural violations, I believe that the medical profession through the AMA and state medical standards and certification boards should deal with these violations. Whenever malpractice involves medical process and/or procedural violations, the AMA and state medical boards must take on the responsibility to investigate the cause(s) of the violations, recommend solutions to the violations, and monitor future performance of the medical providers (both individuals and organizations) to ensure that lasting solutions have been implemented and become habitual.

Finally, I need to address the issue of lost income of patients. There is no doubt that patients who become permanently partially or wholly disabled will suffer a substantial loss of income during the remainder of their lives. This loss of income will affect not only the patient but his/her family. No family should have their entire lives changed by a single errant medical event not under their control. The economic loss to the family should first be calculated by determining the realistic scenario of the patient's career progression. Then, the annual income string should be estimated for the expected duration of the patient's life prior to the errant medical event and outcome. The patient should expect to be reimbursed for that total income, calculated on an annual income basis, for the rest of his/her life. Additionally, any life insurance held on the patient should remain in force for his/her lifetime as well, and if cancelled, should become part of the lifetime liability owed to the disabled patient. Any monthly receipts from private or government disability programs should be deducted from the estimated annual income of the patient were he/she in a completely healthy basis. All life-long health care and/or personal caregiver expenses should be claimed under medical malpractice tort. If the tort case is either not presented by the patient, or not approved by a jury, these expenses should be added to the annual income loss liability of the patient. All net benefits to the patient should be calculated on an annual basis, adjusted for inflation and other employee elements such as promotions and bonuses, payable in monthly installments. There should be no lump sum payments to a patient for lost income. It should be recalculated for each year and then paid monthly. This process should result in the patient receiving an annual income stream essentially equal to what he/she could reasonably expect for their life time, with no deterioration in future medical or life insurance benefits. The question becomes one of who pays the monthly net income loss for these patients who have won a malpractice case in court or settled out of court. In the end, my recommendation is that the gross annual income lost should first be reduced by the government disability insurance, and private disability insurance subsidies paid each year. The annual income loss (including special health care and personal care costs), once reduced by the other private and government disability income payments should be paid by medical malpractice insurers. In this way, we translate all medical malpractice awards to a predictable annual expense to the malpractice insurance company, and allow them to set up good estimated annual total malpractice outgo estimates with modifications for forecast expenses based on actuarial estimates.

After all these economic and philosophical policies are implemented for malpractice reform, the annual cost of malpractice insurance should reduce substantially. This cost reduction to medical professionals and medical organizations should result in directly relatable annual price decreases to patients across the board.

3.   *Neither Obamacare, nor the new House Health Care Plan make any active, direct policies to enhance either cost or price visibility to the American public. You cannot control and reduce costs unless you get accurate visibility into the actual costs incurred for medical care provided by procedure, care facility, and care department(s). I don't believe that I have seen a widespread program of audits of medical care practices and facilities that provide the true actual costs that dictate the level of charges made by medical care providers and medical care organizations. Neither have I seen evidence of audited direct costs versus indirect costs of medical care providers and organizations. I propose that the Congress develop a Federal Medical Costs Government Audit Group (FMCGAG) whose initial job will be to collect actual costs against prices charged patients (customers) by whatever procedure practice charge accounts are used. Additionally, the Audit Group needs to ensure that medical organizations capture the resource types and quantities that are associated with each procedure practice cost. Of course, in order for the FMCGAG to collect these costs, the medical practices and organizations will have to begin to routinely segregate their costs in such a manner as to be traceable to procedures and rates charged patients. The FMCGAG should also be charged with the responsibility to establish cost accounting standards for the entire medical provider industry so that cost and fee comparisons can be made by organization and practice by location, region, and nationally. For those who think this will create a nightmare of paperwork, let me ask a question. Do we really want to continue to spend approximately one-sixth of our GDP each year without knowing what the real cost is, where we might reasonably expect to reduce cost, and how healthcare pricing/ charges to*

patients relate to those costs? Ultimately, a goal of the Federal Government should be to ensure that the pricing/charges to patients are within reasonable bounds of being the same across the entire U. S. Finally, the FMCGAG should gain and provide Americans the visibility of how each medical organization translates actual costs to prices charged patients for each procedure. Where prices are largely dissimilar in one local area or among regions, the Federal Government needs to determine why those dissimilarities exist and get them more similar. For anyone who considers this an unreasonable task, let me ask this. Do you purchase a car without knowing the sticker price of the basic auto plus all the options? Do you purchase a house without knowing the asking price and compare the price of one house to others of similar size and quality in the same area? Do you take your pets to a veterinarian for shots, an examination, boarding, or a medical procedure without asking the price? Furthermore, would you purchase a car, a home, or vet services without determining the reputation of the individual/firm from whom you wish to make the purchase? If you answered "NO" to any or all of these questions, why would you have a medical procedure done without knowing the price and qualitative reputation of the medical facility and doctor(s) who are treating you?

4.   A final area of current costs incurred in the USHCS which are substantially higher than they should be are administrative costs. Hospitals and insurance companies spend a lot of time bickering over the expenses/rates charged by health care organizations for services performed. This bickering involves, the health care organizations adequately convincing the insurance companies of the accuracy of the medical services performed and the allowability of each of the categories of expenses/charges submitted by the health care organization. Additionally, the health care organizations and insurers oftentimes argue about the charges submitted by the health care organization being consistent with negotiated rates for those services with each particular insurance company involved in the covered medical care of each patient.

Oftentimes, questions arise over which insurance company has primary responsibility and which additional insurance companies of the patient are secondary. The advantage in all of this confusion and back and forth communication of payment for health care are always to the benefit of the insurance companies, because delayed payments allow them to collect days and weeks more interest on their delayed cash outlays. The medical organizations are penalized because they wait weeks and sometimes months for the insurance companies to fully pay them for their medical care rendered. Both insurance companies, and especially medical provider organizations have significantly bloated administrative staffs just to transfer money between the insurance companies and the medical provider organizations for medical procedures conducted on patients. I have seen estimates that over 40% of the annual medical expenses in our USHCS center on the administrative process of getting medical providers organizations paid for their medical services performed. This is an outrageous waste of resources and money. I propose that the rates charged by medical providers' organizations be the same for all patients and all insurance companies. These standard prices, once publicized should then hold for at least a year. Additionally, the prices should be set for all procedures and the task content for each procedure. Once a medical professional has prescribed, treated, and completed a specific procedure, the insurance company should promptly pay the medical organization for whom the medical professional worked. Any copays or deductions should immediately be billed to the patient for payment. Deferred payments owed by patients would be negotiated between the patient and the medical organization. There is no justification for any medical procedure not to have a standard price for each patient and insurance company. Once we achieve standard pricing, the need for large administrative staffs at all insurance companies and medical organizations simply goes away because we have cancelled the routine bickering that arises with virtually every procedure done on every patient.

The second major area of the economic process that the current USHCS violates is the market. In fact, there simply is no market in the current USHCS. Why? First, the consumer (patient) is not in control of his or her health care. Instead, the insurance company(ies) to which the consumer pays premiums is in charge of the patient's health care. Secondly, the patient is never aware of the real price of the treatment/procedure, and thus has no basis of comparing medical value received versus the price paid for medical care. Furthermore, the patient (consumer) has no ability to "shop around" for medical care because neither qualitative differences among health care providers nor price comparisons can be made. In short, the least informed individual among the health care professional, the patient (consumer), and the insurance company is the consumer. Yet, in our market driven, free market, capitalist economic system, it is the consumer who is supposed to have the upper hand in determining their medical care, their medical care professional, and their medical provider facility based on full knowledge of price and qualitative comparisons. This lack of a true market place where consumers and producers meet and agree on price and output quality simply does not exist in our current U. S. Health Care System. Furthermore, neither the ACA nor the current House revision to the ACA do anything to change this most egregious of capitalist systemic failures.

1. *The current health care treatment model works something like this. The medical professional determines the procedure/treatment for the patient, then sends that procedure/treatment to the insurer of the patient. Next, the insurer determines whether or not each task in the treatment/procedure will be allowed and therefore paid by the insurance company. Communication of covered versus uncovered tasks within a procedure may or may not be discussed between the medical organization and the insurance company. The medical provider usually sets a date for treatment or procedure with the patient. The medical professional provides the procedure/treatment with little negotiation/explanation with the patient, and particularly excludes any discussion of the price of the treatment/procedure. Once the patient gets treated, the medical organization submits the charges for treatment to the insurance*

companies for payment. Once the medical organization has received remuneration from the insurance companies, they then bill the patient for any and all deductions and copays not paid by the insurance companies. Some several weeks to several months later, the consumer/patient finally sees the "true price" of the bill and how much they have to pay. The astounding tragedy of this situation is that the consumer is absolutely clueless as to the price of the treatment/procedure and incurs a potentially devastating financial liability without being informed during the front end of the decision-making for the medical treatment/procedure. This wrong-headed violation of our basic capitalistic system of market structure and decision-making must be stopped if our USHCS is ever going to work properly. How we might correct this condition is addressed in the next paragraph.

2. *First, each health care provider, both individuals and organizations should establish and publish their prices (rates) for every procedure, task, and treatment which they propose to provide to patients. These prices should be made public and should be singular in that all patients and all insurance companies (and all payers) pay the same price for each procedure, task, and treatment advertised for service. Second, prior to the delivery of every treatment, procedure, and task, the medical professional and or administrative staff member of the treatment facility should, by law, state the specifics of the total price for the treatment, procedure, or task proposed by the health care professional with a full disclosure of how much of the total bill will be paid by the primary insurance company, secondary insurance company(ies), and the patient. The patient, after having been provided this price information can then either approve the treatment proposed, or request the health care professional to provide a list of alternative treatments and their prices. The patient, after having been provided the alternative treatments can then choose which treatment alternative they prefer—including no treatment at all. The full disclosure of price associated with all treatment, procedure, and task alternatives is an absolutely essential*

element of our U. S. Health Care System. This is the only way to provide the patient with the necessary comparison of value of treatment and anticipated results and the price associated with each treatment. We have spent the last half century desensitizing the patients (consumers) to making this comparison of the value of healthcare treatment outcome versus price. Reintroducing the real price per treatment option into the patient's decision-making process directly between the health care professional and the patient (consumer) brings the concept of the market of capitalism into play because it forces the patient (consumer) and the health care professional to agree on the most appropriate treatment, the price of the treatment, and anticipated results of the treatment. If this recommendation, or something very similar is not adopted in the new/replacement USHCS signed into law, this major economic process flaw will remain, because the ACA continues to ignore this necessary element of patient/provider agreement on price, output expectations, and the value of the expected results of the procedure/tasks/treatment. From the market shortfall of the ACA, we now address the final major issue of demand for health care.

What remains in developing the structure of a new U. S. Health Care System is to deal with a few major consumer (demand) issues aimed at reducing the cost of health care, and providing a universality to health care economic decisions by all Americans. Let me make a couple of preface comments before addressing the specific demand issues I see in our current USHCS. First, given the most recent discussions provided by the liberal media and their various statistical organizations, there is a sense of the American public that all Americans should be covered for health care in some fashion. This does not mean, nor do I, a conservative economist interpret this that all people living within the borders of the United States of America should be covered for health care. Specifically, illegal aliens should not be covered unless they purchase their own health care insurance personally or through an employer. Additionally, as a conservative economist I do not support providing able-bodied Americans who can work, but do not with long term health care. I do support providing Americans who transition between jobs whether for brief layoffs or unemployed and seeking new employment, short term health care. Finally, for at least the next decade, I prefer the economic structure of a combined private and public medical insurance program to provide the universal coverage of American citizens. These provisos having been stated, below are my proposed public policy structural aspects for a new U. S. Health Care System.

The final shortfall of the ACA's approach to the current U. S. Health Care System is that it fails to address the overarching issue of the economic concept of demand. If you remember demand is the amount of a good or service that an individual is both willing AND ABLE to purchase. Clearly the ACA, and the proposed House replacement health care legislation fail to fully deal with this issue. One reason I state this is that neither the ACA, nor the replacement legislation deal with the inability of a sizable segment of the U. S. population to afford health care—before or after the imposition of either the ACA or the current House legislative models. The ACA dictates that "all" people should obtain health care insurance, with tax penalties to be applied to those who fail to acquire insurance deemed "adequate" by the Federal Government in that the insurance provides all coverage content required by the ACA. Also, the ACA dictates that every person who previously was denied insurance coverage due to pre-existing conditions can no longer be denied coverage. However, the ACA ignored the substantially higher price levels of health care insurance to all consumers in order to pay the associated high costs incurred by insurers as they bring those with pre-existing conditions under their (the insurance companies') umbrellas. Additionally, the amount of health care premium subsidies paid by the Federal Government were far higher than anticipated by the original estimated costs of ACA. Finally, the anticipated cost of adding 24 million more Americans to the funded demand for health care was greatly misunderstood and grossly underestimated. Let me be clear here. As a conservative economist, I do not object to developing a public policy that brought 24 million more Americans into the health care insurance umbrella. But, I do object to the fact that both the Administration's ACA estimated funding impact, and the Congressional Budget Office's (CBO) estimates of the dollar impact underestimated the cost to the U. S. Treasury by tens of billions of dollars a year. Additionally, neither the Administration nor the CBO estimated the significant premium, copay, and deductible increases initiated by private insurance companies to their business and individual client's resultant from the incorporation of the mandatory dictates from the ACA. In fact, I would go so far as to say that neither the Administration nor the CBO addressed the impact of the ACA on private insurance rates at all. Rather, the focus of their estimates was on the Federal Funds that would be involved in implementing ACA. Both the Administration and the CBO reached the conclusion that the additional Federal funds required to implement the ACA would be offset by the additional taxes that the Federal Government would receive from ACA tax law changes. This assessment has proven to be horrendously false. Health care premiums for private individuals who purchase their own insurance and those who get their health care insurance through business have seen their premiums, deductions, and copays skyrocket—most by at least 30% over the last three years and some by over 100% in the last 3 years. So, whatever changes we make in the USHCS in terms of demand, we have to restructure the price of health care to segregate pre-existing conditions, new patients/customers, and catastrophic health care. Furthermore, we must accomplish the segregation in such a manner that we can develop private insurance premiums which pay for all but these three major segmented health care areas. My proposals are in the below paragraphs.

1. *First, let's quickly deal with an area of U. S. health care demand, not discussed in the paragraph above—health care insurance for illegal aliens. Simply put, the U. S. Government should not pay one penny for health care for illegal aliens. We should not burden American taxpayers with health care costs incurred by people who reside in this country illegally. As a matter of public policy, the intent of Congress is already present on many previously authorized and appropriated laws— do not pay public monies to illegal aliens. This policy should be extended to any new health care legislation.*

2. *For pre-existing conditions and catastrophic health expenses, I propose that the Congress pass legislation that places a low annual maximum dollar health care expenses to be borne by insurers on behalf of their beneficiaries. This catastrophic expense should be at low levels such as $1,500 per treatment per individual, and $5,000 total for each year.*

This should immediately bring the cost of private insurance down substantially because private insurers will no longer face high medical costs. The Federal Government should set up two separate accounts for direct reimbursement to health care providers and organizations—one for Federal payment of pre-existing conditions, and the other for Federal payment of catastrophic conditions. Insurers, not having to face these two major health care cost risks, should be able to offer much lower, highly competitive rates to their business and individual clients resulting in lower premiums, copays, and deductibles.

3. *Those Americans who cannot get health care through their own private means, place of business, or Medicare, should get fully subsidized health care insurance from the Federal Government. The concept of Medicaid should be changed from one of reimbursement of health care costs to one of becoming a Federal Government Insurance Company (FGIC). This FGIC would provide free health insurance cards to those who can only get insurance through this program. And, of course the FGIC would pay all medical bills incurred by this group of individuals. The reason to keep segregated financial records of the cost of pre-existing conditions, catastrophic care, and FGIC insured costs is to be able to determine potentials for cost/price cuts in the future, and/or the success or failure of new treatments.*

4. *The Federal Government should also pass legislation to allow private medical insurance companies to sell medical insurance across state lines and, indeed nationally. The hope here is to reduce medical insurance premiums, copays, and deductibles by spreading the risks of medical expenses over a larger number of people with age and health diversity. Another advantage of regional and national health insurers should be to equalize health care rates over broader geographical areas.*

5. *Demand for drugs as a part of health care has increased substantially during the last 2 decades. We have more drug treatments for many more health infirmities which oftentimes reduce the need for expensive surgical procedures. However, the cost of drugs has also taken a larger share of annual health care costs. The monopoly power of drug companies who bring new drugs to the market enables them to charge high costs for those*

new drugs for some period of time. And current patent laws may need revision to shorten the time for drug companies to retain monopoly rights to bring competition and the resultant lower prices into the market.

CHAPTER SEVENTEEN
Economic Impacts of U. S. Climate Change Policies

The numerous major climate change policies of the Biden administration have, I believe, placed the U. S. into an unknown abyss and each day we continue down into the abyss, the more difficult it will be for the U. S. to correct itself. Why do I dare say that we are in an abyss for our climate change policies? In a nutshell, because the current policy-makers in Washington DC, and every other government agency within the 50 U. S. states, (1) have yet to set realistic goals, (2) captured the ultimate cost to the U. S. both as taxpayers and consuming citizens, (3) recorded the amount of money the U. S. both privately (consumption) and publicly (government expenditures) has spent to date and by year, (4) determined the infrastructure needs to attain the currently unstated goal, (5) provided credible estimates of the cost of current climate change policies on the American public both from a private ownership of carbon dioxide "polluters," and the probable total and annual government expenditures of all governments to achieve the unstated goal, and (6) provided any guidance or money to the private sector to invent new technologies to replace fossil fuels as our major energy source. I will address each of these shortfalls in more detail below.

What is Climate Change

There are two aspects of the definition of climate change. The first is the simple change in temperature around the Earth from one period of time to another period of time. The second aspect of climate change is a general change in weather patterns in one or more areas of the Earth. Most climate change discussions throughout the world and in the U. S. have to do with the "fact" that the Earth's temperature has risen by approximately one degree Fahrenheit since 1800. However, in the U. S. just since May of 2023, I have noticed a significant change in the weather pattern in the U. S. I live in the Northeast Georgia mountains, and have been here for 12 years. This year, at least so far (from 1 May to the end of August 2023), there has been a significant change in the weather pattern for the entire southern states that border the Gulf of Mexico.

We always expect our weather to come from the Gulf and travel from Southwest to Northeast—especially in the May through October time frame when major storms begin to form from the West Coast of Africa towards the islands south and east of Florida into the Gulf of Mexico which often heighten to hurricanes. Thus far this year (2023) however, there have been no major hurricanes form and the weather that we have been getting in Georgia has pretty much always come from the northwest which is controlled by the Arctic air stream. Usually, the warm water creates warm air from the Gulf that drives the Arctic air stream north because of the strong storms forming into hurricanes in the Gulf. That simply has not happened this year because there simply have been only a couple of tropical storms come into the Gulf and basically died before they touched land.

What are the Ultimate Goals of U. S. Energy Policy

The true singular goal for reducing the effect of current climate temperatures by our current U. S. President, Joe Biden is to reduce carbon dioxide and methane gases in the U. S. atmosphere. His continued statement is that he plans to reduce the United States' carbon dioxide release into the world's atmosphere by one single policy goal—kill the American fossil fuel industry. And the implementation of this singular policy goal is solely to make electricity the singular U. S. energy mode of energy usage. President Biden has rather optimistically proposed that the U. S. should (will) reach the singular goal of total electrification as early as 2035, or as late as 2050. As a goal of lower carbon dioxide, current energy policy gurus in Washington DC, have decided that the only way to get the American public to totally electrify their households is to dramatically increase the price of all fossil fuels to a point that the use of electricity either becomes cheaper than fossil fuel alternatives, or more directly because fossil fuels are no longer available to business and households. I recently read an article by Bjorn Lomborg, the president of the Copenhagen Consensus Center, that provided the cost of reducing the projected world's climate average temperature in 2100 from increasing 7.4 degrees to as low a climate change increase of only 3.9 degrees Fahrenheit by 2100 will cost 20 trillion dollars. The cost of NOT changing the world's present pace of climate increasing technologies will result in a total cost of $140 trillion. Of course, any climate change reduction achieved in between those two "probable" costs of climate change temperatures would result in increased costs somewhere between those two estimates.

I have not seen a statement on the part of a U. S. Government senior official stating exactly what they want to achieve from our singularly stated goal to "reduce the use of fossil fuels to zero" or make the world, but in particular the United States "carbon neutral" at some time in the future. As I understand the carbon neutral goal, it means that whatever amount of carbon is sent into the atmosphere, we have enough non-carbon-based energy activities that expel no carbon dioxide into the atmosphere from some annual baseline of carbon emission using some sort of calculation process.

Let me make four points in this part of the Climate Change scenario. First, stating the U. S. goal on becoming carbon neutral is NOT a goal on reducing the general change of the world temperature at some future date. We honestly don't really know if this goal will reduce the world-wide change in the world's climate or not. The U. S. goal has to be some recognizable and easy measure of temperature decrease or at least world temperature remaining the same during the next 75 years. And for sure, the current goal of and singular spoken focus on a goal by President Biden to "kill" the fossil fuel industry or dedicated to a carbon neutral U. S. Economy speaks more of method than of a goal against which there must be many other alternatives than the limited few being implemented today. Second, focusing almost solely on reducing the U. S. reliance on our energy needs by changing the method of generating electricity AND making the U. S. Economy totally dependent on the single energy source of electricity, at least at this point in time is both foolish and unrealistic as to its achievability. Third, every policy decision on the implementation of the U. S. goal to help reduce increased climate temperatures has a cost to the ecology. What we do to our planet in our efforts to use non-fossil fuel electric generation processes and methods has to be considered to an equal degree of what we achieve in terms of climate reduction. And, of course we immediately need a new electrical grid throughout the U. S. because our current grid is already overburdened with power usage today.

For those of us who have a religious thought every once in a while, I propose this last point—Doesn't God determine the world's climate? Are we so brazen to think that we can adjust what God has determined the world's climate to be at any and all points in time. Let's deal with each of the four points in greater detail.

Kill the U. S. Fossil Fuel Industry

For the U. S., this is currently not a reasonable policy goal to implement for several reasons. First, we have only 4 mature alternative methods of generating electricity outside fossil fuels. They are nuclear, directed rushing water (via dams), wind mills, and solar panels. There are others like fuel cells, experimental energy creation from the Earth's magnetic field, and vastly improved batteries that hold virtually a lifetime charge. But, apparently, none of these alternatives are proven to meet their stated technical, time of use, and low to zero maintenance goals. Each of these four alternatives to fossil fuel electrical production have major drawbacks.

Increase the use of Nuclear Power. In the case of nuclear power, a natural disaster or a failure in the production process within the nuclear complex can cause a major disaster. This reason is why Germany has shut down all their nuclear reactors. Additionally, I believe it takes 10 or more years to build a nuclear reactor power plant. Building a nuclear power plant is very expensive. Additionally, a nuclear power plant takes a large amount of water to keep the fuel rods and fuel rods production area cool. This need for a large volume of water greatly limits the places where a nuclear power plant can be built. And, closing a nuclear plant down is both hazardous and very expensive. The United States, Russia, and most recently Japan, have each experienced major nuclear plant accidents. Besides the cost in human lives, the surrounding areas of the nuclear plants have required massive amounts of concrete and structural enhancements to attempt to prevent a future melt-down. Additionally, sizable areas of land space around the facilities have been sequestered in order to keep people a safe distance from the area. It is my belief that the use of nuclear power to produce electricity has lost much of its previous luster as an acceptable means of producing electricity throughout the world.

276

Directed Rushing Water. As a method of generating electricity, using directed rushing water to power turbines and large generators to produce energy seems to be a very safe, continuous source of electric power generation. However, creating the directed rushing water source is usually very expensive. Most of the time it requires great sized dams to hold water back in the creation of great water reservoirs (lakes) which then direct the water through tunnels to generate enough rushing water power to power the turbines. Again, the opportunities to build dams of enough size to generate decent quantities of electricity and create a natural lake water basin behind the dam are limited in the United States.

Directed rushing water takes a major dam at a point in a river that will easily be capable of having a major dam built where the river can be diverted away from the build site, and there is a large, deep area behind the dam to form a lake. I have the feeling that the federal and state governments think they have already pretty well scouted all areas where new dams with large generators can be built.

Wind Mills or Wind Turbines. Wind turbines (mills) have sprung up in many of the states within the U. S. However, they all have one or more significant detractors. First, if you build a windmill farm, it takes 1 ½ acre of land for each windmill. When operating, wind turbines are only 30% to 60% efficient depending on the velocity of the wind. Wind turbines are hazardous to both wild life and tame animal life. Additionally, the land is usually too beat up and cluttered to be able to farm. So, when we put up wind turbine fields, if the land was previously grazing land or farm land, it is no longer capable of producing the food products.

Wind turbines have become one of the two darling technologies chosen by the anti-fossil fuel crowd as a major substitute of fossil fuel produced electricity. However, this alternative solution to fossil fuel electrical production has been proposed and pushed by its proponents without giving the American public any of the serious disadvantages that come with it. The first and most obvious disadvantage is that wind turbines only work when the wind is blowing, and then usually take a steady wind of at least 20 miles per hour to turn the turbine. There are many days throughout the U. S. when the wind simply is not at that velocity. Second, wind turbines must be placed a minimum of about one-half acres apart in order for the turbines not to disrupt the air flow on all the neighboring wind turbines. The ideal ranging of a turbine field is to place one turbine for every one and one-half acres. This gets you 2 megawatts of electricity for each turbine. But, that isn't the only negative about wind turbines. Wind turbines completely distort and essentially destroy the ecology around the wind turbine field. Farmers cannot farm around the turbines because of the wind currents they each and collectively produce and because of the amount of land space used to get access to service wind turbines for maintenance, including the number of access roads per acre of land. Wind turbines, when operational basically void the area of the wildlife and birds—again because of the dangers to birds and the wind currents on the ground discouraging the nesting and food supply for wildlife. The disturbance to wildlife has been most punctuated recently by the construction of one or more planned wind turbine farms in the ocean between the U. S. East Coast and the islands just to the East of the Coast. Recent history has seen a several fold increase in the number of beached whales and dolphins. And that is just with the construction of the base of the turbines below the surface of the ocean. Additionally, of course, fishermen have seen a distinct drop in their fish quantities caught.

Wind turbines cause a major hazard to the ecology as well. The turbine blades are non-biodegradable. That means they must be buried as trash somewhere after they have become unusable. And blades are large—usually 80 meters (262 feet) long. So, it takes aa lot of land space to bury these blades after they have been damaged or met their useful life. And, wind turbine farms have to be on relatively flat ground space. This targets U. S. farm land as the most useful land for wind turbine farms. However, farm land has a significant alternative use—to grow food for the people of the U. S. and the world. I don't see these trade-offs being discussed in terms of impacts to the U. S. and world food production. For example, how many acres of turbine blades would it take to power New York City, or Washington, DC, or Atlanta, Georgia, or Los Angeles, California? At two megawatts per hour per wind turbine, we are talking hundreds of thousands of acres of farm land traded off for electric power for each of these cities. It is no wonder the kill fossil fuels proponents don't want to talk about wind turbines. And, have you ever wondered why few if any wind turbines have landed anywhere next to the homes where they live?

So, the gig is up on wind turbines. Trade-off food, farmland, and the wild animal population of America to stop production of electricity by fossil fuels. How smart does that seem to you, rural America? I can guarantee the American public this, investing heavily in wind turbines will necessarily result in major food shortages, loss of wildlife throughout much of America, and a continued significance in the price of food for decades to come.

Convert to Solar Panels. There is a major boon in the U. S. to have homeowners install solar panels on their rooftops—if they live in an area where their roofs get a long daily facing to the sun. The promise of solar panels on people's roofs is not that the panels will completely keep them from having the local power company provide them electricity. Rather, it is usually sold as a way to greatly reduce the amount of electricity they have to purchase from their local power company. It may also let them sell back some electricity to their provider. But, once again, all is not well for the ecology, and perhaps for the rooftop solar panel owner.

Let's look at the economic principles being used today to encourage more Americans to purchase solar panels to provide the electricity to their homes, and if they have them, additional buildings requiring electricity. There is a current program available to people across America who live in specific zip codes who can get solar panels and their installation for their homes and potentially additional buildings free of charge. Theoretically, this should get you immediate, significant reductions in your electrical bills as you blissfully save that monthly cash. But wait, what if you have a major wind or hail storm and your panels (some or all) are damaged? You won't be able to get the repairs paid by the state or federal government. So, now the maintenance bill come straight to your door sooner than expected? Additionally, why does it cost so much as part of the replacement of damaged solar panels to have the damaged panels taken from your home? Well, you now face a major unadvertised hidden cost of owning solar panels. Solar panels, just as the blades on wind turbines are an ecological nightmare. They are not bio-degradable and thus, the U. S. will have to find some place to dump these solar panels. Of course, the question will be whose back yard do we dump them in?

Furthermore, solar panels have another gaping limitation. It takes a large amount of acreage to put a large number of solar panels to fill the electricity needs of say, just one skyscraper, or a large hotel, or how about a major factory. Just like wind turbines, once we talk about towns, cities, and factories, solar panels suddenly have two major additional expenses. First, where do you find sufficient land space to put millions of solar panels to provide the electricity for an entire large city? Well, unfortunately, the answer is we take more land space from farm land. And, of course the next question is where do we put used, non-functioning solar panels. At this point, the U. S. has no technology that can decompose old solar panels to reuse the material in the old panel to build a new panel. So, here again, our current technology is simply to bury them.

What's wrong with electric vehicles?

The current state of economics for the U. S. to move heavily towards electric vehicles has several costs. The first and most obvious cost is the purchase price of today's electric vehicles. The price of a family automobile is at least $10,000 greater than a gasoline powered vehicle, and oftentimes more than $20,000 greater than a comparable gasoline powered vehicle. Today's electric powered vehicles can only travel about 300 miles without having to sit at a power station to recharge. And, even with the most powerful recharging station today, you will likely have at least a 30-minute wait, if not closer to an hour. Of course, you could eat a meal at a close restaurant if one is available. But if not, and you are on a long road trip, 30 minutes to an hour of time waiting for your car to charge is mostly a waste of time.

An additional cost to a new electric car purchaser that no car salesman talks about until after the sale is that if you want to charge your car at home, you have to call your electric company to install a home charger. It usually takes a special 220-volt line and a small charging station installed for a couple thousand dollars. Home charging stations traditionally recharge your car at roughly 3 miles added per hour. You can pay more for a home station that will recharge your car at roughly 6 miles added per hour. And, yes, that is right, your electric car charging mechanism will determine the number of miles added, not at how full your car's tank of electricity is. Of course, the home auto charging stations are not an expense paid by the government. In fact, the only "reimbursement" by the Federal Government for your purchasing a new electric car is not a cash reimbursement at all. It is, rather a deduction on your Federal Income Tax, which means that you get somewhere between $1,000 to $4,000 reimbursement from the Federal Government depending on whether your income tax rate is 10% or 40%.

The major failing of today's electric car is its battery. The battery is made of significant amounts of a handful of "rare Earth" minerals. This means that the more electric vehicles made will eventually deplete the Earth's deposit of one or more of these minerals. And, at that point, unless and until we learn how to make a battery that is not laden with rare earth minerals, they will eventually decease in supply. That in turn, will increase the purchase price of electric vehicles. It also turns out that the major known deposits of these rare earth minerals, as of today, are located in Russia and China. From an economic perspective, that places the U. S. in a very perilous, relatively powerless position of weakness in having a stable quantity of these rare earth minerals to make the batteries that power these current electric cars. And, of course, those two countries could easily double or triple the prices of these minerals which would cripple the U. S. Economy rather quickly were we to cap the majority of our fossil fuel supplies.

Another aspect of generating an all-electric vehicle fleet in the U. S. that is still in fledgling experimentation and usage has to do with large and semi-trucks as well as large farm machinery. I expect the finalized products to be larger in size, to some degree, than the current diesel-powered vehicles. I already know that farmers across the U. S. are complaining that they won't be able to drive their farm machinery more than about 10 hours a day before recharging. I suggest that increased size and weight of these large truck rigs and farm machinery may prove to be larger problems than now being considered. For example, imagine if you will, how even somewhat larger semi-trucks would become more hazardous on today's highways. And then, there is yet no guarantee that a fully depleted electric farm machine will be rechargeable in 10 to 12 hours either. During harvest and ground preparation times, farmers usually work literally from dawn to dusk, which in the summer is closer to 14 to 15 hours long. Cutting their usage time to 10 hours a day greatly risks the potential planting difficulties and exposes their crops to ruinous weather for a longer period of time during harvest time. Similar problems befall the trucking industry. Once they hit the road with a load, they need to drive for longer periods with shorter stops in between. But, the probable charging time on a large semi-truck with large batteries could keep them off the road for as long as 24 hours. This would cut the annual income and profit opportunities to truckers and the entire trucking business significantly. Finally, the purchase prices of these electric farm machinery and large truck vehicles will be sky high as compared to the prices they pay today which usually exceeds $100,000 per vehicle burning diesel fuel. Finally, and perhaps the most damning trait is that today's lithium-ion batteries are now showing a major safety tendency to explode and catch fire—not just on automobiles, but also on electric bicycles.

Killing Fossil Fuels Means Killing Americans. We now have to deal with the overarching economic impacts to the U. S. Economy as a whole and the American public as a society. The current U. S. President's policy was to turn off the spigot of fossil fuel products to bring about a major change in the U. S. Economy from fossil fuels to electricity. In short, I call it the rather immediate electrification of the U. S. The only problem was that it was in February of 2021 and still is an unachievable goal in the few years that the President said would be possible. The immediate result was for people to see all their energy costs double in just a couple of months and stay at those prices ever since. The price per gallon of gasoline and diesel fuel remains roughly twice as high today as they were in January of 2021. We have as many as 90,000 fewer semi-trucks on the road today than we had three years ago. Throughout the U. S. natural gas and fuel oil prices are at least twice the price they were just prior to January 2021 when President Biden took office. The inflation rate for 2022 was around 8.5%. It is roughly half that so far in 2023, but with the fossil fuel industry production as uncertain as it is could tip the scales into another major price frenzy.

Immediate electrification of the U. S. is simply impossible. There are a number of show-stopper reasons. I will list a few of the major reasons below.

The U. S. Electrical Grid is outdated, outmoded, and under-sized.

The U. S. electrical grid has been criticized for years as being under-sized and outdated. Every theoretical "expert" in the Biden administration has publicly admitted this. But, as of today, I see no plan to fix it. We need to spend, I'm guessing, a few trillion dollars or more to greatly increase the size of the grid, and while we increase the size of the grid, incorporate new technologies to make it more stable and responsive to changes in power needs across the total United States. We already see severe power difficulties in various parts of the country when some kind of major power production capability fails. California has planned blackouts across the state in order to distribute the state's electricity shortages due to summer weather. We saw a major electrical grid failure in the State of Texas a year and a half or so ago, when a winter storm froze the wind turbines and stopped their electrical production, catapulting their power grid into a major state-wide failure. Our country is already in deep trouble meeting our current electrical requirements and yet we have a President who has taken one of our most bountiful resources away from the American public to counteract the known and uncorrected entire U. S. electrical system. In the last year and a half, many Americans have suffered major problems of simply keeping within a living environmental temperature in their homes and work places.

The Current President, his political party, and the policy-makers in Washington DC must understand the pure physical impossibility of going totally electric or even nearly so in the next ten years in the U. S. via virtually 100% non-fossil fuel produced electricity is simply impossible.

The reality of our technology today in terms of creating large amounts of electricity using our current non-fossil fuel technological methods is simply abject folly. Solar power and wind power is simply significantly less efficient than the use of fossil fuels to generate our electrical power. Additionally, the economic trade-offs are simply far too costly in terms of land space used and the fact that solar and wind power production methods are only 63% as productive as fossil fuel produced electricity. If we are going to increase the usage and produce the necessary additional electricity to meet the current President's plans, we will have to increase that electrical output needed through additional use of fossil fuels.

The economic impact of full electrification of the U. S. will cost many trillions of dollars—especially if attempted by current technology. I suggest that little thought of the cost of fully electrifying the U. S. has been given in terms of the absolute enormity of the multiplicity of the tasks that will need to be accomplished. Let me give you just a sampling of what will need to happen to achieve the full electrification goal by 2050. Let's first start with all the U. S. households. Any home, small business, or major factory with natural gas for cooking, heating, or manufacturing of products will have to change to electrical production. We have the technology for household electric cooking and heating, but electrical substitutes for converting natural gas production methods will not be so easy to accomplish and probably won't be cheap. I submit that convincing the American public to spend thousands of dollars to renovate their homes into electric only energy will be more difficult than most anyone in Washington DC realizes. And what of the millions of apartment buildings, and hotels that have at least some dependence on natural gas—how many of those building and business owners will be willing to spend large sums of money to convert their entire buildings to electric-only facilities?

The fact of the matter is that IF the President and a majority of both houses of the Congress decide that total electrification of the U. S. is both necessary and desirable, we need a completely new technology catalog of mass electrification methods to get there. All of the current technology methods of electrifying this country have significant cost and safety faults that cannot be overcome. Additionally, these limited electrification methods to the American consumers and producers simply switch their energy use from personal fossil fuel use to added fossil fuel use to produce the significant increase in electricity demanded. The result is that we pay twice for a small, if any reduction in the use of fossil fuels. The most horrific result of this plan is that the American consumer pays all the costs. Current policies of the Federal Government have already started the American consumer on this merry-go-round. Higher costs of fossil fuels for autos, farm machinery, and semi-trucks raising costs to the consumer for fuel for their vehicles, natural gas for their home heating and cooking, and fuel oil for home heating. Additionally, the higher fuel costs for producing food, airlines, electric bills, and virtually all consumer products resulted in inflation of roughly 22% from mid-2021 through mid-2023 for American consumers. Fuel costs at the pump cost every user, consumer and producer twice as much today as two years ago. And none of this doubled cost of fuel to the consumer has significantly changed the bubble on the amount of fossil fuels used in the U. S. in those last two years. Why has this happened to the American consumers? Because we have put the cart before the horse. Simply stated, the current U. S. energy policy directed by the President and Congress have intentionally caused immediate pain on the U. S. consumer without offering any reasoned, truly technological advanced alternatives that aren't decades old.

What other technologies might be worth maturing? I have read of other technologies that explore entirely new methods of creating electrical power for homes such as capturing electricity from the Earth's magnetic sphere. We also have a half-century old technology, fuel cells, that might be useful in powering single family homes and small apartment buildings. I don't know how efficient they are using today's technology and how useful and price competitive they would be for homeowners, but this technology might be able to be grown sufficiently in a short period of time to be a reasonable price-tolerant alternative for homeowners to be encouraged to change to. The major technological problem as I see it today is that we need to identify an alternative to fossil fuels for vehicles, and for that matter aircraft as well, that is safe, much less volume and weight, made of materials that are plentiful throughout the U. S. and the rest of the world, easily manufactured and inexpensive to build, maintain, and quickly and easily filled with fuel of whatever type. I believe I recently read that a U. S. aircraft manufacturer was given a contract by the Federal Government to research alternative propulsion technologies for aircraft. This may be an even greater challenge than a reasonable alternative method of powering vehicles.

My point is simply this. We need to spend more money in research and development to discover better technologies to replace the use of fossil fuels.

My final and most sobering thought, at least from my perspective. I remember 60 plus years ago when I used to watch cartoons on television that a favorite topic was for a cartoon character to do something to challenge a natural activity. The result was always a major reaction from "Mother Nature," such as a lightning bolt, a sudden crack in the ground, or a quick earth shake. One of the observing cartoon characters would make the comments something like, "It's not smart to trick Mother Nature." As a Christian these thoughts have stayed with me all these days, but, of course, it is not "Mother Nature" who really controls the world's atmosphere. Rather as a Christian, it is the Lord God, Jehovah (also known by many other names by many other religions). I bring this point up because I believe that we humans need to remember that God is in control of all natural activities that happen on this planet. This means that we must remember that what we humans do in the use of the bountiful resources he has provided humankind on, within, and around the Earth are ultimately under his control, not ours. Our job as humankind is to learn how best to husband those resources for the best outcomes of all humanity at all times. We need to take note when some of our resource uses or alterations fail to achieve the results we expected. At that point, it is time to stop what we are doing, and rethink our approach and search for other answers. I believe that is where we are in the U. S. with our current energy policies. From an economics perspective, I believe we are literally tossing a lot of the American peoples' good money after bad.

CHAPTER EIGHTEEN
Current U. S. Economic Instability

The Purpose of this Chapter. This chapter will briefly identify and describe what I think are the most dangerous problems and issues that still beset the U. S. Economy, or may be on the horizon which will promote some degree of instability. I will place them in order of their greatest significance or most probable negative impact on our economy.

1.   *The continued stranglehold on the supply of our U. S. fossil fuels being released into our economy.* *I see no intention on the current President and the democratic party to release a significant additional amount of fossil fuels into the U. S. Economy as long as President Biden and the democrat party control at least one house of the U. S. Congress. They will continue their plan to restrict fossil fuels into our economy in order to force the American public to change to a total electric lifestyle. This means that the prices of natural gas and gasoline will, at best remain at their current high levels or continue to increase in the future. The problem with this policy is that the vast majority of the American public is financially unable to afford a quick electrification of our total home energy usage. Many households simply don't have the money to switch from natural gas heating, hot water supply, and natural gas cooking appliances. And, in many homes in the northeast, the switch isn't from natural gas home heating, it is from fuel oil heating, which is an even larger changeover cost than natural gas. Nor do most families have the money to purchase the significantly higher priced electric automobiles. And the Federal Government's tax breaks aren't sufficiently large enough to enable homeowners who want to make the changeover from fossil fuels to electric. An additional problem if a sudden change away from fossil fuels is attempted is that the U. S. industrial base is incapable of meeting demand which will just add to the price to the consumers.*

Along with this problem is the fact that we already have an insufficient supply of electrical output for the total usage today. So, we do a nasty double whammy in price increases on the American public for their electrical rates and bills. Somehow, they have to pay the price increases of both the new appliances and autos and higher prices for the electricity to operate them—assuming the electricity is available in the first place.

2. **How is the U. S. agriculture industry supposed to keep the U. S. in sufficient food with the electrification of the U. S. killing them due to significantly increased prices to produce food AND gradually decreasing their land space to produce food?** *The price of new battery-powered farm machinery is going to be so enormous that most farmers will not be able to afford the machinery to continue to farm. Their workdays will be decreased simply because the battery power won't last much more than 8 to 10 hours—at best. Additionally, the farm equipment will have to be moved daily back and forth from the farm home where the battery charger is to the field. This will cause an even greater decrease in work day farm activity in the field.*

The world also uses fossil fuels in producing fertilizer. Use of fertilizer over the last 60 years or so worldwide has allowed the world to feed its population growth during those 60 years to the current estimated world population level of approximately 8.056 billion people. The amount of fertilizer production to help farmers have significantly greater production of food per acre has risen from roughly 50 million tons in 1960 to over 200 million tons in 2020. It is, indeed the use of fertilizer in the major food producing countries (the U. S. included) that allowed the significant production of food to keep up with the rate of growth of the world's population. However, the fertilizer production process is one of the highest (if not the highest) carbon dioxide production process in the world today. Natural gas is turned into a nitrogen solid product with methane gas being the major gas oftentimes released into the atmosphere.

Finally, with the current U. S. policy of producing electricity using the non-fossil fuel technologies of solar panels, and windmills to generate electricity, we have created two new ecological monsters—non-biodegradable turbine blades, and solar panels. Additionally, both windmills (alias wind turbine generators) and solar panels also take a lot of land space to produce rather limited amounts of electrical power. The land space used by both is oftentimes capable of the alternative use of farm products.

The bottom line of the current policy of the destruction of the use of fossil fuels for wind turbines and solar panels takes a sizable amount of land space both to produce the electricity and then to trash the hardware after it becomes useless.

3. **How is the new Federal Reserve System of FedNow going to affect the U. S. Banking System and the entire American population.** *The Federal Reserve is the organization that oversees and provides the policies of how financial institutions implement the U. S. monetary system among the financial institutions and the American public. In July, the Federal Reserve Board instituted the FedNow program. Most of the narrative I have read about the FedNow program basically states that it is going to make all financial transactions among U. S. banks happen in a nano-second (meaning immediately). This sounds harmless enough, but I have read from a number of usually level-headed banking experts and Federal Reserve monitors that the Fed plans to expand its monitoring functions into the banking services provided to the American public. For example, the Federal Reserve has been noted as saying that they plan to do away with our U. S. currency and coins and go to a "digital dollar." The Federal Reserve states that they are in the very early stages of*

conceptualizing a non-paper, non-coin currency, but that the current U. S. dollar currency and coins will be around for a long time yet. Additionally, some of the Federal Reserve expert watchers believe that the Federal Reserve will provide easy and full access of every individual's financial transactions to other Federal Government organizations such as the U. S. Department of Justice and the Internal Revenue Service without the necessity of a warrant.

The one singular policy decision(s) that the Federal Reserve has made during the last 18 months or so is to raise the interest rate they charge banks to borrow money from them. This is known as the discount rate and becomes the basis for all interest rates charged by all financial institutions in the United States. In 2020, the discount rate set by the Federal Reserve was 0.25%. Today, 23 August, 2023, the discount rate is 5.25%. The increased discount rate as greatly affected two major financial activities in the U. S. First, the home loan interest rates are always sensitive to what the Federal Reserve discount rate is. Today, the home loan interest rate hovers around 7.1%. The higher home loan interest rate affects buyers and sellers. Buyers tend to be able to purchase a home only at a lower sales price in order to keep their monthly payment within the level that the financial institution has set. Sellers are also affected because they have to lower the selling price of their home in order to make it available to the same number of buyers that could afford their home say six months ago.

The second major borrower that is affected by the Federal Reserve discount rate is the Federal Government. The interest that the Federal Government has to pay on its debt is completely dependent on and tied directly to the Fed's discount rate. As you might imagine, in 2020, the Federal Government was able to borrow money on its debt for under 1.0% per year. But today, the rate the Federal Government pays to borrow money is just under 5.0%. A recent statement by a Federal Government debt manager told the Congress that virtually all of the

Federal Government's debt of roughly $32.0 trillion will have to be refinanced. The total interest the Federal Government spent on our debt of $30.8 trillion at the end of Fiscal Year 2022 was $544 billion. For that same $30.8 trillion debt, with a discount rate of 5.25% in 2024, the total interest bill for each Fiscal Year beginning in Fiscal Year 2025 will be around $1.6 trillion a year. And that is a low number because the Federal Government plans to increase our debt by approximately $1.5 trillion each year through 2028. By Fiscal Year 2025, our entire annual interest payment on the Federal debt will be the result of the entire annual budget deficit.

4. **The continued southern open border of the United States, will, I predict promote a great deal of political and economic instability.** *The political instability is already highly visible. Nary a day goes by when someone in the political arena and major news networks doesn't have a major news story about some aspect of the open U. S. southern border. Every day, we are made aware of the daily totals of illegal immigrants coming into the U. S. Additionally, the drugs brought into the U. S. by drug cartels and mules of drug cartels are constantly on the news. The fact that fentanyl is killing dozens of Americans every day and the annual number of U. S. people killed by the illegal drugs entering our country through the porous southern border are daily news items.*

In Chapter 15 of this book, I discussed the Federation of American Immigration Reform's latest estimate for the cost of illegal immigrants into the U. S. at $150.2 billion net of tax revenues collected from immigrants. But there are many undocumented costs to the American public that are not included in that dollar figure. Think of all the illegal crimes that are committed by illegal aliens who have found their way into the U. S. People at the southern parts of the southern border states are very vulnerable to have house break-ins and thefts, pets and farm animals slaughtered, sometimes family members injured or killed.

Nor does the Federal Immigration Net at the border catch all previous hard-core criminals who come into the U. S. and, surprise, surprise commit the same or worse felony crimes against American citizens again. Cities in the U. S. who once called themselves "sanctuary cities" for illegal immigrants have now taken a different stance after experiencing the large influx of bussed in or flown in from the southern border. The city mayors are finding the immigrants costly to the cities for food and shelter of these illegal immigrants. Oftentimes the neighborhoods where a city decides to house these immigrants complain bitterly about the immigrants being planted where they live. And most of the cities that now house large numbers of illegal immigrants have found it costing millions of dollars which are decidedly outside their capability to afford. Finally, the cities where illegal immigrants are placed are often hard pressed to find enough foreign language translators to help manage the immigrants in their midst.

Finally, many cities in the U. S. are being inundated with hoards of human trafficked immigrants. These human trafficked immigrants live inhuman lives, usually in poor living conditions, and dangerous encounters with their pimps' clients. This is probably on the lowest end of the morality scale which often scars young people for life, and oftentimes means they won't live long into adulthood.

5.   **A major negative impact to our U. S. Economy is the significant increase in crime in our country, both in quantity of criminal incidences but also the increase in the number of methods of criminal behavior.** *Throughout every major city in the U. S., we see an increase in criminal activity. One of the newest criminal activities is the smash and grab technique where a large number of criminals break into a store and grab what they can and leave the store before police show up. Oftentimes today, smash and grabs are so well organized that the throngs of thieves arrive in vehicles that wait on the streets for the thieves to return in a few*

minutes with their arms full of merchandise. These smash and grab tactics have closed not only mom and pop neighborhood stores, but large national name department stores because the losses are so gigantic that they cannot be sustained for the many return engagements they face by smash and grab mobs.

Another increase in rampant crime in cities are the open street shootings and assaults. These confrontations on the streets may be one individual against another who each have weapons and know each other as enemies. Or, it may be a few individuals on each side who are armed and simply commit open warfare on the sidewalk or in the street. There are also assaults by armed individuals against unarmed, innocent civilians that happen—again on the open sidewalks or streets. The ultimate street and sidewalk violence in cities today are gang shootouts. Finally, carjackings are also on the increase throughout U. S. cities.

Every time I turn on my television today to a news station, national or local, there seems to be some major crime being committed at that moment, or that was committed within the last 30 minutes to an hour. To me the U. S. seems on the brink between the open gangland wars in the cities during the 1920s and 1930s, or something more like the mostly lawless old west days. The point is this. Simply put, the major unrest we find widely throughout the major U. S. cities greatly hurts the commerce of our cities. Businesses close, the city's public is afraid to shop where it is not safe, and with the current defund the police efforts, cities are simply no longer safe for conducting business. The obvious result is going to be a continuation of the permanent closing of city businesses AND decrease in customers because of the lack of both personal and business enterprise safety.

6.   **Although the labor statistics look good on the surface, there are, I believe a number of underlying labor detractors that could quickly tip the labor into a very troubled area of the U. S. Economy.** *The first major impact that we will begin to feel is the lost year of schooling during the COVID shutdown by this and last years' high school graduates. These two classes failed to get at least one complete year of high school, and many of this year's high school graduates probably didn't learn at the pre-COVID pace last year—thereby losing perhaps more like a year and a half of high school just prior to going into the labor market or college both last year and this year. For those who graduated high school last year and this year, it simply means that they are less prepared to work as efficiently and effectively as their predecessors of two years ago. Those students who were in college the last three years had a natural capability to recover simply by restarting their college education last year or this year where they left off before and during COVID. One example of this phenomenon is that the U. S. military is having greater difficulty than usual academically qualifying candidates to enter the military by passing the military entrance exams. At least one of the military services recently announced that they were going to let recruit hopefuls take the entrance exam using a hand-held calculator. As a retired Air Force officer this bothers me somewhat because it indicates to me that today's high school graduates are not skilled in the basic mechanics of mathematics. I consider this a definite deficiency in a basic education skill for our high school graduates.*

Another issue I see with our education system in general is that many of the inner-city high schools have graduation rates slightly over or below the rate of 50%. This places the non-high school graduates statistically at a miserable life long prospect of being employed in jobs that are at or below the poverty level of income. There are a number of reasons that inner city children fail to get a high school degree. Some are within their control, and at least some, if not many are not in their control. But, we must understand as a society, that the basic fact is there and will probably remain for a very long time. People without a high school degree are in for a long perilous life of bitterness and hardship because of the probable income they will earn without a high school degree.

The final labor issue that we economists don't work hard enough to get is good labor data on the labor turnover rate. High labor turnover rates that are persistent over time greatly diminish productivity rates. One of the first things I requested from a company that I was reviewing for low productivity rates was their labor turnover rate. Many companies, especially the small and medium volume and/or sales companies in a particular industry, weren't keeping the data. So, the first thing we did was get a data base set up for them to routinely collect turnover data. What bothers me today is that in virtually all the local businesses I frequent as a customer, it seems that I don't remember seeing any of the faces today that I saw a day or so ago, or a week or two ago. High turnover rates are a surefire indication that people have lost goals of their life's work, don't have a goal for their life's work, or have yet to learn that work is... well work. It' probably not going to be enjoyable all the time, you aren't going to like some of the people with whom you work or for whom you work. But, you have to have a vision of what you want to do with your life and earn money while you do it. I fear that this high turnover rate I see in my small part of the U. S. Economy may be hiding a deeper problem among our overall labor force, especially our younger folks. This does not bode well for the U. S. Economy if a high labor turnover rate becomes widespread among all geographical areas of the U. S. and in most or all industries in the U. S.

7.   **The final major U. S. economic problem has to do with shortages and non-home-produced goods.** *As a practicing and long-time experienced economist, I get daily email notices of specific*

final product, or intermediate product, or parts shortages. The reports seem over the month to pretty much hit most consumer goods the American public buys. The economic indicator that quickly shows shortages exist to a large segment of Americans is the inflation rate— in this case not just the overall inflation rate such as the Consumer Price Index, but the inflation rate of specific commodities or parts or products. There are certainly shortages in the U. S. today and we are paying significantly higher prices because of those shortages. Number one on the list is the deliberate reduction in output of fossil fuels driven by President Biden's policy of destroying the fossil fuel industry. Not a day goes by that I don't see someone sending a panicky email to me about a coming severe food shortage. The U. S. at this time, produces more food in general than the U. S. population consumes in a year. Food is one of our major exports. I grew up in the dead center of Kansas in a small farm community. I have a lot of friends who are part of farm families, and I have yet to have any of them tell me that they have been unable to plant their fields for next years yields. There are definitely areas of the U. S. who have suffered and are still suffering droughts, but I have yet to see any of my farm friends in the Midwest plains states of the U. S. say that this summer's droughts have stopped them from planting crops. I live in rural Northeast Georgia where hay and corn are the two main crops. We have had an abundance of rain this spring and summer and I expect to see bumper crops of corn, strawberries, and hay. On the other hand, do not make the mistake that the war on fossil fuels by our current President is NOT hurting farmers in terms of significantly increased costs and decreased profits for the crops and various types of meat they grow.

The second aspect of potential shortages that can be made comes in the area of parts and products made for key products manufactured throughout the U. S., or purchased by the U. S. as the major customer. Let me give you a couple of examples. China and Taiwan produce the vast majority of computer and electronic chips. The chips are used in almost everything a consumer owns today. Some products with chips are obvious—computers, phones, counter appliances. But computer chips are also a key part of major appliances like refrigerators, washer and dryers, and cooking ranges. During the last year the U. S. auto industry could not produce as many cars as they wanted because they couldn't get the computer chips necessary to run all the electronics of the autos from the engines to radios, all the lights, and so on and so on. China produces some 70% or more of the world's steel. They produce roughly 90% of all drugs consumed by Americans. Many DOD equipment parts are produced outside the U. S. In short, the U. S. is dependent on a few other countries to supply some very important final products or parts of final products. Over the last half century, the U. S. has gradually handed the manufacturing of virtually entire product lines to foreign producers. Our entire kitchen and household products we use are made in China. We handed our entire consumer electronics industry to various other parts of the world—Japan, China, Europe. The U. S. makes very few of our TVs, stereo systems, and other entertainment electronics. Many of our computers and printers are assembled outside the U. S. Most of our phones are made in China. Virtually everything we wear (clothing, shoes) are made in Southeast Asia. By now, I hope you get the message. The United States is highly dependent on a sizable part of our non-food products from other countries. China is a high-risk producer because we are at best fairly cut throat economic competitors or more realistically military and political adversaries. The truth is that the United States is extremely vulnerable to Chinese blackmail, or simple murder. Imagine if China told the U. S. they would no longer make and sell drugs to the U. S. unless we let them have Taiwan. Or suppose China simply decided they wanted to bring the U. S. to its knees by killing a large number of us through poisoning our drugs. How patient do you think the people of the U. S. would be if we could no longer buy Chinese made computers, phones, or consumer electronics, or the computer chips for us to make our own phones, computers, and electronics. The United States is greatly exposed to a death knell with/from China from a national security perspective and certainly an economic perspective. I suggest that the U. S. has to get out from under the real-world threat from China and do it quickly. We cannot be so naïve to think that China won't use their economic power over us when (not if) they decide to do so. This situation with China, at least from an economic policy perspective is a definite **Existential Threat.**

8.   ***Summary Statement.*** *In summary of this chapter let me simply state that the current U. S. Economy has a number of very risky situations running within it, that taken on an individual basis, might be considered an acceptable threat. But looking at the seven risk areas as a sum total within our current U. S. Economy, as a professional economist, I am greatly alarmed. I see the U. S. Economy in a perfect storm where each of the conditions mentioned in this Chapter MUST be addressed and addressed quickly, or we will see horrible consequences in the not-too-distant future. But, of course all I have said is poppycock according to the current President. He has stated frequently of late that the U. S. Economy is GREAT.*

CHAPTER NINETEEN
Why Not Socialism or Communism

The form of the economic system in the United States since its history began as a nation in 1776 is capitalism. The major reason for this is that the U. S. Constitution, especially the first 10 Amendments promote individual freedoms, limit government authorities over people, and establishes a government of checks and balances among three separate branches. The newly established U. S. Government and its relationship to its people it governs found itself immediately in kinship with a new economic system that could perform best in a political environment that cherishes and promotes individual freedoms above all else. In fact, the structure of capitalism is the only economic system ever devised by mankind that promotes and enhances the individual freedoms of our U. S. Constitution. All other economic systems developed by mankind have had great aspects of a lack of individual freedom for a large segment of their societies.

There are two other economic systems recognized throughout the world that are called either socialist or communist. The communist system was designed by and documented in a book, entitled, the Communist Manifesto written by Karl Marx and Friedrich Engles in 1848. The book was written as a critique of and alternative to capitalism. The book also spends most of its wordage discussing communism as an economic system with a description of the structure of the political system that would make it work best. Communism is defined as "a society in which all property is publicly owned, and each person works and is paid according to his/her abilities and needs. From an economic perspective, publicly owned property is easily defined and subject to little interpretation. Publicly owned means owned and operated by the state/government. Where things get dicey from an economic definitional and implementation perspective is defining how the state/government determines the abilities of each individual in the country and the needs of each person in the country. The state/government obviously is meant to be the decision authority, but the question of who in the government gets to be the decision authority and the scope of the decision authorities' decision powers are the major issues. It is this second part that depends on the rubric of the political structure in the country that controls and makes all the economic decisions in the country. Simply put, the people have little control over their own economic lives, and absolutely no control over the decisions of what is to be produced and how those outputs (products and services) are to be distributed among the populace. In short, under communism, the people have absolutely no individual freedom of choice either in terms of their job and their place of work, or in terms of what is distributed to them in terms of the goods and services they feel they need and want. Their job is assigned to them, and so too is their output of goods and services. The political system is composed of a group of people who make the input decisions in terms of quantity, quality, and place of production, and in terms of the production processes, quantity and quality of the goods and services provided within the economy. There is no influence on the part of roughly 90% of the population who are not members of the Communist Party. This economic and political structure are most obvious and apparent in China and Russia today.

The definition of socialism as an economic system in today's modern terms is that the people who do the work determine what gets produced and how it gets produced. But, there is a system of social organization in which private property and distribution are subject to government/social control. The "system of social organization" that controls some part of economic income and output of individuals and families is the political part of economic determination.

So, what we see among these three economic systems is that the basic political definition and/or issue is how much government controls the inputs and production processes that provide the quantity and quality of the total goods and services available, and more noticeably how much the government controls the distribution of those goods and services. We can thus, look at every country's combined economic and political system to see how each compares in relation to who controls how much of the assignment of inputs, production processes, and quality of the goods and services throughout the total economy. Second, we also need to judge how the output is distributed and in what quantities that are in the hands of the government authorities versus the individual members of the society. Today, our determinations of which economic system fits each country around the world is adjudged using a continuum among the three descriptive economic/political systems that prevail in each country. The spectrum is defined as capitalism on one end of the spectrum with communism on the other end of the spectrum and socialism as anything that is between the two "extremes" on the spectrum. In truth, there is no country of which I know that has a pure capitalist economy. There are at least two countries, China, and Russia that have mostly communist economic and political characteristics on the far end of the opposing side of the capitalist economic and political definition. Today's countries who lean towards capitalism have some number of socialist characteristics—definitely including the U. S.

So, let's evaluate the U. S. economic system based on the issues of individual versus U. > governmental/institutional control of the various pieces and parts of the U. S. economic system. Let' first deal with the control of the inputs (resources). In the U. S. the human resources are given almost 100% latitude in making their own decisions about what type of work they want to do, the employer for whom they want to work, and the part of the U. S. where they want to work. Additionally, people generally are not forced to work by the government. Finally, individuals have the right and great discretion in negotiating their pay for a job they desire to do or accept to work. Some people may even join labor unions to give them a larger voice in what they are paid and fringe benefits they receive. The production process which involves determining the types, quantities, and qualities of resources, except for jobs offered and needed by government agencies in the U. S. are determined by private companies run by private, non-government management teams. The decisions on what each company will produce, the quantity and quality of the products or services are all determined by the company's management team, not the government. The role of the government generally lies in ensuring the incorporation of national employment standards, producing safe products or services in a safe work environment, and making the product or services available to all American consumers. The government seldom directs the quantity of production of goods or services by a private company. U. S. governments also place few inhibitive regulations or laws against what consumers can buy, where they can buy them, or when they can buy them. Additionally, consumers generally have great freedom in making unfettered choices of what they buy and when they buy it.

U. S. governments at all levels do provide goods and services that were recommended by Adam Smith. First, the Federal Government provides for the common defense of the entire country. Secondly, all the U. S. governments provide some level and aspect of protecting the "sovereign" by enforcing laws that protect the American public from physical harm, laws that enforce the implementation of the basic economic concepts of capitalism, and protecting consumers from individual or corporate predators. The Federal Government also has the specific role of both encouraging and assuring competition throughout the U. S. Economy because of its major function as the invisible hand to prevent, discourage, and if necessary to punish firms for the illegal practice of non-competitive economic activities or policies. The first of several laws implemented by the Federal Government to break up monopolies that promote and implement price-fixing of output or the elimination of competitors first arose in 1890 with the Sherman Antitrust Act.

The U. S. does have a history of creeping socialism as the U. S. governments, particularly the Federal Government have taken control of some programs in the name of helping certain segments of U. S. society be better served than was previously shown to be accomplished from the private sector of the U. S. Economy. The first of these was the gradual take-over of the K through 12 education systems by state and local governments particularly during the first two decades of the 20th Century. Additionally, state governments have gradually expanded state funding to more and more colleges especially after World War II veterans returned from the war and the GI Bill was introduced. This is an area that Adam Smith would probably not object to given the noticeably strong importance he placed on educational achievement as a necessity for a society's economic health and the improved welfare of the entire country as educational prowess becomes more generally spread throughout our country. The methods and gigantic intrusions that both the federal and state governments have incorporated in the college educational system have probably become more broad-based and harmful to the efficient allocation of higher education. And, those policies have certainly skewed significant financial resources in directions that are not equitable to all segments of the U. S. These financial misallocations; however, appear to be on the wane as they are challenged in the U. S. Court system.

The greatest amount of socialistic policy intrusion into the U. S. economic system has occurred since the mid-1930s. Capitalism throughout the world was seen to falter as the Great Depression that began in 1929 and grew into a personal, politically and economically painful decade of the 1930s. In the U. S. the Gross Domestic Product fell to half what it was in 1929 by the end of the first two years of the 1930s. Unemployment in the U. S. increased to 25% by the end of 1932. A British economist by the name of John Maynard Keynes proposed a radical intrusion into the economic system by political policies that promoted significant increases in federal government spending, causing significant sizable annual federal budget deficits to provide economic relief to virtually all people in the economy who were financially devastated by the Depression. The U. S. Federal Government created a number of programs in the 1933 through 1935-time frame that have remained as funded programs from those days until today's current times. The entire concept of welfare programs which today pay tens of millions of people life sustaining incomes for food, clothing, shelter, and transportation began in the early 1930s and remain today supporting a much larger cadre of people than the programs of the 1930s did. Of course, the U. S. population is much larger today than it was in the 1930s, so the total number of people supported by the welfare programs today are much more expensive today in inflation adjusted programmatic terms than we spent in 1933. One significant program that was started in 1935 was the Social Security program which has grown from less thana $2 billion dollars in 1935 (in FY 2022 dollars) to $1.222 trillion in 2022. In 1965, Medicare and Medicaid were established by the Federal Government and have grown from a 1965 expenditure of $6 billion (in FY2022 dollars) to $1.643 trillion (in FY2022 dollars). The impact to the Federal Government and the American public is that the annual budget deficit in 1940 was $2.9 billion (in FY 1940$) to $1.376 trillion (in FY 2022 dollars). Our Gross Federal debt has increased from $50.696 Billion dollars to $30.839 trillion in 2022.

The penchant for the U. S. Government to implement long-term, permanent social income supplement programs has become fiscally and financially disastrous. In statement of fact, our continued political hunger to boost incomes of the American public have placed the U. S. in perilous danger of becoming insolvent to those who traditionally have purchased our annual deficits. Furthermore, the surpluses built over the last 40 years for Social Security and Medicare are quickly being depleted. In fact, the probability is that the Medicare surplus is already depleted. The Social Security surplus is expected to be depleted no later than 2033. Both these programs need to be healed by either increasing the annual amount of Medicare and Social Security taxes paid by today's working Americans or the annual amount of Medicare and Social Security payments to those who have paid into these accounts for their entire working lives will have to be decreased. Neither alternative is going to be particularly acceptable to either of the two segments of our citizenry who will be affected, but such is the nature of a government establishing social programs as political policy that always turn into economic crises.

My bottom-line conclusion as an economist on the socialization of economic basic capitalistic economic systems is that ultimately, the social programs will grow either in the number of programs, and/or the dollar growth of the dollars spent on each social program and will eventually place the entire economy in a fiscal/financial crisis that causes severe political unrest. And, oftentimes that unrest may be virtually impossible to quell peacefully. Secondly, with every social program that is instituted in any country, including the U. S., the American public loses personal choice to governmental dictates. It is one thing for a social program to be totally voluntary, such that each individual has the choice to be a part of it or not. But, as we can see by our own history, what the various levels of government within the U. S. may implement as an "opportunity" to participate in a social program, will almost certainly become a social program which we are demanded to join at some later point in our country's history. This used to be called "creeping socialism." Today, it is simply a gradual increase in socialism.

CHAPTER TWENTY
Grave Danger?

Our beloved USA is in trouble. In the military, we would equate this state of affairs, "grave danger." I have attempted to annotate all of the significant economic status and public policy positions that have placed our country in my assessed current state. Let me briefly hit the major points as a summary.

First, we have a Federal Government debt that exceeds $30 trillion today. By any measure that figure is staggering. If anyone thinks that we can sustain that $31 trillion debt, they are smoking rope. Why? Because we were at the lowest interest rates experienced by this country since the Great Depression of the 1930s. The interest rates are now rising with the current Federal Funds Rate somewhere between 5.0% and 5.25%, with no indication by the Federal Reserve that they plan to decrease the interest rates in the near future. Rather, the probability is that the Federal Reserve will increase the interest rate for the foreseeable future. A 5% interest rate paid on $30 plus trillion dollars' worth of debt will raise the annual interest payments of the U. S. Government to $1.5 trillion a year or more. The Federal Reserve has already signaled this rise in interest rates by increasing them twice in the last 9 months. Every 1% rise in the interest rates costs the American public, through the Federal Government, an additional annual expense of $300 billion. And, of course, as our total debt rises, so also does our incremental annual interest expense to pay for it. Unless we begin to pay down our federal debt soon, we will become bankrupt—perhaps not in the sense that the creditors of our public debt will demand immediate full payment of our debt they hold, or that we will be legally be placed into world-wide receivership. But, at some point, the U. S. Treasury will offer U. S. debentures for sale and no one will purchase them at any interest rate. We cannot predict when this date will occur, but rest assured that if our debt continues to rise, it will. When it does, it will be without warning and the U. S. Government will suddenly have to reduce spending to meet the revenue collected. When that day happens, we will have low ranking bureaucrats deciding who gets paid, how much, and when. The U. S. financial system will quickly collapse, and the U. S. Economy will go into crisis mode quickly. Finally, with severe economic unrest and most of the population and businesses in the country in financial distress, the economic calamity will quickly drive severe political unrest. Suddenly, panic, riots, and self-serving actions by all Americans will become the norm. The social stability of the USA will disintegrate and lawlessness, and anarchy will rise quickly. None of our residents will recognize what we will have become.

Second, since the beginning of the New Deal of 1933, continuing to the present, the economic policy of the Federal Government has been to significantly increase the influence and control of our U. S. Economy by governments at all levels, but particularly at the Federal Government. For the last eight decades, the Federal Government has deliberately expanded its regulation of people and business, controlled more of our country's resources through tax policy, and created a growing sense of "entitlement" among our population. The result is that capitalism as an economic system envisioned by Adam Smith has greatly morphed into an economic system that becomes more and more characteristically like socialism and communism. Furthermore, it seems that more and more Americans are persuaded that communism, and particularly a more centrally-controlled economic system is a better fit for today's United States of America culture. As a conservative economist, I strongly believe that any perceived failings of the U. S. capitalist economic system to adequately serve all Americans is not the fault of the basic concepts and principles of capitalism. Rather, it is the decades-long public policies that have eroded and infringed upon the continued implementation of those original capitalist economic system principles established by Adam Smith.

Third, Federal Government public policy over the last 8 decades has been Keynesian in nature. This policy favors increasing the total demand for goods in the U. S. rather than aiming public policy towards increasing supply. For the last 85 years this policy has sometimes translated into good annual GDP growth, but it is not guaranteed. Oftentimes the implementation of Keynesian demand management policies resulted in significant inflation and stagnant growth in GDP output. This, in turn brought about increased inflation. Federal tax and spending policies have resulted in annual Federal deficits much more often than surpluses, creating an expectation on the part of the American public that they can spend large sums of money without making hard decisions on what not to implement from public policy perspectives. We now have a Federal Income Tax System where almost 50% of the American public pays no Federal Income Tax. We have a large portion of the American public who collects some form of welfare (excluding Social Security and Medicare). We have created a sub-culture in the United States that believe they are owed a good paying job, no matter their education or skill level achieved, and failing being given a good paying job, they are owed a middle-income standard of living. Many people with these expectations no longer feel that they have any responsibility to prepare themselves for those good paying jobs via learning and achieving good skill sets in order to "earn" those good paying jobs.

The alternative public policy proposal, supply-side economics, emphasizes business growth over consumption. It is businesses who provide the goods and services for Americans to consume. Additionally, it is businesses who provide the jobs for Americans that gives them the income to purchase the goods and services. Governments at all levels need to provide businesses incentives to increase investment in new products and equipment to manufacture goods and services. Governments also should develop public policies that reward businesses for increasing the number of people employed and increases in output. The USA has only limited experience and economic data to determine definitively whether or not supply-side, conservative economics provides a better outcome to our U. S. Economy. Certainly, the statistical data of the Reagan era of Federal policy development and implementation shows robust economic activity across the U. S. Economy during the eight years of his presidency. The effects of supply-side economics on the U. S. Economy during the following 12 years of Republican presidents beyond President Regan provides less persuasive data to support positive effects of supply-side economics from a statistical standpoint. And, certainly, general, non-targeted tax cuts have been a cause of sizable Federal budget deficits historically. But what is clear is that increasing supply is the only economic policy that will increase output, increase jobs, and reduce product and service prices. Additionally, the U. S. has literally handed entire industries to other countries to produce and sell to us. One of those countries, China, is not our friend. They could disrupt the entire U. S. by simply withholding all that they produce for us and/or they could send us faulty products that are at best useless, and at worst deathly. Additional to that threat is the very real situation that China steals much of our intellectual property which is the first step in our capability to grow our wealth. In short, China is simply stealing our wealth as well as endangering our supply of many necessary goods.

Fourth, as a conservative Christian, I fear that many Americans no longer accept the mandate of God that our existence on this Earth as individuals and collective communities necessitates that we serve God and the people of Earth. Additionally, God's mandate to all able-bodied humans is that we have an individual responsibility to determine and hone our best traits and abilities towards the singular goal of service to mankind. In my 7 decades of life in this country and on the Earth, I believe that I have observed a gradual and steady divestiture of the American public from these Christian beliefs and doctrine of service to mankind.

Fifth, today we have several economic issues that need to be dealt with AND solved. These are far ranging, and each alone is a serious issue. But together, the economy is in great danger. These issues are illegal immigration—especially the care, housing, feeding, and educating of those people. Along with those illegal immigrants we incur 100,000 drug deaths of our citizens each year. And we also have tens of thousands of humans trafficked into the U. S. Interest rates are rising, the Federal Reserve just introduced the "digital dollar" without much explanation for its creation. The U. S. dollar is in great danger of no longer being the world's stable, go-to currency for all goods and services by virtually every nation in the world. This will greatly destabilize the federal, state, and local governments and citizens' ability to conduct business and purchases goods and services from overseas countries. Inflation is not yet under control, the U. S. labor market is in turmoil because of high turnover rates, and an ever-growing illegal immigrant population that remains largely unemployed. Our entire educational system lost at least one year, and more probably two years of education during the COVID years at all levels, but particularly in grades K-12.

The annual tests taken last spring for "no child left behind," are coming back with horrible scores. This means that today's students entering college are unprepared for the transition of both knowledge and learning skills that they will need to perform in college—assuming the colleges retain their academic standards. This situation will ultimately hit our businesses and government agencies as the K-12 students are already entering our work force and college graduates of all years for the next four years will probably not be as skilled as those who graduated two years ago. It will take some time for the COVID crisis impacts on education to be overcome in our economy. Many Americans doubt the efficacy of the inflation and unemployment data being calculated by government agencies today. The unemployment data doesn't measure the turnover rates many industries are experiencing, and the inflation rate certainly does not seem to measure the inflation rates Americans continue to face for EVERYTHING they buy. Restricted U. S. fossil fuel production is driving the prices of everything up and substitute energy solutions will never produce the amount of electricity that the federal government plans to force upon Americans. The answer to more electricity production in the U. S. will necessarily require a large number of fossil fuel driven generation plants.

The bottom lines of this entire book are two-fold. First, I believe the long-term economic policies followed by the Federal Government over the last 85 years or so have seriously degraded the positive effectiveness of the design of the capitalist economic system created and envisioned by Adam Smith. Much evidence exists that the long-term dominance of Keynesian economic policies has established cumulative effects that currently have placed the United States Economy in dire peril. We have a crushing Federal debt with no clear public policy to reverse our 8 decades-old Federal budget deficits. We have, for the last 50 years seen heavy declines, if not complete disappearances of many industries where the U. S. once dominated the world. We have gradually brought significantly more regulation into the lives of producers and consumers, and American businesses and households as taxpayers that economic activity has been noticeably stunted. And, the Federal Government passes more and more laws that greatly inhibit the basic economic freedoms essential to the very core operation of our capitalist economic system.

Second, if we do not make radical changes in our laws and public policy to get us back to the basic principles and concepts of our capitalist economic system as designed, described, and envisioned by Adam Smith, the United States will suffer an apocalyptic economic system disaster in the future. This economic disaster will be closely followed by a chaotic reaction in the cultural, social, and general national stability that our national political policy-makers have promised ever since the close of the decade of the 1930s. Remaining on the same road of the deterioration of the U. S. Economic System away from capitalism to a blend of a socialist/communist economic system will destroy the U. S. as we know it today. And the new economic system and its attendant political system will not be to the liking of our general population. Furthermore, if we continue the present public economic policies of government control of our economic system, my beloved country could literally self-destruct. And finally, the current economic policies in place from the Administration and the Congress have long term promises for improvement in our U. S. Economy, but those promises seem to be woefully optimistic in terms of time of arrival for the" good times," and the promised significant improvement in the economic conditions of the U. S. Thus, my assessment of the direction of the U. S. Economy is that the United States of America as I know and love it is in **GRAVE DANGER** of becoming a country I no longer recognize and revere.

EPILOGUE

I made every effort to bring you, the reader as many facts as I could on each issue and policy failures and recommended correctional policies. I hope that I was persuasive to draw you to the conclusion that the United States Economy, and therefore, our personal, family, and national standard of living are in dire jeopardy. Many of the economic policies being carried out today have been around for decades, indeed since 1933. These policies have led the U S. to the brink of financial disaster that could easily destroy our country and our American way of life. Today, our country is pitted one group against another. The split can be defined in a number of ways—liberal/progressive versus conservative, democrat versus republican, rural versus urban, and yes, still today, black versus white.. Some new cultural distinctions have also arisen: LGBTQ, Woke cultural tolerance, illegal aliens versus intolerant American citizens, violence for change and equitability versus violence for destruction of property and historical culture.

Our federal government in Washington, D. C. is evenly divided—virtually a 50 democrat versus 50 republican splits in the U. S. Senate, and a 5 to 8 seat majority of republicans versus democrats in the House of Representatives. Our current president and vice-president have been everything but nimble at describing their policies, let alone carrying them out. Even the current Supreme Court seems to have lost its way on many important economic issues in terms of meeting the true sense of our capitalist economy. The result is, in my mind, nothing short of chaos in the U. S. Economy. I find many more negative policy influences for our economy sending us largely in the wrong direction with far too few economic policies pushing our economy in the right direction. Furthermore, the negative policy influences in our economy in the last 20 years and certainly in the last two and three quarter years have placed our economy and the vast majority of the American public in deeper jeopardy than when this four year presidential term began in January of 2021.

But, the truth of the matter is that the American public has no one to blame for the economic ills in this country other than ourselves, our country's collective citizenry. We have grown complacent in educating ourselves about the facets of capitalism, the corner stone of our U. S. Economy, and in learning and getting a detailed understanding of the United States Constitution and how our Federal Government is both intended to work on behalf of the American public, and how we, as American citizens must exercise our will to bring about favorable outcomes to the majority of our citizens. Sadly, my observation is that people talk not about the policies of the political party they support, but rather what gimmies they will get from the party of their choice. Strengthening the federal government's execution of policies and actions that benefit all Americans is much less important than the WIFM (what's in it for me) viewpoints. As a result, the body politic of the legislative, executive, and judicial branches of the U S. Government now seem mired in how many people will be complacent about the decisions by each person in the branch, rather than determine what best fits the true meaning of the issues at hand. I adamantly oppose decisions made in Washington DC that are devoid of establishing right over wrong, good versus evil, morality over immorality, and the greatest good for the many over greed for the few. The way, we Americans determine the roads that those in DC who direct and guide our country is through voting. Yes, WE choose the people who represent us, our values, our patriotism towards our country and the American community as a whole—OR NOT. So, I tell you now that I had two goals for every reader of this book. First, have you learned enough about the original structure of Capitalism to measure the decisions that come from Washington DC to know when those DC decisions violate the concepts of Capitalism at its core? And, secondly, have you learned that the decisions made by the three branches of the U. S. Government may often seem very complex, but usually get down to moral and fiscal issues that can be meshed against the original concepts of Capitalism described by Adam Smith? When asked whether I am a republican or democrat, my answer is that I am first and foremost a conservative—particularly a conservative.

May your decisions not be made by political party affiliation, but on the policies and the values of each person running for political office—for the rest of your lives.

Dr. John C. Bredfeldt

BIBLIOGRAPHY

1. Adam Smith, The Wealth of Nations, the Modern Library, New York, NY,1965.

2. John Maynard Keynes, An Open Letter to President Roosevelt, New York Times, 31 December 1933, newdeal.feri.org/misc./Keynes2.htm.

3. U. S. Code, Title 31, Subtitle IV, Chapter 51, Subchapter I, Section 5103.

4. Fiscal Year 2024 President's Budget, Historical Tables..

5. Annual Federal Budget Analysis Report, Dr. John C. Bredfeldt, 17 April 2023.

6. Economic Indicators—August 2023, President's Council of Economic Advisors.

7. Anatomy of a Meltdown, John Cassidy, The New Yorker, December 1 2008 Issue.

8. 6.5 Billion Hours, $260 Billion: What Tax Complexity Costs Americans, April 17, Demian Brady, National Taxpayers Union Foundation.

9. The Fiscal Burden of Illegal Immigration on United States Taxpayers—2023 Cost Study, Federation for American Immigration Reform, March 2023.

10. Federal Regulations Cost $1.9 Trillion Annually, Competitive Enterprise Institute, May 10, 2018.

11. Hart-Scott-Rodino Annual Report—Fiscal Year 2021, Federal Trade Commission (Bureau of Competition), and Department of Justice (Antitrust Division).

12. FTC and DOJ Propose Significant Changes to US Merger Review Process, Kenneth Knox, K&L Gates HUBB, June 29,2023.

13. Historical U. S. Federal Individual Income Tax Rates & Brackets, 1862-2021, Tax Foundation.

14.   Imprimis April/May 2023, Thinking Smartly About Climate Change, Bjorn Lomborg.

15.   How Much Land is Needed for Wind Turbines, Richard Gaughan, Sciencing.com, May 10, 2018.

AUTHORS BIOGRAPHY

John was born in 1947, and raised in a small town in dead center Kansas (Bushton). He attended grades 1-12 in Bushton, then obtained a Bachelor in Business Administration with a major in economics and a minor in accounting (1969). He was commissioned a 2nd Lieutenant in the U. S. Air Force (via Air Force ROTC), and immediately continued his education at Wichita State University to obtain a master's degree in economics (1971). John served 24 years in the U. S. Air Force in various strategic financial planning and aircraft acquisition financial roles (eight of which were in Washington, D. C.), retiring as a Lt. Colonel. He was immediately hired as a contractor to continue his efforts of working with heavy equipment manufacturers to help them reduce their costs and improve their logistics support to the Air Force. Shortly after retiring from the Air Force, John began 2 years of work to complete his Doctorate in Public Administration and Economic Public Policy (completed in 1995). John also has taught college business and economics courses for over 32 years a various colleges and universities as an adjunct professor.

John is currently retired and still continues to teach courses at local colleges whenever his schedule allows. This is John's fourth book on economics and the U. S. Political Economy.

Me And My Pets

Lexi (gray-faced red) and Mena (red and white)

www.ingramcontent.com/pod-product-compliance
Lightning Source LLC
Chambersburg PA
CBHW032049020426
42335CB00011B/256